Teaching Strategies GOLD®

Objectives for Development & Learning: Birth Through Kindergarten

Cate Heroman; Diane C. Burts, EdD; Kai-leé Berke; Toni S. Bickart
English Language Acquisition Objectives by Patton Tabors, EdD
Foreword by Diane Trister Dodge

Contributing Authors:
Hilary Parrish Nelson, Laurie Taub, Kelly Boyle

TeachingStrategies® · Bethesda, MD

The publisher and the authors cannot be held responsible for injury, mishap, or damages incurred during the use of or because of the information in this book. The authors recommend appropriate and reasonable supervision at all times based on the age and capability of each child.

Teaching Strategies, LLC
7101 Wisconsin Ave., Suite 700
Bethesda, MD 20814

www.TeachingStrategies.com

978-1-60617-312-1

Teaching Strategies, The Creative Curriculum, and Teaching Strategies GOLD names and logos are registered trademarks of Teaching Strategies, LLC, Bethesda, MD.

Library of Congress Cataloging-in-Publication Data

Teaching strategies GOLD : objectives for development & learning : birth through kindergarten /
Cate Heroman ... [et al] ; English language acquisition objectives by Patton Tabors ; foreword by
Diane Trister Dodge ; contributing authors, Hilary Parrish Nelson, Laurie Taub, Kelly Boyle.
     p. cm.
  ISBN 978-1-60617-312-1
 1. Education, Primary--Curricula. 2. Early childhood education--Curricula. 3. Individualized instruction. 4. Cognitive styles in children. I. Heroman, Cate.

  LB1523.T43 2010
  372.13--dc22
                        2010017604

9 10 11 12 13	19 18 17 16 15 14
Printing	Year Printed

Printed and bound in the United States of America

Acknowledgments

We give special thanks to the people who use this book. The successes and frustrations that you shared helped us understand your challenges. We have tried to respond to your needs.

We would also like to acknowledge many people for their essential role in developing this tool. Foremost, we would like to recognize the leadership and inspiration of Diane Trister Dodge, our president and founder. Thank you to Hilary Parrish Nelson and Laurie Taub for their tireless dedication to this product. We appreciate the thorough research work of Kelly Boyle, Jeffrey Capizzano, and Jennifer Mosley, who oversaw extensive field testing. Dr. Richard Lambert of the University of North Carolina deserves recognition for his evaluation and research work as does Dr. Renee Casbergue for drafting language and literacy items.

We would like to thank our content reviewers for the first draft. They provided insightful and valuable advice: Dr. Laura Berk, Illinois State University; Jenna Bilmes, MEd, author and early childhood consultant; Dr. Renee Casbergue, Louisiana State University; Dr. Juanita Copley, University of Houston; Dr. Rosalind Charlesworth, Weber State University; Dr. Cynthia F. DiCarlo, Louisiana State University; Dr. Linda Espinosa, University of Missouri-Columbia; Dr. Beth Graue, University of Wisconsin-Madison; Dr. Craig Hart, Brigham Young University; Candy Jones, MEd, author and early childhood consultant; Dr. Faith Lamb-Parker, Columbia University; Dr. Lea McGee, Ohio State University; Dr. Jennifer Park, early childhood consultant; Dr. Susan Sandall, University of Washington; Dr. Steve Sanders, University of South Florida; Dr. Anne Stonehouse, Monash University (Melbourne); and Monica Vacca, early childhood consultant.

Teachers at our field-test sites played an essential role by providing feedback about *Objectives for Development & Learning: Birth Through Kindergarten*. They helped us make it as applicable and reliable as possible. We thank the leaders and users at the following field-test sites: Chicago Public Schools: Karen Carradine, EdD, Director of Assessment and Accountability; Easter Seals Child Development Center of Silver Spring, MD: Marion A. Entwisle, Director; Easter Seals Child Development Center of Washington, DC: Kate Jordan-Downs, Director; Innovation Station Child Development Center/Bright Horizons Family Solutions: Greta M. Duncan, Training and Curriculum Specialist; Howard Area Community Center, Family Center and its staff: Cindy Coudek, Yan Ferguson, and Becky Rube.

The University Child Development Center of North Carolina had three participating sites: North Cross: Gina Jones, Director; University Park: Stella L. Fogle, Director; Highland Creek: Phillippe Locke, Director. Thanks to the Louisiana State University Child Development Lab Preschool and Michele D. Fillastre, Director. Community Action Head Start of Washington County, Oregon's Part Day, Pre-K Program had nine sites participating: Beaverton, Hiteon/Mill, Tigerton, Tigard-Tualatin, Hillsboro, Newhill, Hillsboro Child Development Center, Beaverton Child Development Center, Part Day/Full Year Early Head Start.

Thanks to Lori Balch, Education Coordinator, for her cooperation. Acelero Learning, Monmouth County, NJ had five participating sites: Head Start Freehold Center; Head Start Neptune Center; Head Start Redbank Center; Head Start Keyport Center; and Head Start Howell Center. Thanks to Rachel Bragin, Vice President, Education & Training, and Linda Foutch, Director of Curriculum and Instruction Development at Early Childhood Program, Tulsa Community Action Project, Tulsa, OK.

The Louisiana State University Child Development Laboratory Preschool, which is affiliated with the School of Human Ecology in the College of Agriculture, participated in the Phase 1 Instrument Review Pilot. We would like to thank the following people who were so very helpful in this pilot: Carol Aghayan, Rachel Crockett, Dr. Cyndi DiCarlo, Michele D. Fillastre, Undrea Kwain Guillory-Smith, Susanna Melikyan, and Lindsay Sanches.

We also extend a special thanks to the teachers and staff of the Women's League Child Development Center in Hartford, CT. Based on their feedback, we further refined our materials for the next instrument review. We especially appreciate the participation of the following teachers and staff at the Fairfax County Employees' Child Care Center: Shadawna Brown, Tonya Nolen, Shirley Palmer, Asria Rafiqzad, Ruth Stover, and Keo Zelaya. Their insightful feedback was invaluable to us during the Phase 2 Instrument Review.

We thank Dr. Dina Castro, Dr. Linda Espinosa, Antonia Lopez, Dr. Lisa Lopez, and Dr. Patton Tabors of our Latino Advisory Council and Dawn Terrill for their assistance in developing our dual-language learning component. We deeply appreciate the contributions of Dr. Espinosa and Dr. Lopez for their work on the Spanish literacy and language objectives. We are also grateful to the Oregon Child Development Coalition, Donalda Dodson, Executive Director, for piloting the Spanish materials of *Teaching Strategies GOLD*®. Diane Meisenheimer, Lead Education Specialist, and Clarissa Martinez, Education Specialist, oversaw the pilot test at two sites. For providing direct support to teachers during the pilot, deep thanks are extended to Berni Kirkpatrick, Education Manager for the Polk County site, and Patricia Alvarado, Education Coordinator for the Washington County site.

The creation of *Teaching Strategies GOLD*® was an ambitious undertaking that would not have been possible without a unified effort. We recognize the entire staff of Teaching Strategies who used their relentless energy to make this product the best for our users. A special thank you to Margot Ziperman, Production Manager, and our Creative Services team, who were so focused on designing a beautiful and engaging product. We also thank Rachel Friedlander Tickner for her detailed work on the references.

Contents

Foreword

It gives me great pleasure to introduce *Teaching Strategies GOLD*®, our innovative assessment system for children birth through kindergarten. Developing this system has been a long and exciting journey with many contributors who passionately share our belief that ongoing, authentic, observational assessment can be part of meaningful everyday experiences in the classroom and that it supports effective teaching.

We began by identifying the objectives that are most predictive of future school success and that are linked to state early learning standards. Now teachers can be assured that they are focusing on the objectives that are most important to children's development and learning, and they can read summaries of the extensive research findings that explain each objective. This new assessment system, available online and in print, can be used with any developmentally appropriate curriculum.

There are many special aspects of *Teaching Strategies GOLD*®:

- It is a seamless system that spans birth through kindergarten, so teachers do not have to struggle with the question of when to change from a system for infants, toddlers, and twos to a system for preschool children. Information about a child can be passed to the child's next teachers as he or she moves from an infant room all the way through the kindergarten classroom.

- There are two objectives for English language acquisition, and it offers guidance on assessing children who do not speak English.

- It includes Spanish language and literacy objectives for children whose home language is Spanish. This enables teachers to assess and support the children's home language and literacy development while promoting learning in all domains.

- Objectives address all areas of development (social–emotional, physical, language, and cognitive) as well as content learning in literacy, mathematics, science and technology, social studies, and the arts.

- The color-coded progression for each objective helps teachers see the full range of development and learning at once, enabling them to work with any child, at whatever level, including children with disabilities.

- For each objective, a list of teaching strategies shows teachers how to help children make progress.

- A variety of purposeful tools help teachers gather assessment data in quick and meaningful ways.

- *Assessment Opportunity Cards*™ support integrated, play-based experiences that enable teachers to focus their observations more accurately for particular literacy and numeracy objectives.

- Model portfolios enable teachers to establish interrater reliability, so teachers know they are using the assessment system accurately.

This is not our first assessment venture. Since I founded Teaching Strategies in 1988, we have recognized that, to plan instruction that supports the learning and development of every child successfully, teachers need a system of ongoing assessment that helps them gather important information about each child. While *Teaching Strategies GOLD*® is an innovative assessment system, several aspects are consistent with our previous work:

Authentic, observation-based assessment–The best way to capture what children know and can do is by observing them in the context of their everyday experiences and by documenting how these observations relate to objectives. The skills that many teachers have already gained are also used with *Teaching Strategies GOLD*®.

Assessment as an ongoing cycle–Teachers 1) observe and collect facts; 2) analyze the documentation they have collected and then respond by scaffolding children's learning and planning instruction; 3) evaluate each child's progress; and 4) summarize, plan for, and communicate children's progress to families and others.

A progression of development and learning–Our new assessment system continues to explain the typical sequence in which children's knowledge, behaviors, and skills advance.

The role of objectives–Objectives for development and learning are the starting point for assessment, as they have always been. Teachers use them to focus their observations, think about what they learn, and respond appropriately.

Progress checkpoints–Although assessment is ongoing and teachers use what they learn each day, teachers pause three (or four) times a year to review what they have learned and to summarize a child's skills and behaviors at those points in time.

The teacher is the most important factor in how children experience the care and education they receive in early childhood programs. Your knowledge of each child and your ability to support each child's optimal development and learning helps you achieve positive outcomes for all of the children in your program. Every day in the classroom, in all of your interactions with children, you have opportunities to address the 38 objectives in the *Teaching Strategies GOLD*® assessment system and to help children become enthusiastic, engaged, and successful learners. Every day, you make hundreds of decisions about what to teach, when to teach it, what instructional strategies to use, the materials that will interest and appropriately challenge children, and how to respond to the individual strengths and needs of each child.

Objectives for Development & Learning: Birth Through Kindergarten is the foundation of *Teaching Strategies GOLD*®. It shows the learning progressions in each developmental area from birth through kindergarten. It is your essential resource to use with any developmentally appropriate curriculum. The assessment system enables you to follow each child's development and learning and to use what you learn to ensure that every child does progress. I feel confident that the use of this new assessment system will go far in helping all early childhood educators to support children's learning and development and to build a foundation for each child's success in school and in life.

Diane Trister Dodge
Founder and President
Teaching Strategies, LLC

Introduction

Teaching Strategies GOLD® is an authentic, observational assessment system for children from birth through kindergarten. It is designed to help you get to know children well—what they know and can do, and their strengths, needs, and interests. With this information, you can guide children's learning by planning engaging experiences that are responsive to individual and group needs.

The *Teaching Strategies GOLD®* assessment system blends ongoing, authentic, observational assessment for all areas of development and learning with intentional, focused, performance-assessment tasks for selected predictors of school success in the areas of literacy and numeracy. This seamless system for children birth through kindergarten is designed for use as part of meaningful everyday experiences in the classroom or program setting. It is inclusive of children with disabilities and children who demonstrate competencies beyond typical developmental expectations. It can also be used to assess the knowledge, skills, and behaviors of children who are English-language or dual-language learners. *Teaching Strategies GOLD®* recognizes that young children's development is uneven, that it changes rapidly, and that development and learning are interrelated and overlapping. The assessment system may be used with **any** developmentally appropriate curriculum; it is not linked exclusively to a particular curriculum.

The **primary purposes** of the *Teaching Strategies GOLD®* assessment system are to help teachers

- observe and document children's development and learning over time
- support, guide, and inform planning and instruction
- identify children who might benefit from special help, screening, or further evaluation
- report and communicate with family members and others

The **secondary purposes** are to help teachers

- collect and gather child outcome information as one part of a larger accountability system.
- provide reports to administrators to guide program planning and professional development opportunities.

Teaching Strategies GOLD® is not designed as a screening or diagnostic tool, a readiness or achievement test, or a teacher- or program-evaluation tool. For accountability purposes, the information obtained should be used as just one part of a larger system of data collection for decision making.

The following pages provide an overview of *Teaching Strategies GOLD®* assessment system, descriptions of each component of the assessment system, and a discussion of how to use the components of *Teaching Strategies GOLD®* during the assessment cycle.

Overview of *Teaching Strategies GOLD®* Assessment System

When you implement an assessment system, you follow a systematic process, or cycle. Think of the steps of the *Teaching Strategies GOLD®* assessment cycle as a way to find answers to these questions:

- What does this child know, and what is he or she able to do?

- How does this relate to important objectives for development and learning? How do I scaffold this child's learning?

- Is this child making progress? How do this child's skills and behaviors compare to those of most children in his or her age-group?

- How can I summarize what I know about this child and use it to plan and communicate with others?

These questions are the focus of each part of the *Teaching Strategies GOLD®* assessment cycle. Each part of the cycle requires teachers to undertake a different task:

1. **Observe and collect facts** through observation and documentation.

2. **Analyze and respond** to children by considering their skills in relation to specific objectives and then scaffolding their learning.

3. **Evaluate** by comparing a child's skills and behaviors to research-based indicators of learning and development.

4. **Summarize, plan, and communicate**, making use of the collected information to plan experiences and share with others.

Teaching Strategies GOLD® includes four components, or tools, to use during the assessment cycle:

- *Objectives for Development & Learning: Birth Through Kindergarten*

- *Child Assessment Portfolio*

- *Assessment Opportunity Cards™* (optional)

- *On-the-Spot Observation Recording Tool* (optional)

Objectives for Development & Learning: Birth Through Kindergarten is the background, or reference, document that you use to learn about the related research and typical progression of development and learning for each objective, the expectations for each age-group, and examples of strategies that promote learning. The *Child Assessment Portfolio* is used to record and document assessment information throughout a year. *Assessment Opportunity Cards™* offer 10 carefully selected, developmentally appropriate activities that can be integrated into everyday classroom experiences to help you focus your observations and collect information related to particular objectives. The *On-the-Spot Observation Recording Tool* is a practical checklist that captures information about children quickly, thereby streamlining the documentation process.

The Components of *Teaching Strategies GOLD*®

Objectives for Development & Learning

Birth Through Kindergarten

Child development and learning is complex. It would be overwhelming to try to measure every skill and behavior that children demonstrate in these early years. The *Teaching Strategies GOLD*® assessment system measures the knowledge, skills, and behaviors that are most predictive of school success. In addition, *Teaching Strategies GOLD*® helps you focus on competencies valued in state early learning standards and standards of professional organizations. The tool has 38 objectives, including 2 objectives related to English language acquisition.

Thirty-six **objectives** are organized into nine **areas of development and learning.** The first four are major areas of child development and learning:

- Social–Emotional
- Physical
- Language
- Cognitive

The content learning that is usually identified in early learning standards are organized in the following five areas:

- Literacy
- Mathematics
- Science and Technology
- Social Studies
- The Arts

The objectives in a tenth area, English Language Acquisition, help you follow a child's progress in acquiring receptive and expressive skills in English.

Many of the objectives include **dimensions** that guide teachers' thinking about various aspects of an objective. For example, dimensions of the Objective 1, "Regulates own emotions and behaviors" include "Manages feelings," "Follows limits and expectations," and "Takes care of one's own needs appropriately."

A list of the objectives and dimensions can be found on pages xxx–xxxi.

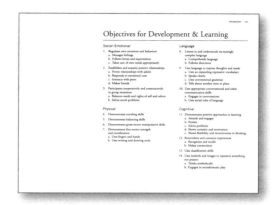

A further breakdown of the large-muscle physical objectives can be found on pages 203–206. Sometimes teachers have questions or concerns about a child's physical development. You may be curious about the way a child walks or runs or how a child is trying to kick a ball. A child might seem to struggle, so you want to know how to support development appropriately, understand the usual sequence of development, and find out what teaching strategies will be most effective. In such instances, it is helpful to examine the development of gross-motor skills in more detail. These optional dimensions for Objectives 4–6 show the sequence of development for walking, running, galloping and skipping, jumping, hopping, throwing, catching, and kicking.

Objectives for Development & Learning: Birth Through Kindergarten is based on an extensive review of the most current research and professional literature in the field of early childhood education. This resource includes several sections:

The **overview of each area of development and learning** explains the research about why the area is important. The objectives included in the area are listed in a shaded box.

The **research foundation** page for each objective summarizes the important research findings related to the objective. It provides a broad picture of development and learning from birth through kindergarten, and it explains what is being measured and why. Cultural and linguistic considerations, as well as considerations for children with disabilities, are included in this foundation.

Progressions of development and learning include indicators and examples based on standard developmental and learning expectations for various age-groups and for classes or grades.

The rating scale (numbers above each box) is used to assign a value to the child's level on a particular progression. The "in-between" boxes allow for more steps in the progression, so teachers can indicate that children's skills are emerging in this area but not yet solid. These in-between ratings also enable you to indicate that a child needs adult support (verbal, physical, or visual) to accomplish the indicator.

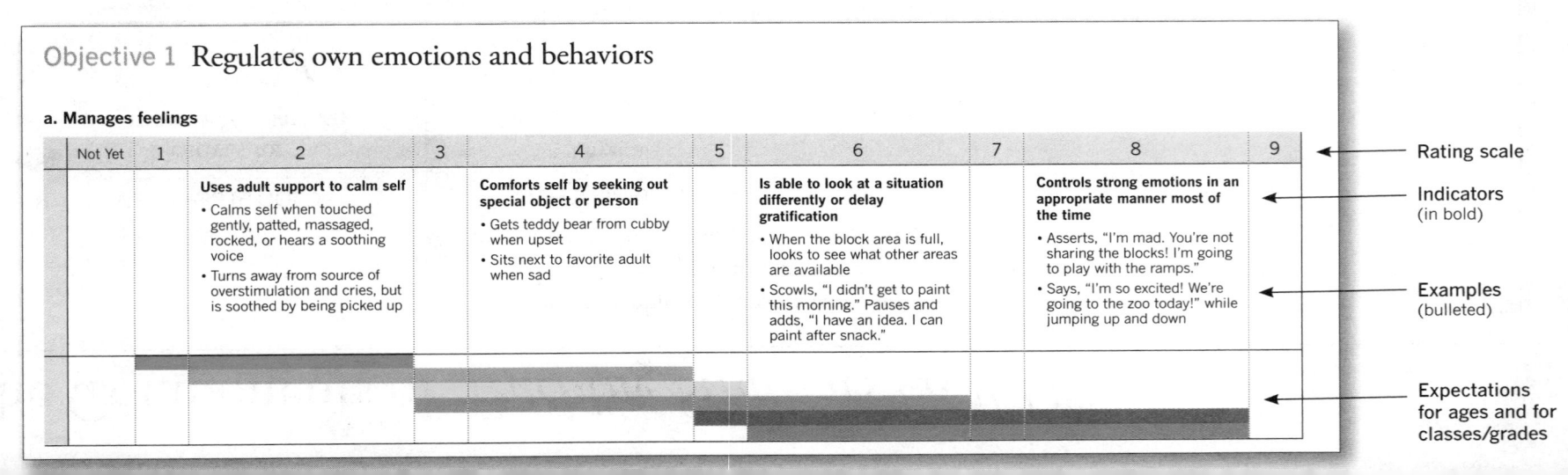

Colors are used to indicate the age or class/grade ranges for these expectations. Red, orange, and yellow code each year of life for the first 3 years. Green, blue, and purple code classes/grades for the next 3 years.

Birth to 1 year

1 to 2 years

2 to 3 years

Preschool 3 class

Pre-K 4 class

Kindergarten

Notice that some colored bands of a progression are longer or shorter than others. Some bands begin in the "Not Yet" category. While there is a typical progression for each objective, it is not rigid; development and learning are uneven, overlapping, and interrelated. Sometimes a skill does not begin to develop until a child is 2 years old, and another skill may not emerge until age 3 or 4. For example, the colored bands might show you at a glance that it is typical for children to enter the pre-K year with a particular skill emerging at level 5 and then for the children to progress to level 8 by the end of the year if they are given appropriate support and experiences.

Finally, the **strategies** page for each objective offers ways to promote development and learning in relation to the objective.

Child Assessment Portfolio

You collect and store documentation and evidence (e.g., samples of work, audio and video clips, photographs, and observation notes) that the child has demonstrated particular behaviors related to the objectives. Information for reports is recorded in the *Child Assessment Portfolio* and can be included with a larger portfolio of children's work. You use one *Child Assessment Portfolio* for each child. This can become part of the child's record that is passed along to next year's teacher.

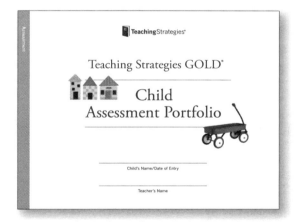

The pages mirror the progressions in *Objectives for Development & Learning*. The examples are not included in the *Child Assessment Portfolio*. Mark the boxes to indicate a child's level at three or four checkpoints during the year.

Use the *Child Assessment Portfolio Summary Form* to summarize ratings at the objective level, in order to share that information with administrators.

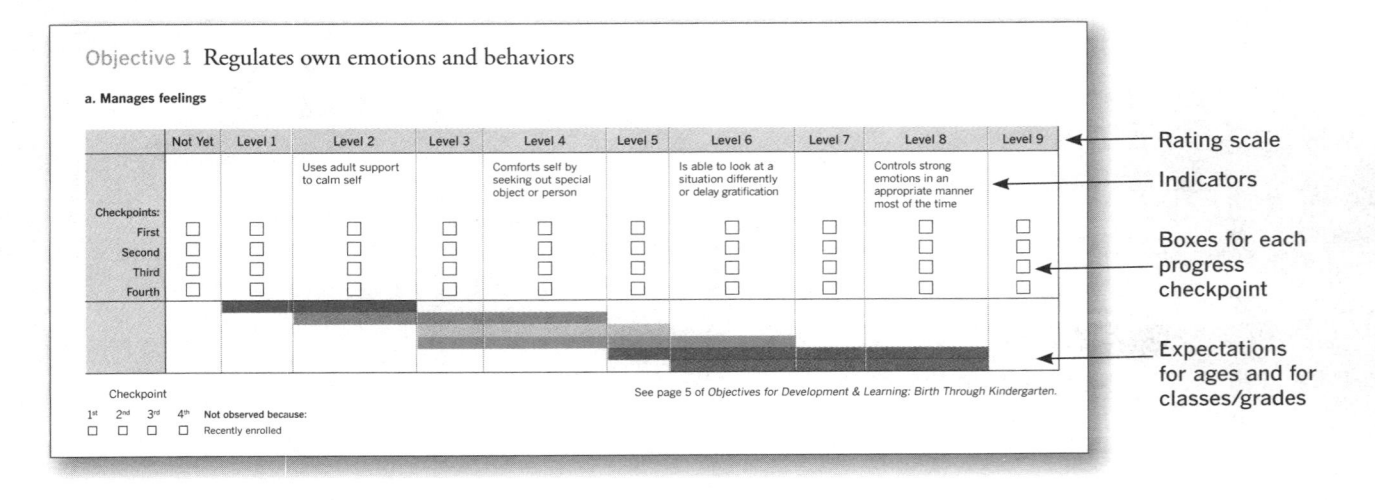

On-the-Spot Observation Recording Tool

The *On-the-Spot Observation Recording Tool* is a checklist that enables you to collect information quickly, either for one child or a group of children. It is designed to streamline the overall process of recording information about physical development, literacy, and mathematics. Use this tool when you are involved with children in the classroom or outside and need to note a date when a behavior or skill was observed.

Use it this way:

1. Focus your observations on particular objectives.

2. Turn to the appropriate objectives in the tool and write the date or a check mark under the indicator that best describes the child's skills and behaviors.

3. At progress checkpoints, refer to both the *On-the-Spot Observation Recording Tool* and your other forms of documentation before making your final ratings.

Assessment Opportunity Cards™

Teaching Strategies GOLD® supports *authentic assessment.* You observe and document children's learning as they use their skills during meaningful experiences. Sometimes it is more effective and efficient to plan a small-group or individual experience to capture the information you need. For example, observation notes alone might not be an accurate way to determine which letters of the alphabet a child knows. It may also be very difficult to capture children's strengths in phonological awareness as they play. For some objectives, you need additional chances to conduct focused observations. Conducting a focused observation during a learning experience planned for that purpose is called *performance assessment.*

The 10 *Assessment Opportunity Cards™* explain how to structure additional opportunities for children to demonstrate what they know and can do in relation to particular literacy and numeracy objectives. These experiences for preschool and kindergarten children are integrated into everyday classroom activities. Because these activities are not removed from the children's general classroom experience, they are authentic. Teachers should scaffold children's learning during these activities, not simply observe without interacting as necessary.

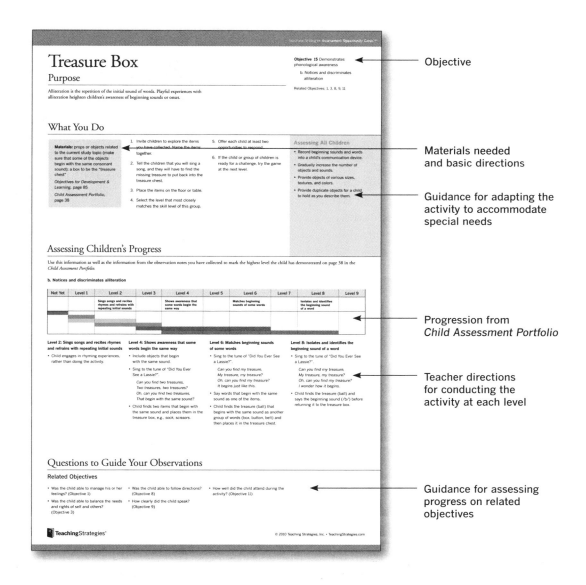

- Objective
- Materials needed and basic directions
- Guidance for adapting the activity to accommodate special needs
- Progression from *Child Assessment Portfolio*
- Teacher directions for conducting the activity at each level
- Guidance for assessing progress on related objectives

Using *Teaching Strategies GOLD®* to Assess Children With Disabilities

The assessment process should be the same for all children. Using the same widely held developmental and learning expectations for all children helps teachers encourage every child to reach his or her full potential. In addition, such an assessment process enables teachers to identify learning and developmental lags and gaps in order to provide appropriate interventions and learning experiences.

The *Teaching Strategies GOLD®* assessment system illustrates the predictable sequence of development and learning of most young children. To ensure that all children—including those with disabilities—are making progress, teachers recognize the many emergent skills that precede the development of typical skills from birth through the end of kindergarten. *Objectives for Development & Learning* shows wide ranges of progressive skills and behaviors for the objectives. The progressions serve as a guide to determine how all children are progressing in nine areas of development and learning, while acknowledging that children show what they know in different ways. The progressions emphasize to teachers that all children have knowledge, skills, and behaviors upon which to build.

Teaching Strategies GOLD® helps you identify children who may be struggling in some areas of development and learning. In general, the developmental rates of children with disabilities tend to be more unpredictable than the rates of children without disabilities. Children demonstrate their abilities in various ways as well. You can identify supportive strategies, such as offering small-group work or other materials, to make it easier for children to participate and make progress through daily experiences.

Using *Teaching Strategies GOLD®* to assess children with disabilities provides significant benefits for a number of reasons:

- It includes the important indicators for appropriate assessment as recommended by the Division for Early Childhood (DEC) of the Council for Exceptional Children and the National Association for the Education of Young Children (NAEYC). It has all of the attributes of high-quality assessment described by DEC, i.e., it is used for specified purposes, is authentic; and has good psychometric qualities.

- It is comprehensive. For the purpose of planning instruction, information is gathered across all areas of development and learning.

- It involves families in the assessment process.

- It identifies a child's skills and abilities and minimizes the impact of the disability on the results.

- It emphasizes what a child can do. Because incremental rates of progress are documented within a broad range of development and learning tasks, it guides teachers to understand next steps in development.

- It is a strengths-based tool. A child can demonstrate skills and behaviors within the various levels of each objective and its dimensions. It provides an ongoing record of what a child can do at every checkpoint.

- It uses universal language that reflects an understanding that children show what they know in various ways. Discrete skills are replaced by functional objectives.

Because the *Teaching Strategies GOLD*® assessment system provides a picture of predictable development over more than 6 years, children whose skills and abilities are emerging and developing at an uneven or less-predictable rate are able to show progress. When using the *Objectives for Development & Learning* to assess children with disabilities, consider the intent of each objective as it applies to individual children. Observe how each child progresses toward meeting the objective while using individualized modifications, assistive devices, or adult supports as necessary. For example, a child with a physical impairment might use a walker or a wheelchair to move around the classroom. The intent of Objective 4, "Demonstrates traveling skills," is that the child is able to move or propel him- or herself to get where he or she wants to go. Any means that a child uses (e.g., adaptive equipment, scooting, or crawling) meets the intent of the objective. Children with significant disabilities may appear to stay on a single level for a long time. The use of a supplemental assessment instrument may help the child's team identify incremental changes that are taking place. For example, a child with a physical disability may need a more specific checklist for gross-motor development so you are better able to intervene and show progress. On all of the other objectives, the child may be developing typically, so collecting the same documentation as you would for other children may be fine. The use of supplemental tools to address specific questions and concerns can provide additional information for planning instruction and monitoring progress. Gathering data from multiple sources at different points in time gives a better picture of each child's development and learning.

Teaching Strategies GOLD® can be used to support tiered models of supportive instruction and individualize intervention by identifying a child's strengths in relation to classmates. You can design learning experiences and group children in ways that support skill building and practice. For some children, *Teaching Strategies GOLD*® can help identify areas of strength and need so that collaborative teams of educators, professionals, and family members can design more explicit interventions to assist with skill attainment and expansion.

You can use *Objectives for Development & Learning* to guide the development of Individualized Education Program (IEP) goals for children. The objectives are not IEP goals, themselves, but they can be used to identify the skills that a child needs to strengthen in order to meet IEP goals. IEP goals are often similar to the objectives in that they identify interrelated and progressive skills that help a child participate and progress in the general curriculum.

Assessing English- and Dual-Language Learners

English- and dual-language learners are children who are developing the ability to understand and speak more than one language. Some children begin learning English for the first time when they enroll in preschool, while others have been introduced to English from an early age by family members. To assess the knowledge and development of English- and dual-language learners accurately, it is important first to determine the primary language(s) of the children.

The "Home Language Survey" that follows is designed to help teachers gather and record useful information about the language(s) children have been exposed to in the home environment and the language(s) children use at home and at school. This information assists teachers in planning ways to support children's language and literacy acquisition and in basing instruction on children's strengths and needs. Teachers discuss the questions with parents or other family members (with the assistance of interpreters if necessary), and they determine the answers to the questions together. The survey should *not* be completed by teachers without input from parents or other family members.

The data gathered with this "Home Language Survey" should not be used to label children or identify them for special services. It should be used to help the teacher determine how to assess children most accurately and support their development and learning. The "Home Language Survey" is a resource of the *Teaching Strategies GOLD*® assessment system, not a requirement. If parents do not wish to provide this information or complete the survey with you, their wishes should be respected.

Respond to each question by using the scale ranging from "only English" to "only home language." Add the numbers you circled and put the sum in the space provided. Then divide this sum by the number of questions you were able to answer, not counting any questions for which you circled "N/A." The value you obtain will help you determine whether to use the objectives for English language acquisition. If the value is 2 or greater and the child is in a preschool 3, pre-K 4, or kindergarten class, assess this child's receptive and expressive language skills by using Objective 37, "Demonstrates progress in listening to and understanding English," and Objective 38, "Demonstrates progress in speaking English." If the value is less than 2, English can be considered the child's primary language, and it is not necessary to use Objectives 37 and 38.

The "Home Language Survey" may provide information that will assist you in planning and individualizing learning experiences for infants, toddlers, and 2-year-olds. However, Objectives 37 and 38 are only used for English- and dual-language learners in preschool 3, pre-K 4, and kindergarten classrooms. This is because preschool and older children are in the process of learning English after already establishing a beginning foundation in their family languages.

For all of the objectives other than those for language and literacy, it is ideal to assess children's skills by documenting their knowledge and skills when they respond in their *preferred languages*, the languages they choose at particular times to show what they know and can do. For example, if a child can count to ten in Spanish and counts five objects accurately, using one number name for each object, then he or she is considered as being at level 4 of Objective 20a, "Counts."

While it is preferable to assess in a child's home language, it is not always possible because of limited program resources and the multitude of languages spoken the classroom. When you do not speak the child's home language, it is even more important to partner with family members and other trained volunteers who speak the child's language to gather information. While you are still responsible for collecting assessment information, the observations shared by those who speak the child's language can be invaluable in helping you assess the child's development and learning accurately.

In addition, you can gather data about many objectives by observing, even if you do not speak the child's home language. These objectives are considered *language-free* objectives because they do not require children to comprehend or produce English to demonstrate what they know or can do. For example, you may gather information related to Objective 1b, "Follows limits and expectations," when a child begins cleaning up in response to a musical cue. During cleanup, you could also observe to see whether the child sustains attention to a task over time (Objective 11a, "Attends and engages").

Some of the math objectives are also language free. When a child creates or extends a simple repeating pattern, you can collect information related to Objective 23, "Demonstrates knowledge of patterns." Review the objectives and dimensions to determine those for which you can gather data without speaking the child's language. This will also help you identify the *language-dependent* objectives for which you need assistance from family members or trained volunteers.

The language objectives (8–10) and literacy objectives (15–19) are measured from an English-language perspective. For example, is the child able to understand and follow directions in English? Does the child recognize letters of the alphabet when they are named in English? For children whose home language is Spanish, a Spanish-language version of these objectives is presented on pages 207–219 to help teachers track language and literacy development in Spanish. These objectives are very similar to the English version of these language and literacy objectives, but adaptations were made to reflect patterns of development unique to Spanish language and literacy.

Language and literacy objectives are included only for Spanish and English. Data about children's use of languages other than English and Spanish must therefore be gathered informally if its collection is a program requirement.

Home Language Survey[*]

☐ Check here if the child's parents or legal guardians decline to provide information for this survey.

A. What language do family members use when speaking to the child in the home?

	1	2	3	4	5
	only English	mostly English but sometimes home language	both equally	mostly home language but some English	only home language (not English)

(Write in home language: _____)

B. What language does the child use when speaking to family members in the home?

N/A	1	2	3	4	5
Not applicable	only English	mostly English but sometimes home language	both equally	mostly home language but some English	only home language (not English)

C. What language does the child use when speaking to other children in the classroom?

N/A	1	2	3	4	5
Not applicable	only English	mostly English but sometimes home language	both equally	mostly home language but some English	only home language (not English)

D. What language does the child use when speaking to teachers?

N/A	1	2	3	4	5
Not applicable	only English	mostly English but sometimes home language	both equally	mostly home language but some English	only home language (not English)

Sum of circled numbers	Number of questions answered			
_____	/	_____	=	_____

If this value is 2 or greater and the child is in a preschool 3, pre-K 4, or kindergarten class, assess the child by using Objectives 37 and 38.

[*]These research reports helped guide our thinking in the development of the "Home Language Survey."

Aikens, N. L., Caspe, M. S., Sprachman, S., López, M. L., & Atkins-Burnett, S. M. (June 2008). *Paper Symposium: Development of a language routing protocol for determining bilingual Spanish–English speaking children's language of assessment*. Biennial Head Start Research Conference. Washington, DC.

Puma, M., Bell, S., Cook, R., Heid, C., López, M. L., et al. (2005). *Head Start impact study: First year findings*. Washington, DC: U.S. Department of Health and Human Services, Administration for Children and Families.

Gutiérrez-Clellen, V. F., & Kreiter, J. (2003). Understanding child bilingual acquisition using parent and teacher reports. *Applied Psycholinguistics, 24*(2), 267–88.

Following an Assessment Cycle

Assessment is a continuous cycle of observing and collecting facts; analyzing and responding; evaluating; and summarizing, planning, and communicating to others. This section helps you understand how to take each step of the cycle and to link curriculum and assessment seamlessly to support children's development and learning.

Step 1: Observe and Collect Facts

The first step in the assessment process is to learn about the children you teach: what they know and can do in relation to each of the objectives. Ongoing observation is an essential part of connecting assessment and curriculum. In order to respond to children appropriately, use *Objectives for Development & Learning: Birth Through Kindergarten* to focus your observations on particular objectives and to understand the development and learning progressions that children typically follow.

To help you remember and use what you learn from your observations, you need a systematic way to document the information. In addition to your observation notes, you can collect concrete evidence of what children are able to do by maintaining portfolios that include samples of their work over time.

Setting Up a System

Before you begin to observe and collect facts about children's learning, take the time to set up a system for taking notes and organizing your documentation on each child. That way you can avoid having to organize a large collection of unsorted observation notes and other forms of documentation all at once.

Think about what you need to store and how you will store it. Observation notes may be stored in each child's *Child Assessment Portfolio,* a notebook, or file folders labeled with the children's names. Samples of children's work may be stored in larger envelopes, pizza boxes, or cardboard magazine holders.

Set up a system to name and organize digital photos of children as well as audio and video clips. Decide how you will name and store the files you can access them easily.

Observing and Documenting Children's Learning

Observation is the basis of all good teaching and the foundation of any assessment system. To learn about a child, you look and listen objectively to what he or she does and says (Jablon, Dombro, & Dichtelmiller, 2007). For some objectives, seeing a child perform a skill once is sufficient to make an informed decision. Other objectives need more evidence and documentation. **There is no set number of observations or amount of documentation that must be collected in relation to each objective.**

Documentation can take many forms:

- Observation notes—These are short, objective, factual notes about what you hear and see. Include direct quotations of language and descriptions of actions, gestures, facial expressions, and creations.

- Photographs—Take pictures of children's constructions, artwork, or examples of how they are demonstrating knowledge and skills related to an objective. Label each photo with the date and a brief note that explains the context In which it was taken.

- Video and audio clips—Keep clips short. Capture just enough information to show an example of what the child knows and can do. Lengthy clips are difficult to store and locate.

- Samples of children's work—Don't save everything! Select the writing and art samples that relate best to particular objectives.

- Diagrams or sketches—In the child's portfolio, include sketches of his or her block structures or other constructions.

- Checklists, participation lists, and frequency counts—Use procedures to count behaviors and skills in order to capture information quickly. For example, keep records of which interest areas a child visited and the letters a child recognized. A simple checklist to mark skills can also be included as part of the documentation of children's learning. The *On-the-Spot Observation Recording Tool* is such a checklist.

Two excellent sources for learning more about observation and documentation are *The Power of Observation* (Jablon, Dombro, & Dichtelmiller, 2007) and *Observation: The Key to Responsive Teaching* (Stetson, Jablon, & Dombro, 2009).

Systems for Taking Notes

Keep your documentation simple. If your notes are too elaborate, you will have to take valuable time away from interacting with children. You don't want to feel so burdened that observation becomes a chore. Set up simple systems to make collecting observation notes as convenient as possible. Here are some ideas that have worked for other teachers.

Ideas for Recording Observation Notes

- Use mailing labels or sticky notes to record your observations. At the beginning of the day, place on a clipboard three or four notes or labels with the names of three or four children whom you wish to observe. Keep the clipboard handy.

- Keep sticky notes in your pocket or in each interest area. Keep a simple folder in each interest area. Draw a grid on the folder with as many squares as there are children in your class. Write a child's name in each square and store your notes about the child there until you want to transfer them in the child's portfolio.

- Use a digital pen. Many digital pens have voice recorders that enable you to interact with a child while the pen records voices.

- Develop your own system of shorthand so you can write quickly. Stick to brief notes, use short phrases, and abbreviate whenever possible. You can underline particular words to indicate emphasis.

You can store your observation notes in the *Child Assessment Portfolio* near a related objective or you may choose to have a separate notebook or file for your notes.

Be assured that you do not have to write an observation note on every child every day. That would be unrealistic. Try to set a goal of writing three or four brief notes a day. As a reminder to yourself, write the names of the children you plan to observe on your weekly plan so no child is overlooked. Remember that you don't need to record everything that happens and every word a child says.

Using *Assessment Opportunity Cards*™ for Focused Observations

Your ongoing observations should provide you with information about every objective. For some objectives, you may find it more difficult to capture information for all children. It may be more efficient to plan a learning activity during which you can collect information efficiently and accurately. For example, while you may be able to observe some of children's use of letters as they play, it may difficult to document more specifically all that a particular child knows about letters. Playing a game or engaging in an activity about letters will help you focus your observation and document what you see. Here are some general guidelines to follow:

- Read the *Assessment Opportunity Card*® first.

- Gather the necessary materials.

- Determine which children you want to collect additional information about during the activity. Not all children need to participate in each activity at each checkpoint.

- Read through the levels and determine a good starting point for the child or children with whom you are working.

- Follow the general procedures in the "What You Do" section.

- Select and follow the adaptation of the activity that most closely matches the child's skill level.

- If the child demonstrates abilities at a given level, offer a more challenging experience by adapting the activity for the next level. If the child is not successful at a given level, try the activity at a less challenging level.

The *Assessment Opportunity Cards*™ should be used flexibly. At the first progress checkpoint, if you have determined that a child is at level 4 on a given objective, you do not need to go back to the activity described at level 2.

While the prompts have been standardized to help you assess children more reliably, you have choices about the types of materials or examples you use. For example, if your class has been studying clothes, you might have a child identify the first sound of clothing words (e.g., sock, button, belt, hat, or pants) during the "Treasure Box" game.

Although the *Assessment Opportunity Cards™* explain primarily literacy and numeracy experiences, you will also be able to observe skills and behaviors related to objectives in other areas of development and learning. The section "Questions to Guide Your Observations" points you to those related objectives and helps you gather assessment information.

Step 2: Analyze and Respond

The next stage in the assessment cycle involves organizing your documentation and making informed judgments about what the information tells you about a child's progress toward each of the objectives. As you observe children, ask yourself, "What does their behavior mean?" Often you will respond appropriately in the moment. You will use your knowledge and understanding of the progressions in *Observing Development & Learning: Birth Through Kindergarten* to provide just the right strategy, material, or support to scaffold the child's learning.

At other times you will step back and reflect on the documentation you have collected. Many teachers find it useful to record the objective numbers directly on their observation notes or samples of work. That way, you can quickly see the related objectives when you are ready to evaluate a child's progress.

A child's learning and development is very integrated. When you analyze your documentation, keep in mind that one rich observation note can relate to several different objectives.

Step 3: Evaluate

Evaluating children's progress means deciding what level each child has reached in terms of the objectives. To evaluate, you first need to gather and think about all of the documentation you have collected. Then, using the *Objectives for Development & Learning: Birth Through Kindergarten* and the *Child Assessment Portfolio*, you can begin evaluating each child's progress.

How to Use the *Child Assessment Portfolio*

The *Child Assessment Portfolio* is the place to record and preserve important information about the child's progress. This is your record-keeping tool for each child.

With an ongoing assessment system, you are continually watching, observing, and documenting. At certain times, you pause, reflect, and take a snapshot of how a child is progressing in relation to the objectives and dimensions. These points in time are called **progress checkpoints**. Here's what to do at each progress checkpoint:

1. Gather and review all of the documentation you have collected.

2. Gather your copy of *Objectives for Development & Learning* and the child's *Child Assessment Portfolio*.

3. Read the objective and its dimension(s), if any.

4. Think about and review the documentation you collected in relation to each objective.

5. **Colored bands** on the form show reasonable expectations for development and learning

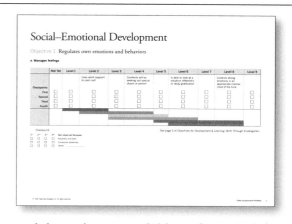

and show where most children of a particular age-group or class/grade are likely to be at the beginning and end of a program year. In the first 3 years, you will want to carefully adjust your expectations according to the child's age. In the next 3 years, there are more standard expectations for each year in group programs. A teacher with a preschool class designed for 3-year-olds would first focus on the green indicators and consider children's skills, knowledge, and behaviors in comparison to those expectations. This would be so even if a few of the children in the group are a few months shy of age 3 in September or turning 4 during the program year. Then, if those indicators do not describe a particular child's skills, knowledge, and behaviors, the teacher would look to the indicators of other colored bands for guidance. A teacher with a pre-K 4 class designed for 4- to 5-year-olds would first focus on the blue indicators. A kindergarten teacher would instruct and evaluate with the purple band in mind, whether the children are 4, 5, or 6 years old.

6. For each objective and dimension, begin by focusing on the indicator(s) (at levels 2, 4, 6, or 8) above the colored band that matches the child's age or class/grade. For example, for a pre-K 4 child (whether 3, 4, or 5 years old), begin with the indicator(s) above the blue band. Sometimes the colored band will span one indicator and an "in-between" level. Sometimes the band will span two or three indicators. Those indicators are your starting point for deciding which one best describes the child's knowledge, skill, or behavior.

7. To make sure you are selecting the correct level, read the indicators to the right and left of your starting point. Choose the indicator that most closely matches the child's skills and behaviors. Indicators often include multiple expectations (separated by semicolons). In order to rate a child's skills as being at a particular level, the child must demonstrate skills related to all elements of the indicator. Also consider whether the child can best be described as being at an "in-between" level.

8. A colored band in the "Not Yet" column shows that a child of that age or class/grade is not yet expected to demonstrate a particular skill or behavior. The "Not Yet" level might also be useful when you evaluate information about a child with a disability or developmental delay who is not yet demonstrating a skill or behavior that is expected of a child who is developing typically.

9. Levels 1, 3, 5, and 7 should be used to indicate that a skill or behavior is just beginning, or emerging. The child may not be demonstrating the indicator consistently or regularly, or the

child may needs a certain amount of adult support. This support may be verbal, physical, or visual.

10. Use Level 9 for the child whose knowledge, skills, and behavior exceed expectations for the end of kindergarten and go beyond the scope of the progression for a given objective.

11. Use "Not Observed" only on rare occasions, such as when the child has been in the program for only a few weeks or has had significant absences during the checkpoint period.

12. Place a mark (a check or an X) in the box that most accurately describes this child's level.

The levels are used for the social–emotional, physical, language, cognitive, literacy, and mathematics objectives as well as the English language acquisition objectives. Colored bands on the form illustrate reasonable expectations for development and learning and show where most children of a particular age-group or class/grade are likely to be at the beginning and end of a program year. The colored bands are not used for the English language acquisition objectives.

For the objectives in science and technology, social studies, and the arts, record highlights from your observations that provide examples of a child's learning in these areas. You may choose to use only narrative notes to document what children know and can do in these areas, especially if your program wants you to document evidence related to these objectives in some way. You have the option of checking "No evidence yet," "Emerging," or "Meets program expectations" if you need to make a rating on these objectives.

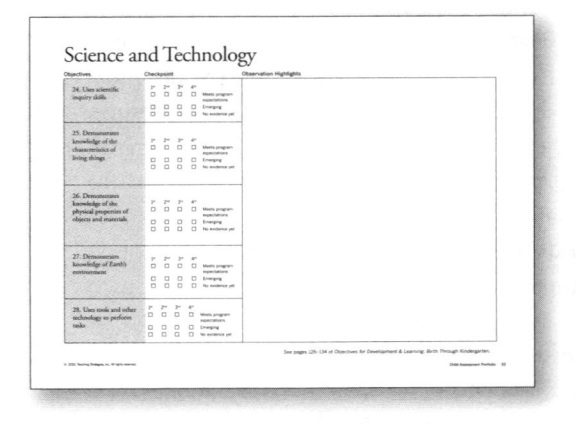

The system can be used to determine how a child's knowledge, skills, and behaviors align with standard expectations at given points in time. It can also be used over time to determine whether the child has made significant progress over the course of one or several years. As a child transitions to another class or setting, his or her *Portfolio* can be passed along to the next teacher.

Step 4: Summarize, Plan, and Communicate

The final step of the assessment cycle is one of the most important steps, but it is often neglected. It involves summarizing what you know, basing plans for individual children and the group as whole on that knowledge, and communicating with those outside your classroom to explain what children are learning. At this point, you link curriculum and assessment directly.

Plan

You make many decisions each day as you observe children and respond in appropriate ways. New questions will arise as you reflect on what you learn about a child and consider how best to provide support. *Teaching Strategies GOLD®* is a powerful tool for helping you identify each child's developmental level for each objective and how to scaffold children's learning. Because this assessment system covers all areas of development and learning, it gives you a comprehensive picture of the child.

Planning for children on the basis of assessment information is an art. There are no formulas or quick solutions. It would be wonderful to be able to say that a child will progress to the next level if you do a particular activity. However, it takes time, practice, and reflection to determine what support a child or group of children needs.

As you make your daily, weekly, and long-range plans, refer to your assessment information. Your interpretation of evidence informs the types of experiences you offer to children.

Plan for the particular strengths, needs, and interests of individual children. Consider what you know about each child and the expected outcomes identified by *Teaching Strategies GOLD®* and by your state early learning standards. Use this information to shape what you do each day. Your assessment information and the progressions of development and learning guide how and when to adapt an activity to make it simpler or more complex.

Involve others in planning for the children in your class. Review assessment information with your assistant, with families, and with your colleagues to consider how best to guide children's learning.

Consider assessment information as you plan changes to your physical environment. Are the materials you include challenging yet manageable for the children in your group? Has assessment information revealed that a child has a particular interest you want to nurture? Do you need to adapt some materials so that children can use them more easily? Might a child who is an English-language learner demonstrate additional competencies if the materials were more linguistically appropriate?

Family Conference Form

Another important task at a progress checkpoint is to summarize information to share with the child's family during a conference. To do so, look at the samples of the child's work you collected and the ratings, or levels, you assigned to describe the child's development and learning. Now step back and think about the big ideas you want to share with the family members about each area of development and learning.

On a "Family Conference Form," highlight the child's strengths. Using examples, describe what the child *can* do in the different areas of development and learning. Consider your audience when writing these summaries. Your language should be clear, concise, and family-friendly. This should be done before meeting with the family members.

1. Record a few learning goals and next steps you have in mind for the child.

2. At the family conference, discuss your observations and invite families to share information and contribute to the assessment data. Talk about their goals for children's learning and record them in the space provided on the conference form.

3. Together, discuss and record next steps for school and for home.

4. Always end the conference on a positive note. Ask family members to sign the "Family Conference Form." Keep one copy for your records and give the family members a copy. Your administrator may want a copy as well.

Assessing Throughout the Year

This chart provides you with a big picture of using the *Teaching Strategies GOLD*® assessment system over the course of a program year.

Month	All Year Long	
1st month	**Observe** children in the context of everyday experiences.	
2nd month		
3rd month		**1st Progress Checkpoint** – Review documentation. Assign each child a level on each applicable objective. Summarize your findings on the "Family Conference Form." Share information with families.
4th month	**Document** what you see and hear as evidence of development and learning.	
5th month		
6th month		**2nd Progress Checkpoint** – Review documentation. Assign each child a level on each applicable objective. Summarize your findings on the "Family Conference Form." Share information with families.
7th month	Use the *Assessment Opportunity Cards*™ as needed.	
8th month		
9th month		**3rd Progress Checkpoint** – Review documentation. Assign each child a level on each applicable objective. Summarize your findings on the "Family Conference Form." Share information with families.
10th month		
11th month		
12th month		**Optional 4th Progress Checkpoint** – Review documentation. Assign each child a level on each applicable objective. Summarize your findings on the "Family Conference Form." Share information with families.

Objectives and Dimensions	Birth to 1 year	1 to 2 years	2 to 3 years	Preschool 3 class	Pre-K 4 class	Kindergarten
SOCIAL–EMOTIONAL						
1. Regulates own emotions and behaviors						
a. Manages feelings	■	■	■	■	■	■
b. Follows limits and expectations	■	■	■	■	■	■
c. Takes care of own needs appropriately	■	■	■	■	■	■
2. Establishes and sustains positive relationships						
a. Forms relationships with adults	■	■	■	■	■	■
b. Responds to emotional cues	■	■	■	■	■	■
c. Interacts with peers	■	■	■	■	■	■
d. Makes friends		■	■	■	■	■
3. Participates cooperatively and constructively in group situations						
a. Balances needs and rights of self and others		■	■	■	■	■
b. Solves social problems		■	■	■	■	■
PHYSICAL						
4. Demonstrates traveling skills	■	■	■	■	■	■
5. Demonstrates balancing skills	■	■	■	■	■	■
6. Demonstrates gross-motor manipulative skills	■	■	■	■	■	■
7. Demonstrates fine-motor strength and coordination						
a. Uses fingers and hands	■	■	■	■	■	■
b. Uses writing and drawing tools		■	■	■	■	■
LANGUAGE						
8. Listens to and understands increasingly complex language						
a. Comprehends language	■	■	■	■	■	■
b. Follows directions	■	■	■	■	■	■

Ranges (color-coded):
- Birth to 1 year
- 1 to 2 years
- 2 to 3 years
- Preschool 3 class
- Pre-K 4 class
- Kindergarten

Objectives and Dimensions	Ranges (color-coded)					
9. Uses language to express thoughts and needs						
a. Uses an expanding expressive vocabulary	■	■	■	■	■	■
b. Speaks clearly	■	■	■	■	■	■
c. Uses conventional grammar	■	■	■	■	■	■
d. Tells about another time or place		■	■	■	■	■
10. Uses appropriate conversational and other communication skills						
a. Engages in conversations	■	■	■	■	■	■
b. Uses social rules of language	■	■	■	■	■	■
COGNITIVE						
11. Demonstrates positive approaches to learning						
a. Attends and engages	■	■	■	■	■	■
b. Persists	■	■	■	■	■	■
c. Solves problems	■	■	■	■	■	■
d. Shows curiosity and motivation	■	■	■	■	■	■
e. Shows flexibility and inventiveness in thinking		■	■	■	■	■
12. Remembers and connects experiences						
a. Recognizes and recalls	■	■	■	■	■	■
b. Makes connections	■	■	■	■	■	■
13. Uses classification skills		■	■	■	■	■
14. Uses symbols and images to represent something not present						
a. Thinks symbolically		■	■	■	■	■
b. Engages in sociodramatic play		■	■	■	■	■

Objectives and Dimensions	Ranges (color-coded)						Assessment Opportunity Cards™
LITERACY							
15. Demonstrates phonological awareness							Listening Cords; Duck, Duck, Goose Word Play; Around and Around; Treasure Box
a. Notices and discriminates rhyme		■	■	■	■	■	
b. Notices and discriminates alliteration		■	■	■	■	■	
c. Notices and discriminates smaller and smaller units of sound				■	■	■	
16. Demonstrates knowledge of the alphabet							Alphabet Recognition Game
a. Identifies and names letters			■	■	■	■	
b. Uses letter–sound knowledge				■	■	■	
17. Demonstrates knowledge of print and its uses							Let's Read Together
a. Uses and appreciates books	■	■	■	■	■	■	
b. Uses print concepts			■	■	■	■	
18. Comprehends and responds to books and other texts							
a. Interacts during read-alouds and book conversations			■	■	■	■	
b. Uses emergent reading skills			■	■	■	■	
c. Retells stories			■	■	■	■	
19. Demonstrates emergent writing skills							Class Book
a. Writes name		■	■	■	■	■	
b. Writes to convey meaning		■	■	■	■	■	

Objectives and Dimensions	Ranges (color-coded)	Assessment Opportunity Cards™
MATHEMATICS		
20. Uses number concepts and operations		Counting Collectibles; Shazam!; Number, Please!
a. Counts	▪ ▫ ▪ ▪ ▪	
b. Quantifies	▪ ▫ ▪ ▪ ▪	
c. Connects numerals with their quantities	▫ ▪ ▪ ▪	
21. Explores and describes spatial relationships and shapes		
a. Understands spatial relationships	▪ ▫ ▪ ▪ ▪	
b. Understands shapes	▪ ▫ ▪ ▪ ▪	
22. Compares and measures	▪ ▫ ▪ ▪ ▪	
23. Demonstrates knowledge of patterns	▪ ▫ ▪ ▪ ▪	
SCIENCE AND TECHNOLOGY		
24. Uses scientific inquiry skills	No evidence yet	
25. Demonstrates knowledge of the characteristics of living things	Emerging	
26. Demonstrates knowledge of the physical properties of objects and materials	Meets program expectations	
27. Demonstrates knowledge of Earth's environment		
28. Uses tools and other technology to perform tasks		
SOCIAL STUDIES		
29. Demonstrates knowledge about self	No evidence yet	
30. Shows basic understanding of people and how they live	Emerging	
31. Explores change related to familiar people or places	Meets program expectations	
32. Demonstrates simple geographic knowledge		

Objectives and Dimensions	Ranges (color-coded)
THE ARTS	
33. Explores the visual arts	No evidence yet
34. Explores musical concepts and expression	Emerging
35. Explores dance and movement concepts	Meets program expectations
36. Explores drama through actions and language	
ENGLISH LANGUAGE ACQUISITION	
37. Demonstrates progress in listening to and understanding English	Progressions included, but not age-level designations
38. Demonstrates progress in speaking English	

Objectives for Development & Learning

Social–Emotional

1. Regulates own emotions and behaviors
   a. Manages feelings
   b. Follows limits and expectations
   c. Takes care of own needs appropriately

2. Establishes and sustains positive relationships
   a. Forms relationships with adults
   b. Responds to emotional cues
   c. Interacts with peers
   d. Makes friends

3. Participates cooperatively and constructively in group situations
   a. Balances needs and rights of self and others
   b. Solves social problems

Physical

4. Demonstrates traveling skills

5. Demonstrates balancing skills

6. Demonstrates gross-motor manipulative skills

7. Demonstrates fine-motor strength and coordination
   a. Uses fingers and hands
   b. Uses writing and drawing tools

Language

8. Listens to and understands increasingly complex language
   a. Comprehends language
   b. Follows directions

9. Uses language to express thoughts and needs
   a. Uses an expanding expressive vocabulary
   b. Speaks clearly
   c. Uses conventional grammar
   d. Tells about another time or place

10. Uses appropriate conversational and other communication skills
    a. Engages in conversations
    b. Uses social rules of language

Cognitive

11. Demonstrates positive approaches to learning
    a. Attends and engages
    b. Persists
    c. Solves problems
    d. Shows curiosity and motivation
    e. Shows flexibility and inventiveness in thinking

12. Remembers and connects experiences
    a. Recognizes and recalls
    b. Makes connections

13. Uses classification skills

14. Uses symbols and images to represent something not present
    a. Thinks symbolically
    b. Engages in sociodramatic play

Literacy

15. Demonstrates phonological awareness
    a. Notices and discriminates rhyme
    b. Notices and discriminates alliteration
    c. Notices and discriminates smaller and smaller units of sound
16. Demonstrates knowledge of the alphabet
    a. Identifies and names letters
    b. Uses letter–sound knowledge
17. Demonstrates knowledge of print and its uses
    a. Uses and appreciates books
    b. Uses print concepts
18. Comprehends and responds to books and other texts
    a. Interacts during read-alouds and book conversations
    b. Uses emergent reading skills
    c. Retells stories
19. Demonstrates emergent writing skills
    a. Writes name
    b. Writes to convey meaning

Mathematics

20. Uses number concepts and operations
    a. Counts
    b. Quantifies
    c. Connects numerals with their quantities
21. Explores and describes spatial relationships and shapes
    a. Understands spatial relationships
    b. Understands shapes
22. Compares and measures
23. Demonstrates knowledge of patterns

Science and Technology

24. Uses scientific inquiry skills
25. Demonstrates knowledge of the characteristics of living things
26. Demonstrates knowledge of the physical properties of objects and materials
27. Demonstrates knowledge of Earth's environment
28. Uses tools and other technology to perform tasks

Social Studies

29. Demonstrates knowledge about self
30. Shows basic understanding of people and how they live
31. Explores change related to familiar people or places
32. Demonstrates simple geographic knowledge

The Arts

33. Explores the visual arts
34. Explores musical concepts and expression
35. Explores dance and movement concepts
36. Explores drama through actions and language

English Language Acquisition

37. Demonstrates progress in listening to and understanding English
38. Demonstrates progress in speaking English

Areas of Development and Learning

Social–Emotional

Young children's social–emotional development involves learning how to understand their own and others' feelings, regulate and express their emotions appropriately, build relationships with others, and interact in groups (Rubin, Bukowski, & Parker, 1998). Social–emotional development flourishes when children have close, supportive, and trusting relationships with adults (Howes & James, 2002). When adults are responsive, when they express pleasure about children's accomplishments and discoveries, and when they create an environment in which children can participate actively in daily routines and experiences, children know that adults consider them to be important, interesting, and competent.

Children's interactions with others are crucial to their learning. Problematic childhood relationships with adults and peers have been linked to negative outcomes such as emotional and mental health problems, lower school achievement, higher dropout rates, peer rejection, and delinquency. When their interactions are positive, young children are more likely to have positive short- and long-term outcomes (Rubin et al., 1998; Smith & Hart, 2002). The strong connection between early relationships and later behavior and learning makes it especially important for teachers to assess children's social–emotional development accurately and to support their growth and competence in this area.

SOCIAL–EMOTIONAL OBJECTIVES

1 Regulates own emotions and behaviors

2 Establishes and sustains positive relationships

3 Participates cooperatively and constructively in group situations

Regulates own emotions and behaviors

1

In order to manage emotions and regulate his or her behavior, a child must learn to control impulses, tolerate frustration, cope with strong emotions, follow limits and expectations, and delay gratification. A crying infant calms when rocked by a loving adult. A 2-year-old sits in a quiet place hugging a stuffed bear after his mother leaves for work. A preschooler acts out a birthday party, thanking her guests for coming. A 5-year-old tells you when others are not following the rules.

To be able to regulate their emotions and behaviors, children must: 1) develop a basic understanding that actions have positive and negative consequences, 2) know what behaviors are acceptable, 3) be aware that they are capable of controlling their behavior, and 4) know that they have the power to manage their emotions (Bilmes, 2004). Children learn how to manage their emotions and regulate behavior in an environment that is warm and nurturing, and where the adults are trustworthy and responsive to each child's needs. Discussing the reasons for limits and the consequences of behavior helps children know why limits and rules are necessary. Teachers usually provide reasons for moral rules that apply in every setting, such as not hitting or taking another child's toy. They usually do not explain the social reasons for rules such as putting blocks back on the shelf neatly (Charlesworth, 2007; Smetana, 1984).

Children who regulate their emotions positively do better in school (Blair & Razza, 2007; Bronson, 2000) and have an easier time getting along with peers (Copple & Bredekamp, 2009; Ponitz, McClelland, Jewkes, Conner, Farris, & Morrison, 2008). Noncompliant, problematic behavior in preschool tends to continue in later school years (Charlesworth, 2007; Campbell, 1995; Campbell, Pierce, March, Ewing, & Szumowski, 1994). Self-regulation is ranked as the most important characteristic necessary for school readiness by kindergarten teachers, who also indicate that over half of their children lack effective self-regulatory skills (Rimm-Kaufman, Pianta, & Cox, 2000). Children who have warm, supportive, secure relationships with their teachers exhibit fewer behavioral problems than children who do not have positive relationships (Bronson, 2006; Howes & Ritchie, 1998), so teachers' role in helping children follow limits and expectations is important to children's future school success.

Objective 1 Regulates own emotions and behaviors

Various factors, such as a disability, life experiences, and family practices, influence the way children express their feelings and emotions. Some children are taught to avoid expressions of emotion, while others are encouraged to express their feelings openly (Trawick-Smith, 2006). Difficulty in learning to manage emotions may be an early warning sign of a disability or future psychological problems (Diamond, 2002; National Scientific Council on the Developing Child, 2004). Infants who have trouble remaining calm may need special help to develop self-regulatory skills (Cook, Klein, & Tessier, 2004). Children who cannot control their emotions at age 4 are likely not to be able to follow the teacher's directions at age 6 (Bodrova & Leong, 2005).

Differences in family beliefs and expectations affect the way children respond to classroom limits. The ways people express opinions, discuss ideas and feelings, and take turns in conversations differ from one culture to another and often from one family to another. Children from some cultural backgrounds look others straight in the eye during conversations while other children are taught to avoid eye contact (McAfee & Leong, 1994). There are also differences in the strategies families use when children do not follow the established limits (Trawick-Smith, 2006). Frequent communication between teachers and families is therefore necessary to guide children's behavior and to work toward shared goals.

Children's ability to meet their own needs appropriately is valued and typically expected by some cultures (Pierce & Schreibman, 1994). When children take care of themselves in these cultures, they build their confidence, and this influences their emotions and behaviors. Children who feel competent, or who have belief in their abilities, are better able to face life's challenges (Curry & Johnson, 1990). Children develop confidence by participating successfully in everyday activities. When children can communicate their needs, move from place to place, use tools, and participate in classroom routines, they have more opportunities to build self-confidence.

Children with physical disabilities may be viewed by their nondisabled peers as being less able to perform certain tasks or to participate fully in everyday classroom activities (Diamond & Hestenes, 1996). It is therefore important for teachers to support children with disabilities appropriately in their efforts to do things for themselves and to give them, whenever possible, the same opportunities to participate in classroom activities as their typically developing peers. Teachers may need to provide children with disabilities as well as English-language learners with pictorial examples depicting various sequences of a routine or activity. The pictures support children's abilities to complete tasks by themselves (Macrina, Hoover, & Becker, 2009; Pierce & Schreibman, 1994).

Objective 1 Regulates own emotions and behaviors

a. Manages feelings

Not Yet	1	2	3	4	5	6	7	8	9
		Uses adult support to calm self • Calms self when touched gently, patted, massaged, rocked, or hears a soothing voice • Turns away from source of overstimulation and cries, but is soothed by being picked up		**Comforts self by seeking out special object or person** • Gets teddy bear from cubby when upset • Sits next to favorite adult when sad		**Is able to look at a situation differently or delay gratification** • When the block area is full, looks to see what other areas are available • Scowls and says, "I didn't get to paint this morning." Pauses and adds, "I have an idea. I can paint after snack."		**Controls strong emotions in an appropriate manner most of the time** • Asserts, "I'm mad. You're not sharing the blocks! I'm going to play with the ramps." • Says, "I'm so excited! We're going to the zoo today!" while jumping up and down	

b. Follows limits and expectations

Not Yet	1	2	3	4	5	6	7	8	9
		Responds to changes in an adult's tone of voice and expression • Looks when adult speaks in a soothing voice • Appears anxious if voices are loud or unfamiliar • Touches the puddle of water when adult smiles encouragingly		**Accepts redirection from adults** • Moves to the sand table at suggestion of adult when there are too many at the art table • Initially refuses to go inside but complies when the teacher restates the request		**Manages classroom rules, routines, and transitions with occasional reminders** • Indicates that only four persons may play at the water table • Cleans up when music is played • Goes to rest area when lights are dimmed		**Applies rules in new but similar situations** • Walks and uses a quiet voice in the library • Runs and shouts when on a field trip to the park • Listens attentively to a guest speaker	

See pages 1–2 of *Child Assessment Portfolio*.

Objective 1 Regulates own emotions and behaviors

c. Takes care of own needs appropriately

Not Yet	1	2	3	4	5	6	7	8	9
		Indicates needs and wants; participates as adult attends to needs • Cries to show discomfort, hunger, or tiredness • Opens mouth when food is offered • Raises knees to chest when on back for diaper changing • Pulls off own socks • Raises arms while being lifted out of buggy		**Seeks to do things for self** • Asserts own needs by pointing, gesturing, or talking • Holds hands under faucet and waits for adult to turn on water • Tries to zip jacket, but throws to ground in frustration • Attempts to clean up toys		**Demonstrates confidence in meeting own needs** • Washes hands and uses towel to dry • Stays involved in activity of choice • Uses materials, utensils, and brushes appropriately • Takes off coat and hangs it up • Puts away toys • Volunteers to feed the fish		**Takes responsibility for own well-being** • Completes chosen task • Waits for turn to go down slide • Creates a "Do not touch" sign for construction • Tells why some foods are good for you • Takes care of personal belongings	

See page 3 of *Child Assessment Portfolio.*

Objective 1 Regulates own emotions and behaviors

Strategies

- Stay nearby when babies are lying or sitting close to each other. Gently separate them if they touch each other too roughly, showing them how to be gentle.

- Use clear, simple language to communicate which behaviors are acceptable, e.g., say, "Pat Tamika's arm gently."

- Establish and practice consistent routines.

- Only put acceptable play materials within reach. This will limit the number of times you have to say *no*.

- Acknowledge when children show self-discipline, e.g., say, "You wanted to grab Tommy's car, but you waited until he was finished playing with it."

- Use simple, clear language and facial expressions to communicate acceptable behaviors.

- Create clear boundaries to help children learn to control themselves. Use visual aids, such as carpet squares or floor tape, to mark boundaries with preschool children.

- State rules positively rather than negatively. Tell children what behavior is expected, e.g., say, "Walk when you are inside," instead of saying, "Don't run."

- Give children alternative ways to express their anger, e.g., tell the child, "If you feel angry, tell us. Say, 'I'm angry!' That way we can help you."

- Set clear, reasonable, age-appropriate expectations that children can understand. When children do not behave in acceptable ways, assess whether the adult expectation is appropriate in the given situation. Respond by consistently structuring consequences that are related to the behavior, e.g., have the child help clean up dumped paint instead of using time-out.

- Model taking deep breaths, counting to five, or doing relaxation exercises when situations are stressful. With toddlers, talk about how you are taking deep breaths to help you relax. With older children, engage them in doing relaxation exercises with you.

- Explain the reasons for rules, and help children understand why particular behaviors are not acceptable, e.g., "Be kind to others. Hitting hurts people's bodies." Or, "Only three children may play at the sand table. When there are too many children, some can't reach the toys."

- Use gestures and other visual cues while telling children the rule or limit.

- Respond positively and firmly when a child's behavior is challenging. To help a child change his or her behavior, observe systematically, talk with others who know the child, develop a plan of action, and implement and evaluate the plan.

- Provide opportunities for children age 2 and older to help create the rules for their classroom.

- Ask families about the self-care activities in which the child participates at home.

- Describe what you are doing during caregiving routines, so children can learn the sequence of actions to care for themselves.

- Serve food that children can feed to themselves. Be prepared for messes.

- Use picture cues so non-verbal children or children with certain disabilities can communicate their needs through photos such as, "Hello," "I'm thirsty," or "I'm sleepy." Children point to the pictures until they learn the words in English or until they can do the activities for themselves.

- Talk with children about their feelings during routine activities. For example, you might say, "I know you're unhappy having your diaper changed now, but soon I'll be done and you can play. Here's a ball to hold."

- Provide opportunities for preschool and older children to engage in extended make-believe play in which they can act out strong emotions.

- Provide picture and word cues to assist toddlers and older children as they participate in self-care tasks, e.g., use a recipe for making a snack or post cue cards with the steps of feeding the class pet.

Objective 1 Regulates own emotions and behaviors

Strategies, *continued*

- Model using self-talk with older children to help them verbalize their thoughts and guide their own behavior. For example, tell them "Say to yourself, 'Stop. Calm down. I'm getting mad, but I don't need to hit anyone'."

- Discuss photos of people showing various emotions. Encourage older preschool and kindergarten children to create stories about the source of the person's feelings. Guide them to come up with appropriate ways the person might respond to the situation.

- Provide child-sized cleaning materials such as sponges, mops, brooms, and dust pans so children can assist with meaningful classroom cleaning.

- Include clothing of various sizes so children can practice dressing themselves. Slightly larger-sized clothes and those with large fasteners are easier for young children and children with certain disabilities to manipulate.

- Display posters made by kindergarten children that depict things they do to take responsibility for their own well-being. Posters might focus on healthy eating habits, exercise, or personal hygiene. Create individual calendars and have each child record their healthy behaviors during the week. Review at the end of the week and determine which habits need more attention.

- Allow plenty of time to let children take responsibility for self-care routines.

- Provide a variety of self-care materials for children to explore, e.g., dolls to dress and undress, shoes to lace and tie, dress-up clothes with fasteners of varying difficulty.

- Provide only as much help as necessary for children to accomplish tasks, e.g., put socks on the child's toes and then encourage him or her to pull them up the rest of the way.

- When appropriate, encourage families to involve their children in simple household tasks, as appropriate, e.g., hanging clothes, pouring beverages, and setting the table.

Objective 2

Establishes and sustains positive relationships

2

Being able to establish caring relationships and to enter successfully into ongoing social interactions are essential skills for school and for success in life. There are four dimensions to this objective: establishing and sustaining positive relationships with adults; making and keeping friends; relating to other children in groups; and interpreting the emotional cues of others and responding appropriately.

Relationships With Adults

The ability to establish caring relationships between a child and the important people in his or her life is called *attachment*. An infant squeals with laughter as a trusted adult plays with him. A toddler struggles to say good-bye to her mother at drop-off time. A 2-year-old runs into the room and hugs her teacher hello every morning. A preschool child works and plays with friends but knows when to ask an adult for help. A kindergartner engages a teacher in a conversation about their shared interest in horses.

Children's ability to form positive relationships with adults is important to their social development and academic success (Berk, 2006; Bronson, 2006; Howes, 2000; Howes et al., 2008; Palermo, Hanish, Martin, Fabes, & Reiser, 2007; Pianta, 1999). The model for all future relationships begins with the infant's early interactions with parents and other primary caregivers (Lamb, Bornstein, & Teti, 2002; Rubin, Bukowski, & Parker, 1998). Responding to infants' signals is critical to the development of a trusting, secure relationship with their primary caregivers (Peterson & Wittmer, 2008).

Various factors can interfere with a child's ability to form secure attachments with adults. Risk factors such as poverty, disabilities, or stress may influence the formation of secure attachments (Diamond, 2002; Ray, Bowman, & Brownell, 2006; Sigman & Ruskin, 1999; Trawick-Smith, 2006). Family socialization practices, such as encouraging dependence, may also affect how the child separates from the primary caregiver, how the child responds to other adults, and how other adults respond to the child (Chen, 1996; Harwood, Miller, & Irizarry, 1995; Trawick-Smith, 2006).

The classroom is an important setting for the development of positive relationships with adults outside the family (Pianta, 1999). Just as in the parent–child relationship, the quality of the teacher–child relationship can support or limit children's development and learning (Howes et al., 2008; Palermo et al., 2007; Schmidt, Burts, Durham, Charlesworth, & Hart, 2007). Teacher–child relationships may be close and affectionate, distant and formal, filled with conflict, or overly dependent (Coplan & Prakash, 2003; Howes & Matheson, 1992; Pianta, 1999). Overly dependent relationships and teacher–child relationships marked by lots of conflict can interfere with children's learning and academic achievement (Coplan & Prakash, 2003; Palermo et al., 2007; Ray et al., 2006). Teachers must build respectful and trusting relationships with children and their families. This is particularly true when the family's home culture and socioeconomic background differs from the teacher's (Ray et al., 2006).

Objective 2 Establishes and sustains positive relationships

Supportive relationships with teachers can help children overcome the challenges associated with living in high-risk circumstances and help children whose early relationships have not been positive (Pianta, 1999). Children who have secure attachment relationships with primary caregivers and teachers have an easier time interacting with peers, forming positive relationships, and being a part of the group.

Interpreting the Emotional Cues of Others and Responding Appropriately

Learning to recognize and respond to the emotional cues of other people involves learning a set of skills that adults model. When an infant smiles back at a smiling face and a toddler moves near a crying child, they are beginning to recognize and respond to the emotions of others. Two-year-olds respond to others with empathy and understanding when they offer a crying child a special toy and tell the teacher, "He's sad." Preschoolers and kindergartners understand the reasons for people's emotions and begin to learn that feelings are complex, for example, that someone can be happy and disappointed at the same time.

Emotional understanding is critical to positive social relationships and peer acceptance (Denham, von Salisch, Olthof, Kochanoff, & Caverly, 2002; Eisenberg et al., 1997; Hubbard & Coie, 1994; Hyson, 2003). Social acceptance depends on a child's ability to understand, predict, and interpret the emotions of others (Mostow, Izard, Fine, & Trentacosta, 2002). Children who can accurately interpret emotional signals are more likely to respond appropriately to others and less likely to become angry or aggressive. Children who exhibit challenging behaviors may not recognize what others are feeling (Webster-Stratton & Herbert, 1994). But some children who bully others may "read" emotions correctly, but respond inappropriately. Adults must combat bullying behavior by being proactive and taking preventive actions.

Families introduce young children to cultural rules about ways of feeling and displaying emotions (Denham et al., 2002). Some children are taught to openly express their emotions, while others are encouraged to avoid outward expressions (Day, 2006; Trawick-Smith, 2006). Children who have suffered abuse or witnessed abuse often have difficulty managing their own emotions (Beland, 1996; Ontai & Thompson, 2002).

Some disabilities may affect children's sensitivity to emotions. For example, some children with autism spectrum disorders have difficulty reading the emotions of others (Baron-Cohen, 1995). They may not recognize the meaning of basic emotional signals such as facial expressions, tone of voice, or words (Ayoub & Fischer, 2006). The more adults acknowledge children's emotional reactions and describe emotional signals, the better children become at interpreting them (Berk, 2006; Denham & Kochanoff, 2002).

Interacting With Peers and Making Friends

The ability to enter successfully into ongoing social interactions is an important social skill. This ability begins with an infant's early interactions with a primary caregiver and quickly grows into an interest in watching other children at play. A toddler who laughs with another child as they both finger paint with their own materials becomes a 2-year-old who takes turns dipping his fingers in a shared pot of paint. The preschooler who talks about friendships becomes a kindergartner who establishes and maintains relationships over time with special friends.

Children's ability to build positive relationships with peers affects their social competence, school adjustment, academic success, and mental health in adulthood (Berk, 2006; Katz, Kramer, & Gottman, 1992; Ladd, Birch, & Buhs, 1999; Ladd, Buhs, & Seid, 2000; Peisner-Feinberg et al., 1999; Raver & Zigler, 1997; Shonkoff & Phillips, 2000; Wentzel & Asher, 1995). Some children's interactions put them at risk for developing negative relationships with peers. Once children develop negative reputations, they are likely to be rejected by their peers unless adults intervene (Black & Hazen, 1990; Kaiser & Rasminsky, 2003). Children who are not well liked often exhibit expressions of anger, hostility, or aggression (Cillessen & Bellmore, 2002; Denham et al., 1990; Hartup & Abecassis, 2002). Aggressive behaviors are not only physical. Aggression also may be verbal, e.g., name calling; nonverbal, e.g., mean faces; or relational, e.g., excluding children from an activity (Ostrov, Woods, Jansen, Casas, & Crick, 2004).

Objective 2 Establishes and sustains positive relationships

Both the aggressor and the victim need adult intervention and support to develop positive peer relationships.

Children who are successful in their peer relationships use strategies such as making comments that are appropriate to the ongoing interaction. Children who are not well liked use behaviors such as calling attention to themselves or trying to control the interaction (Cillessen & Bellmore, 2002; Dodge, Schlundt, Schocken, & Delugach, 1983; Putallaz & Gottman, 1981). Many children need adult assistance to learn how to enter group play successfully. Children with disabilities may need help to enter the group or to initiate social contacts with potential social partners (Buysse, Goldman, & Skinner, 2003; Hart, McGee, & Hernandez, 1993; Kantor, Elgas, & Fernie, 1993; Pettit & Harrist, 1993; Robinson, Anderson, Porter, Hart, & Wouden-Miller, 2003).

Through interactions with peers over time, children begin to form friendships. These friendships can help children acquire positive social skills and develop more complex social competence (Katz, Kramer, & Gottman, 1992; Shonkoff & Phillips, 2000). Friend relationships are different from other relationships that children have with peers.

Friends are more likely to be the same sex, ethnicity, and have similar behaviors, both positive and negative. They spend more time with one another (Hartup & Abecassis, 2002). Most children with disabilities who are in programs with typically developing peers have at least one friend (Buysse, 1993).

Play is an important context for developing close relationships. Creative learning activities such as fantasy play, block play, and open-ended art activities provide opportunities for children to build positive relationships with peers (Wishard, Shivers, Howes, & Ritchie, 2003).

Objective 2 Establishes and sustains positive relationships

a. Forms relationships with adults

Not Yet	1	2	3	4	5	6	7	8	9

Demonstrates a secure attachment to one or more adults

- Appears uneasy when held by a stranger but smiles broadly when mom enters room
- Calms when a familiar adult offers appropriate comfort
- Responds to teacher during caregiving routines

Uses trusted adult as a secure base from which to explore the world

- Moves away from a trusted adult to play with a new toy but returns before venturing into a new area
- Looks to a trusted adult for encouragement when exploring a new material or physical space

Manages separations without distress and engages with trusted adults

- Waves good-bye to mom and joins speech therapist in a board game
- Accepts teacher's explanation of why she is leaving the room and continues playing

Engages with trusted adults as resources and to share mutual interests

- Talks with teacher every day about their pets
- Brings in photos of home garden to share with teacher who also has a garden

b. Responds to emotional cues

Not Yet	1	2	3	4	5	6	7	8	9

Reacts to others' emotional expressions

- Cries when hears an adult use an angry tone of voice
- Smiles and turns head to look at person laughing
- Moves to adult while watching another child have a tantrum

Demonstrates concern about the feelings of others

- Brings a crying child's blanket to him
- Hugs a child who fell down
- Gets an adult to assist a child who needs help

Identifies basic emotional reactions of others and their causes accurately

- Says, "She's happy because her brother is here." "He's sad because his toy broke."
- Matches a picture of a happy face with a child getting a present or a sad face with a picture of a child dropping the banana she was eating

Recognizes that others' feelings about a situation might be different from his or her own

- Says, "I like riding fast on the trike, but Tim doesn't."
- Shows Meir a picture of a dinosaur but doesn't show it to Lucy because he remembers that she's afraid of dinosaurs

See pages 4–5 of *Child Assessment Portfolio*.

Objective 2 Establishes and sustains positive relationships

c. Interacts with peers

Not Yet	1	2	3	4	5	6	7	8	9

Plays near other children; uses similar materials or actions
- Sits next to child playing an instrument
- Imitates other children building with blocks
- Looks at other child's painting and chooses the same color

Uses successful strategies for entering groups
- Watches what other children are doing for a few minutes and then contributes an idea
- Asks, "Can I run with you?"

Initiates, joins in, and sustains positive interactions with a small group of two to three children
- Sees group pretending to ride a bus and says, "Let's go to the zoo on the bus."
- Enters easily into ongoing group play and plays cooperatively

Interacts cooperatively in groups of four or five children
- Works on tasks with others toward a common goal
- Plays and works together for extended periods of time

d. Makes friends

Not Yet	1	2	3	4	5	6	7	8	9

Seeks a preferred playmate; shows pleasure when seeing a friend
- Leaves library area to greet another child upon his arrival
- Seeks preferred child to sit next to at group time

Plays with one or two preferred playmates
- Builds block tower with another child during choice time and then looks at books with same child later in the day
- Joins same two friends for several days to play a running game outside

Establishes a special friendship with one other child, but the friendship might only last a short while
- Talks about having friends and what friends do together
- Seeks out particular friend for selected activities on a regular basis

Maintains friendships for several months or more
- Finds her friend's favorite purple marker and gives it to her
- Works through a conflict and remains friends after a disagreement

See pages 6–7 of *Child Assessment Portfolio*.

Objective 2 Establishes and sustains positive relationships

Strategies

- Learn to distinguish an infant's cries so you can respond appropriately, e.g., know if he or she is hungry, tired, lonely, or needs a diaper changed.

- Exaggerate your response to an infant's behavior, e.g., widening your eyes and changing the pitch of your voice to show excitement over a new accomplishment.

- Engage in experiences that help infants and toddlers understand how to interact with others, e.g., play peek-a-boo.

- Acknowledge children's positive interactions, e.g., comment as two children interact, "You touched Omar's face very gently."

- Label and talk about emotions and their causes, e.g., "Christina is angry because you took her truck," and "Willard is sad because he dropped his sandwich."

- Read simple books showing different emotions. Discuss why the people look and feel the way they do, e.g., say, "She's smiling because she is happy. She's happy because her mommy is home."

- Discuss and read books about friendships, e.g., how friends treat one another, the things they do for each other.

- Build positive relationships with each child by making purposeful observations every day, talking to each child respectfully, being sensitive to the child's feelings, and validating accomplishments and progress.

- Assist parents or caregivers as they leave. Help them understand that separation may be more difficult for toddlers than it is for infants and preschoolers.

- Interact one-on-one with children daily, playing and talking with them.

- Display family pictures in the classroom to validate children's most important relationships.

- Respond promptly and consistently to children's needs.

- Show respect in handling children, e.g., say, "I'm washing your face to get the food off."

- Smile frequently at children as you interact with them. This helps to establish positive relationships.

- Show appropriate affection, e.g., rub backs at nap time, hold children's hands as you walk around the playground, give hugs as children arrive in the morning.

- Talk to children at their eye level.

- Make each child feel special. Make time for him or her to share special interests with you, e.g., show you a favorite book or tell you about a recent experience. Tell children about your interests, e.g., things you like to do, what you liked to do as a child.

- Model respectful relationships with other adults in the program, e.g., tell children how other adults help. Say, "Mr. Jonas keeps our play yard clean and safe," or, "Thank you, Ms. Kelly, for getting the trikes out for us."

- Provide duplicates of favorite toys.

- Model cooperative behavior.

- Make accommodations for children with disabilities. You may need to pair a child with a disability with a peer partner, hold a prop for the child to use during group play, or give guidance and language for entering a peer group.

- Pay close attention to a child who is likely to act aggressively. Help the child control his or her emotions and behavior before another child gets hurt.

- Help children detect and interpret cues about how someone feels, e.g., say, "He looks angry. His forehead is wrinkled, his mouth turns down, and his fists are tight."

Objective 2 Establishes and sustains positive relationships

Strategies, *continued*

- Read stories to preschool and older children about various emotions. Discuss why the characters in the story look, feel, and act the way they do.

- Observe children as they try to enter group activities both indoors and outdoors. Help children who need assistance find play partners. Teach them positive strategies for entering and participating in group activities.

- Address all types of aggressive behavior. With twos and older children, assist the victim and the aggressor to develop prosocial behaviors such as helping, sharing, and including others in group activities and play. Call attention to positive changes in the child's behavior. Guide the other children toward responding to the child in new, more positive ways.

- Create spaces in the room for two preschool children to work together.

- Help preschool children learn how to enter a group by

    1) waiting, watching, and listening without speaking;

    2) imitating the actions of the children in the group; and

    3) saying something positive that relates to what the group is doing such as suggesting roles they could play.

- Explain that people have a variety of emotional responses to particular events (loss, injury, pain, birthday, going home, etc.) and they do not always react the same way.

- Explain that people express the same emotion in different ways, e.g., sometimes when people are sad they cry; sometimes they turn the corners of their mouths down like this and furrow their brows like this, but they do not cry.

- Engage children in informal conversations about your life and theirs. Listen attentively while they speak.

- Label your own feelings as you share experiences from your life and how you felt. Talk about things that made you happy, sad, or excited. Explain and model some of the ways you expressed your emotions.

- Provide opportunities for kindergarten children to work together on group projects over time. Model how children can help each other and work through conflict situations.

Objective 3

Participates cooperatively and constructively in group situations

3

Functioning as a member of a group requires an understanding of the feelings and rights of others and the ability to balance personal needs and desires with those of other people. When an infant babbles to the children at the lunch table, he is showing his interest in belonging to the group. When a 2-year-old waits for a turn on a bike, she is learning that other people's needs are important, too. When a preschool child works with others to paint a class mural, he is cooperating and sharing materials and ideas. And, an experienced kindergartner knows how to negotiate a trade of toys so that he gets what he wants. The foundational skills for being a productive member of social and learning groups are established during the early childhood years, and they are important for early school success (Chadd et al, 1999).

Being a productive member of a group involves complex interactions. Children must gradually learn to cooperate, negotiate, lead and follow, and express their feelings and ideas in socially acceptable ways. Positive group participation includes work-related skills like listening, following directions, behaving appropriately, staying on task, and organizing work materials. Poor work-related skills in kindergarten are related to behavioral difficulties and lower academic achievement in the primary grades (McClelland, Morrison, & Holmes, 2000).

Children who are socially competent interpret social situations and match their behavior accordingly. They comply with group expectations, and they work and play collaboratively. Social, cultural, and ethnic differences may create a mismatch between the kinds of behaviors expected at school, e.g., working independently to complete a task, and those expected at home, e.g., working together to complete a task (Ray, Bowman, & Brownell, 2006). Adult guidance helps children learn how to act and adapt to the different expectations they encounter in diverse group settings.

Younger children and children with poor peer relationships may use negative strategies, such as grabbing or hitting, to meet their needs (Berk, 2003; Downey & Walker, 1989; Yeates, Schultz, & Selman, 1991). Children with peer difficulties often assert their needs in ways that drive friends away (Erdly & Asher, 1999; Youngstrom et al., 2000). Some children come from homes where violence is the most frequently used problem-solving strategy. Children who experience difficulty processing social information often give up easily and resort to aggression (Kaiser & Rasminsky, 2003). Aggressive children are especially at risk for developing more serious problems throughout childhood and adolescence (Campbell, 1995; Parker & Asher, 1987), but intervention can help (Burton & Denham, 1998; Denham & Burton, 1996, 2003; Shure, 1997). Limited language skills can also be a barrier to social problem solving.

Conflicts are important opportunities for children to learn the give-and-take necessary for mature, successful social interactions that require negotiation and compromise (Kimple, 1991). It is tempting for an adult to fix children's social problems, but children need opportunities to think about and implement their own solutions. Good social problem-solving skills enable children to speak up for themselves, build self-esteem, and develop competence in other areas (Dinwiddle, 1994; Gonzalez-Mena, 2002), and such skills deter aggressiveness (Richard & Dodge, 1982; Spivack & Shure, 1997). Children who think of multiple ways to solve a problem are better able to solve problems without resorting to aggression.

Children are more likely to use prosocial behaviors, such as cooperating or consoling and helping others, when their teachers use positive guidance strategies and a curriculum that emphasizes the values of a community (DeVries, Haney, & Zan, 1991; Schmidt, Burts, Durham, Charlesworth, & Hart, 2007).

In addition, adult guidance helps children develop a repertoire of effective problem-solving strategies. Children benefit from learning a process for solving social problems (see strategies at the end of this section) (Committee for Children, 2002; Gonzalez-Mena, 2002; Kaiser & Rasminsky, 2003; Levin, 2003; Slaby, Roedell, Arezzo, & Hendrix, 1995).

Objective 3 Participates cooperatively and constructively in group situations

a. Balances needs and rights of self and others

Not Yet	1	2	3	4	5	6	7	8	9

Responds appropriately to others' expressions of wants
- Gives another child a ball when asked
- Makes room on the sofa for a child who wants to look at the book with him

Takes turns
- Waits behind another child at the water fountain
- Says, "It's your turn now; the timer is up."

Initiates the sharing of materials in the classroom and outdoors
- Gives another child the gold marker to use but asks to use it again when the other is done
- Invites another child to pull the wagon with her

Cooperates and shares ideas and materials in socially acceptable ways
- Leaves enough space for someone else to work at the table
- Pays attention to group discussions, values the ideas of others, and contributes own ideas in a respectful manner

b. Solves social problems

Not Yet	1	2	3	4	5	6	7	8	9

Expresses feelings during a conflict
- Screams when another child touches his crackers
- Gets quiet and looks down when another child pushes her

Seeks adult help to resolve social problems
- Goes to adult crying when someone takes the princess dress she wanted to wear
- Calls for the teacher when another child grabs the play dough at the same time he does

Suggests solutions to social problems
- Says, "You ride around the track one time, then I'll take a turn."
- Says, "Let's make a sign to keep people from kicking our sand castle like we did in the block area."
- Asks teacher to make a waiting list to use the new toy

Resolves social problems through negotiation and compromise
- Says, "If I let you use the ruler, will you let me use the hole-punch?"
- Responds, "Hey, I know! You two can be the drivers to deliver the pizza."

See pages 8–9 of *Child Assessment Portfolio.*

Objective 3 Participates cooperatively and constructively in group situations

Strategies

- Provide opportunities for infants and toddlers to play and interact with other children, staying nearby to offer redirection and to prevent harm to children.

- Coach toddlers to use the words, *stop* and *no*, when they are in conflict. Respond to the situation and expand a child's language, e.g., "I heard you say *no*. It sounds like you don't want Mica to touch the truck."

- Explain conflicts to children when they take place, describing people's feelings and the reasons for those feelings.

- Carefully watch a situation that is becoming a conflict. Allow children the chance to work out difficulties for themselves if no one will be hurt, but be prepared to offer support if needed.

- Coach children to use assertive (not aggressive) language, e.g., say, "Zory, you tell him, 'It's my turn now'."

- Establish respectful and meaningful interactions between families and teachers. Share the objectives and expectations of your program.

- Communicate what you and other adults at school do to support children in group situations. Explain how family members can help their children develop work- and play-related skills, to assume responsibility, and to cooperate.

- Provide opportunities for infants to spend time watching and interacting with other children, e.g., hold the infant on your lap while you watch the toddlers painting, put the child's blanket in a place where he can observe others at play.

- Sing songs, do fingerplays, and read books with small groups of toddlers. Keep these activities short and interactive to hold their interest.

- Give older children, and toddlers as soon as they are able, opportunities to help in the classroom, e.g., setting out the mats at nap time, looking for another child's missing shoe.

- Help twos and older children learn about cooperation by providing ample time, materials, and opportunities for children to engage in play and other cooperative activities with multiple children.

- Use positive strategies to guide children's behavior and to help them learn how to cooperate with others. Encourage cooperative interactions by suggesting turn taking and sharing and by modeling cooperation.

- Use role-play, games, and books to help preschool children to practice conflict resolution when there is not an immediate problem. When a conflict does arise, help children think about the sequence of events that led to it. Guide children through the problem-solving process and help them experiment with possible solutions.

- Teach preschool and older children the steps involved in resolving conflicts: 1) Identify and model how to state the problem, e.g., say, "Juan wants the truck, but you're playing with it." 2) Brainstorm solutions. Discuss possible solutions with the children involved. Accept all ideas as possibilities. 3) Evaluate solutions. Use open-ended prompts to help children predict outcomes, e.g., say, "I wonder what would happen if...." 4) Help children choose and try a solution. 5) Help children evaluate the outcome. Discuss what worked and what did not. Encourage the children to try other solutions if necessary.

- Encourage preschool and older children to watch for and record, through drawings or writing, the cooperative acts of others. Keep them in a special place, e.g., a "kindness jar." Before the day is over, read the children's notes aloud (Whitin, 2001).

- Begin to coach toddlers and twos and older children as needed about taking turns and sharing.

Physical

Physical development includes children's gross-motor (large muscle) and fine-motor (small muscle) skills. Balance; coordination; and locomotion, or traveling, are part of gross-motor development. Motor development progresses predictably, from simple to complex, in a head-to-toe direction. An infant lifts his head, lifts his trunk, rolls, crawls, sits, stands, walks, and then becomes a toddler who runs. Children gain control of their bodies in a predictable sequence as well, from the center of their bodies and outward to their fingers and toes. A child first catches a ball by trapping it against her whole body, then by holding out her arms to catch it, and finally by catching it with her hands. Similarly, fine-motor skills progress from the child's grabbing an object with a whole hand, picking up a small item with thumb and index finger, and eventually controlling the fine hand muscles needed for writing. Children need many opportunities to practice their gross-motor skills, e.g., pulling, climbing, running, kicking, throwing, jumping. and their fine-motor skills, e.g., cutting, drawing, writing.

As they develop physically, children master increasingly sophisticated tasks and are able to meet more of their own physical needs, such as feeding and dressing themselves. Motor and other aspects of physical development are influenced by gender, heredity, nutrition, health, environment, economic level, experience, culture, and disabilities (McKenzie, et al., 1997; Spaulding, Gottlib, & Jensen, 2008; Trawick-Smith, 2006).

PHYSICAL OBJECTIVES

4 Demonstrates traveling skills

5 Demonstrates balancing skills

6 Demonstrates gross-motor manipulative skills

7 Demonstrates fine-motor strength and coordination

Physical development affects other areas of development. Brain research points to the importance of early, positive movement experiences to brain development (Gabbard, 1998; Robert, 1999). Physical development is linked to children's emotional development and their school performance (Pica, 2006; Rule & Stewart, 2002; Sanders, 2002; Son & Meisels, 2006). The ability to be physically active influences social well-being and mental health. Regular physical activity helps children build and maintain healthy bones, muscles, and joints. It helps them to control weight and prevents or delays health conditions such as high blood pressure (McKenzie, et al., 1997; Pica, 2006; Sanders, 2002). The more children can do physically, the more willing they are to interact with other children and to try new and challenging physical tasks (Kim, 2006). This establishes a positive cycle that affects overall learning and health.

Motor development is not automatic. If children are to develop physical competence, they need a variety of equipment and materials; planned, appropriate movement experiences; and opportunities to practice and apply previously learned skills (Barbour, 1999; Epstein, 2007; Gallahue, 1995; Manross, 2000; Sanders, 2006).

Demonstrates traveling skills

4

Traveling involves moving the body through space. When an infant rolls over, a toddler takes a few steps, a preschooler rides a tricycle, and a kindergartner skips across the playground, they are traveling. The early years are critical for the development of the large muscles needed for traveling. Basic traveling movements, like running, galloping, and marching, can be combined in even more complex movements for dance and sports.

Environmental conditions, e.g., lack of space and weather, the demands of the task, family background, and disabilities influence a child's ability to perform a motor task. Some children with motor impairments achieve traveling movements by using a wheelchair or other adaptive technology. Children without independent mobility may become socially isolated if adults do not support their efforts to participate in ongoing activities (Harper & McCluskey, 2002). The strong desire to play with their peers may motivate children with motor impairments to work toward more independent mobility (Kim, 2005). When children with disabilities achieve greater independent mobility, they show improved social and language development (Charlesworth, 2007; Kim, 2005).

Children learn some motor skills primarily through exploration and discovery. In order to develop more proficient movement skills, children need a combination of unstructured play and appropriate, planned movement experiences (Deli, Bakle, Zachopoulou, 2006; Manross, 2000; Pica, 1997). Adult guidance is especially important for learning skills such as marching, galloping, and skipping. Verbal cues and modeling can help children learn to perform the skills more successfully (Breslin, Morton, & Rudisill, 2008; Sanders, 2006).

Objective 4 Demonstrates traveling skills

Not Yet	1	2	3	4	5	6	7	8	9

Moves to explore immediate environment
- Rolls over several times to get toy
- Crawls
- Cruises
- Takes a few steps
- Takes steps, pushing a push-toy or chair
- Moves from crawling to sitting and back again

Experiments with different ways of moving
- Walks across room
- Uses a hurried walk
- Walks backwards
- Pushes riding toy with feet while steering
- Uses a walker to get to the table
- Marches around room

Moves purposefully from place to place with control
- Runs
- Avoids obstacles and people while moving
- Starts and stops using wheelchair
- Walks up and down stairs alternating feet
- Climbs up and down on playground equipment
- Rides tricycle using pedals
- Gallops, but not smoothly

Coordinates complex movements in play and games
- Runs smoothly and quickly, changes directions, stops and starts quickly
- Steers wheelchair into small playground spaces
- Jumps and spins
- Moves through obstacle course
- Gallops and skips with ease
- Plays "Follow the Leader" using a variety of traveling movements

See page 10 of *Child Assessment Portfolio.*

Objective 4 Demonstrates traveling skills

Strategies

- Create a protected space for young infants to explore movement safely while lying on their stomachs and backs.

- Provide push toys, e.g., toy shopping carts and doll strollers, in the classroom and outside to help children who are learning to walk maintain balance.

- Provide time every day for outdoor play. Make sure there is sufficient space for running, jumping, skipping, and galloping.

- Play music during movement activities. Incorporate dances that may be familiar to families in your program. Model, describe, and suggest ways for children to respond to music by using a variety of movements.

- Use traveling movements to transition children from one activity to another. Invite children to walk slowly, quickly, sideways, or backwards.

- Provide riding toys for children to push with their feet and eventually pedal.

- Provide movement activities that involve all children actively. Avoid activities where children spend much time waiting or watching others participate.

- Include activities that have a range of appropriate ways to participate so that every child is successful most of the time.

- Use movement activities to enhance stories, e.g., encourage a wild rumpus as in *Where the Wild Things Are* or together act out *Going on a Bear Hunt*.

- Set up an obstacle course so preschool and older children can practice particular skills, e.g., hopping, skipping, running. Help children who need assistance with a skill or to be safe. Adjust the difficulty of tasks to match and slightly challenge children's current ability levels.

- Involve older children in traveling games where they start, stop, and change directions quickly, e.g., hopscotch or "Travel, Stop, Change." For "Travel, Stop, Change," call out a traveling movement (e.g., spin, jump, gallop, run). When the whistle blows, children immediately stop that movement and change quickly to the next movement called.

- Use traveling cards with kindergarten children to direct their movements. For example, the card might indicate, "Gallop 6 steps with right foot," "Walk backwards 10 steps," or "Skip to the end of the sidewalk."

Demonstrates balancing skills

5

Balancing involves movements to help stabilize the body's position when the person is not at rest (Payne & Rink, 1997). Balance is required for an infant to sit unsupported, for a toddler to stoop to pick up a toy and stand up again without tipping over, for a 3-year-old to jump off the bottom step on the climber and land on two feet, and for a kindergartner to walk across a narrow balance beam.

Turning, stretching, stopping, rolling, jumping and landing, swinging, swaying, and dodging require balance (Sanders, 2002). Balancing is difficult for very young children because of their uneven body proportions. As children become less top heavy, their ability to balance improves.

Balance can be static or dynamic. Static balance involves holding a particular position while the body is stationary, such as standing on one foot or sitting. Dynamic balance requires holding a stable position while the body is moving, such as while jumping and landing (Sanders, 2002).

Children's ability to balance affects their performance of gross-motor tasks (Ulrich & Ulrich, 1985). Appropriate instruction, practice, and safe materials and equipment are needed to help children improve their balancing skills (Bosma, 2000; Wang & Ju, 2002). Children often use materials in unique and sometimes dangerous ways to help them balance (Berger, Adolph, & Lobo, 2005). It is important to be sure that equipment is stable and in good repair.

Various factors influence children's ability to balance. For example, performance on the balance beam is affected by changes in beam width, length, and height and whether the child is moving (Robert, 1999). Certain disabilities also influence children's balance. Children with Down syndrome, visual impairments, or motor disabilities such as cerebral palsy may need adaptations to assist them with balancing tasks, or they may need to participate in activities for shorter periods of time (Gould & Sullivan, 1999).

Objective 5 Demonstrates balancing skills

Not Yet	1	2	3	4	5	6	7	8	9

Balances while exploring immediate environment

- Sits propped up
- Rocks back and forth on hands and knees
- Sits a while and plays with toys
- Sits and reaches for toys without falling

Experiments with different ways of balancing

- Squats to pick up toys
- Stands on tiptoes to reach something
- Gets in and out of a chair
- Kneels while playing
- Straddles a taped line on the floor
- Sidesteps across beam or sandbox edge

Sustains balance during simple movement experiences

- Walks forward along sandbox edge, watching feet
- Jumps off low step, landing on two feet
- Jumps over small objects
- Holds body upright while moving wheelchair forward

Sustains balance during complex movement experiences

- Hops across the playground
- Hops on one foot then the other
- Walks across beam or sandbox edge forward and backwards
- Attempts to jump rope

See page 11 of *Child Assessment Portfolio.*

Objective 5 Demonstrates balancing skills

Strategies

- Provide supervised opportunities for young infants to play on their stomachs to build strength.

- Play games with toddlers to promote balance. Place a few objects, such as beanbags, several feet away from a large bucket. Encourage the child to walk from the bucket to the beanbags, pick one up, walk back to the bucket, and drop it in.

- Modify the environment and learning experiences to accommodate a range of abilities.

- Stay close to catch or support a child if he or she loses balance. Use soft surfaces, such as rugs or mats, to help cushion falls indoors.

- Encourage children to stop, change directions, or walk up and down low ramps to promote their balance as they walk.

- Place masking tape or brightly colored yarn on the floor and encourage children to practice balancing by walking on it. Coach children about how to hold their arms out to steady themselves. Hold their hands as needed to provide support.

- Encourage twos and older children to practice walking with beanbags on different body parts, e.g., on head, shoulder, elbow, or under the chin.

- Introduce balance beam activities to twos and older children by offering a wide, low (not more than 4–5 inches off floor) beam. Have children walk with arms out to the side. Increase the challenge by having children walk forward, backward, or sideways, or walk forward while carrying a light object in their hands. Tilt the beam slightly so children can walk up or down the beam. Provide support as needed, such as holding a hand for the first few times a child walks along the beam.

- Provide opportunities for preschool and older children to practice static balance. Have children stand on one foot. Give the cue *freeze* when you want the children to hold their positions (for at least 3 seconds). When they can do that, ask them to balance on the other foot or with their eyes closed.

- Create balancing cards that show animals, objects, or people in various positions. For example, you might have a stork standing on one foot, a frog squatting, a toy soldier, an airplane, a person in yoga position, etc. Children select a card and then carry out the act. The other children try to guess what they represent.

Demonstrates gross-motor manipulative skills

6

Gross-motor manipulative skills involve giving force to or receiving force from balls or similar objects. A toddler picks up a large ball, lifts it over her head, brings it forward again as fast as she can, and then drops the ball in front of her. A preschooler holds a whiffle ball in one hand, moves the ball back along the side his head, takes a step while moving his arm forward, and propels the ball. Both of these children are demonstrating their gross-motor manipulative skills by attempting to throw a ball. In addition to throwing, these skills include collecting or catching, bouncing, kicking, and striking. Children can throw at advanced levels before they can catch objects.

The early years are important for the development of fundamental gross-motor manipulative skills. Children should explore and experiment with balls and similar objects of various sizes and weights. Equipment that is proportionate to the sizes and weights of the children is critical to developing mature gross-motor manipulative skills (Payne & Rink, 1997).

Developing competence with basic ball skills increases children's potential for learning more advanced skills such as those used in organized sports. These skills may also have a positive effect on self-concept and social skill development. Previous learning experiences; size, shape, and weight of the ball or object; and the presence of a disability can affect how children perform gross-motor manipulative tasks. Some children with motor impairments may need adaptations to participate in gross-motor activities (Gould & Sullivan, 1999).

When children's movements become more consistent and less haphazard, they are ready for more specific instruction in how to perform a particular gross-motor manipulative task. One way to do this is through the use of cue words or phases. For example, when helping children learn to catch, you might say, "Watch the ball. Reach with your hands. Pull it into your body." When you tell children discreet actions to take, you help them focus on the skill so they can perform it more efficiently (Breslin et al., 2008; Sanders, 2002). As children play with balls and similar objects, they also need to learn how to maintain their position in relation to people and objects. This is an important safety component (Breslin, Morton, & Rudisill, 2008). Adults are crucial in helping children build a foundation for later skill development and in the safe use of equipment.

Objective 6 Demonstrates gross-motor manipulative skills

Not Yet	1	2	3	4	5	6	7	8	9

Reaches, grasps, and releases objects
- Reaches for object
- Pushes ball
- Drops objects
- Grasps a rolled ball or other object with two hands
- Bats or swipes at a toy

Manipulates balls or similar objects with stiff body movements
- Carries a large ball while moving
- Flings a beanbag
- Throws a ball or other object by pushing it with both hands
- Catches a large, bounced ball against body with straight arms
- Kicks a stationary ball

Manipulates balls or similar objects with flexible body movements
- Throws a ball or other object
- Traps thrown ball against body
- Tosses beanbag into basket
- Strikes a balloon with large paddle
- Kicks ball forward by stepping or running up to it

Manipulates balls or similar objects with a full range of motion
- Steps forward to throw ball and follows through
- Catches large ball with both hands
- Strikes stationary ball
- Bounces and catches ball
- Kicks moving ball while running

See page 12 of *Child Assessment Portfolio.*

Strategies

- Avoid activities that encourage competition or that eliminate children from participating.

- Provide sufficient equipment for each child to participate. Include a variety of shapes, sizes, textures, and weights to encourage experimentation and active participation.

- Ensure children's safety by helping them adjust their position in space in relation to other children and objects. Some children need particular guidance about how to notice and move around other people and objects. Teach the safe use of each piece of equipment.

- Provide balls of various sizes, textures, and grips to explore. Include balls with chimes, bells, and visible items rolling inside.

- Provide opportunities for toddlers to practice releasing balls into targets such as large baskets, buckets, or a small basketball hoop.

- Use scarves or mylar balloons to practice catching. These items are easier to catch than balls because they move slowly and give children time to position themselves for a catch.

- Provide lightweight clubs or mallets and balls of various sizes for toddlers and older children to practice hitting along the ground.

- Provide equipment that is appropriate in scale. Young preschool children like to throw and catch large rubber or beach balls. Smaller, softer balls are good for kicking. Also provide yarn balls or beanbags for catching or for throwing against a wall with varying force. Use short-handled, oversized plastic or foam paddles or bats for striking.

- Make modifications for children with disabilities or who have less developed manipulative skills. Use lower targets; provide easy-to-see, bright objects to strike; or reduce the distance between the child and target. Offer balls or similar materials that are lightweight. Hang paper balls for children to hit without having to retrieve them.

- Use specific cues with individual children to help them increase proficiency, e.g., "Look at the target before you throw." Use consistent terminology to avoid confusion.

- Provide kindergarten children with plastic cups and tennis or foam balls to practice throwing and catching skills. Increase difficulty by having children throw and catch while sitting, standing, crouching, or walking.

Objective 7

Demonstrates fine-motor strength and coordination

7

Fine-motor skills involve grasping and releasing objects using fingers and hands, as well as using both hands together and often coordinating these movements with the eyes. They require hand and finger strength and dexterity. An infant who slowly picks up Cheerios® one at a time with his thumb and index finger will become a 2-year-old who scribbles with a crayon. A 3-year-old who squeezes and pounds play dough will become a 5-year-old who cuts a picture out of a magazine accurately. Dramatic changes occur in what children can accomplish as they gradually gain control of the small muscles in their hands and fingers. Fine-motor skills improve with regular practice and can be supported through routines and play activities.

Fine-motor skills are important in the performance of daily routines and many school-related tasks. The pincer grasp (using the thumb and index finger, or forefinger, in opposition to one another) develops at the end of the first year, enabling the child to manipulate small objects. Fine-motor development progresses slowly during the preschool years. By kindergarten, children who have often experimented with various materials engage in fine-motor activities for longer periods of time and with less frustration than children who have not had opportunities to handle materials.

Hand and finger strength and control enable children to perform a variety of self-care tasks, such as eating, toileting, dressing, toothbrushing, and nose blowing. These skills give children the experience of doing things on their own and build confidence. Self-care skills are learned gradually and mastered with repetition. Complex skills, such as tying shoes, require children to have an adequate attention span, memory for a series of complex hand movements, and the dexterity to carry them out. Children who have difficulty coordinating the small muscles in their hands have trouble dressing and feeding themselves (Rule & Stewart, 2002).

Gender and family background also affect the development of children's fine-motor skills. Girls tend to be more advanced than boys in fine-motor skills (Sanders, 2006). Some children from at-risk families may have less-developed fine-motor skills. The risk factors were low maternal education, welfare dependency (poverty), only one parent in the home, and having parents whose primary home-language was not English (National Center for Education Statistics, 2000).

Children with disabilities and others who have difficulty coordinating the small muscles in their hands may struggle with using pencils, crayons, and scissors (Rule & Stewart, 2002). They may avoid fine-motor activities because the activities are difficult for them, they tire, or they become anxious and give up in frustration. Modification of activities and materials to fit their developmental levels, as well as more structure and guidance, can help children increase fine-motor skills (Stewart, Rule, & Giordano, 2007).

Young children in some cultures perform self-care tasks and family chores that most children in the United States do not perform until they are older, e.g., preparing food (Trawick-Smith, 2006; Whiting & Edwards, 1988; Whiting & Whiting, 1975). Some children are not expected to perform self-care tasks such as dressing themselves until after their preschool years because their families value interdependence (doing things for each other) over personal independence.

Objective 7 Demonstrates fine-motor strength and coordination

a. Uses fingers and hands

Not Yet	1	2	3	4	5	6	7	8	9

Reaches for, touches, and holds objects purposefully (2)
- Bats or swipes at a toy
- Transfers objects from one hand to another
- Releases objects voluntarily
- Rakes and scoops objects to pick them up
- Picks up food with fingers and puts in mouth
- Bangs two blocks together
- Crumples paper

Uses fingers and whole-arm movements to manipulate and explore objects (4)
- Places shape in shape sorter
- Points at objects and pokes bubbles
- Releases objects into containers
- Uses spoon and sometimes fork to feed self
- Dumps sand into containers
- Unbuttons large buttons
- Rotates knobs
- Tears paper

Uses refined wrist and finger movements (6)
- Squeezes and releases tongs, turkey baster, squirt toy
- Snips with scissors
- Strings large beads
- Pours water into containers
- Pounds, pokes, squeezes, rolls clay
- Buttons, zips, buckles, laces
- Uses hand motions for "Itsy Bitsy Spider"
- Turns knobs to open doors
- Uses eating utensils
- Sews lacing cards
- Cuts along straight line

Uses small, precise finger and hand movements (8)
- Uses correct scissors grip
- Attempts to tie shoes
- Pushes specific keys on a keyboard
- Arranges small pegs in pegboard
- Strings small beads
- Cuts out simple pictures and shapes, using other hand to move paper
- Cuts food
- Builds a structure using small Legos®

b. Uses writing and drawing tools

Not Yet	1	2	3	4	5	6	7	8	9

Grasps drawing and writing tools, jabbing at paper (2)

Grips drawing and writing tools with whole hand but may use whole-arm movements to make marks (4)

Holds drawing and writing tools by using a three-point finger grip but may hold the instrument too close to one end (6)

Uses three-point finger grip and efficient hand placement when writing and drawing (8)

See pages 13–14 of *Child Assessment Portfolio*.

Objective 7 Demonstrates fine-motor strength and coordination

Strategies

- Provide a wide variety of fine-motor activities that interest and appeal to all children in the program. Include items that are easy to manipulate by hand and add more challenging activities as quickly as possible without causing frustration.

- Offer activities that strengthen infants' and toddlers' hand grasp, e.g., transferring an object from one hand to another, pulling scarves from a hole cut in a box.

- Engage children in activities that encourage them to move their fingers individually, e.g., finger plays, pointing at pictures.

- Provide activities to strengthen the hand grasp and release of toddlers and older children, e.g., using squirt bottles, medicine droppers, punching holes, using clothespins, and handling play dough.

- Include activities for toddlers and older children that support eye-hand coordination, e.g., stringing beads on pipe cleaners or laces, picking up objects with tongs or tweezers, placing various sized pegs in holes, and folding paper. Encourage kindergarten children to fold paper into halves, fourths, very small, etc. and/or to create shapes or animals.

- Include activities for twos and older children that require using two hands together, e.g., tearing paper, opening and closing containers, using wind-up toys.

- Have children watch as you demonstrate a task and describe the steps. Vary your language to accommodate different developmental levels.

- Allow plenty of time for children to explore materials and complete tasks.

- Take advantage of self-care activities (e.g., handwashing and scraping plates) throughout the day to support the development of children's fine-motor skills.

- Give simple, clear, verbal instructions and physically guide, model, or use picture cues to help children perform tasks successfully.

Language

Language is the principal tool for establishing and maintaining relationships with adults and other children. Children's desire to communicate their thoughts, ideas, needs, and feelings with others motivates them to develop language (Epstein, 2007). Learning to understand and use words is complex. Language also involves learning about the structure and sequence of speech sounds, vocabulary, grammar, and the rules for engaging in appropriate and effective conversation (Berk, 2003).

Language development begins at birth, but many children do not receive the ongoing experiences that support this learning. By age 3, differences in children's understanding and use of language are enormous (Berk, 2005; Strickland & Shanahan, 2004). Strong language skills are essential for children's success in school and life (Hart & Risley, 2003; Heath & Hogben, 2004; Jalongo, 2008; Kalmar, 2008). Oral language, including grammar, the ability to define words, and listening comprehension, helps provide the foundation and is an ongoing support for literacy (National Early Literacy Panel, 2008; Strickland & Shanahan, 2004). Children use language to think and to solve problems. Because words represent objects and ideas, language development is closely related to cognitive development. Children with certain types of disabilities face particular challenges in learning to understand and use language effectively.

LANGUAGE OBJECTIVES

8 Listens to and understands increasingly complex language

9 Uses language to express thoughts and needs

10 Uses appropriate conversational and other communication skills

Family background and culture also affect how children learn language. There are differences in how much mothers talk with their children and what they talk about. Some parents focus on social norms such as turn-taking; others discuss what people are thinking and feeling. There are major differences in the kinds of questions they ask (Pena & Mendez-Perez, 2006).

Teachers are very important in helping children develop a strong foundation in language. Teachers influence language development through the language they use, the way they set up the environment, and the types of experiences they provide. The opportunities children have for sociodramatic play and the level of that play affects children's language development. Higher levels of play allow for increased language and more complex language structures (Heisner, 2005).

Listens to and understands increasingly complex language

8

Children must be able to comprehend what they hear. *Receptive language* includes listening to, recognizing, and understanding the communication of others. An infant turns to the sound of her mother's voice, a 2-year-old answers simple questions, and a kindergartner follows detailed, multistep directions. To comprehend language, children must focus their attention and listen with a purpose. They must accurately and quickly recognize and understand what they hear (Roskos, Tabors, & Lenhart, 2004). Receptive language starts to develop before expressive language, but they are closely connected (Hirsch-Pasek, Golinkoff, & Naigles, 1996; Strickland, 2006). Expressive language is dependent upon receptive language.

Young children connect what they hear with their background knowledge and experiences (Strickland, 2006). The more children understand about the world around them, the better able they are to make sense of what they hear. Through conversations with adults, listening to stories read aloud, and engaging in meaningful experiences, children develop new concepts and acquire new vocabulary that helps them to understand increasingly complex language.

Some children with hearing impairments may be learning other forms of communication such as sign language or cued speech. Children with receptive language difficulties may have difficulty understanding the meaning of what they hear. They may understand only a word or two and then guess the meaning of the rest of the words.

English-language learners who are not proficient in their home language, may find it harder to learn English (Jalongo, 2008; Tabors & Snow, 2001). Environments that are noisy make it even more difficult for them to recognize English words (Jalongo, 2008). Positive language interactions with skillful English speakers are critical to helping them become proficient in English (Piker & Rex, 2008).

Nonverbal communication is an important part of the listening experience and may have different meanings in different cultures. Some people value direct eye contact while listening, and others perceive eye contact as a sign of disrespect (Trawick-Smith, 2006).

Objective 8 Listens to and understands increasingly complex language

a. Comprehends language

Not Yet	1	2	3	4	5	6	7	8	9

Shows an interest in the speech of others

- Turns head toward people who are talking
- Recognizes familiar voice before the adult enters the room
- Looks at favorite toy when adult labels and points to it
- Responds to own name

Identifies familiar people, animals, and objects when prompted

- Picks up cup when asked, "Where's your cup?"
- Goes to sink when told to wash hands
- Touches body parts while singing "Head, Shoulders, Knees, and Toes."

Responds appropriately to specific vocabulary and simple statements, questions, and stories

- Finds his favorite illustration in a storybook when asked
- Listens to friend tell about cut finger and then goes to the dramatic play area to get a Band-Aid®
- Responds using gestures to compare the sizes of the three leaves

Responds appropriately to complex statements, questions, vocabulary, and stories

- Answers appropriately when asked, "How do you think the car would move if it had square wheels?"
- Builds on ideas about how to fix the broken wagon
- Acts out the life cycle of a butterfly after the teacher reads a story about it

b. Follows directions

Not Yet	1	2	3	4	5	6	7	8	9

Responds to simple verbal requests accompanied by gestures or tone of voice

- Waves when mother says, "Wave bye-bye," as she waves her hand
- Covers eyes when adult prompts, "Wheeeere's Lucy?"
- Drops toy when teacher extends hand and says, "Please give it to me."

Follows simple requests not accompanied by gestures

- Throws trash in can when asked, "Will you please throw this away?"
- Puts the balls in the basket when told, "Put all the balls in the basket, please."
- Goes to cubby when teacher says, "It's time to put coats on to go outside."

Follows directions of two or more steps that relate to familiar objects and experiences

- Washes and dries hands after being reminded about the hand-washing sequence
- Completes a sequence of tasks, "Get the book bin and put it on the table. Then bring the paper and crayons."

Follows detailed, instructional, multistep directions

- Follows instructions for navigating a new computer program
- Follows teacher's guidance: "To feed the fish, first get the fish flakes. Open the jar and sprinkle a pinch of food on the water. Finally, put the lid on the jar and put it back on the shelf."

See pages 15–16 of *Child Assessment Portfolio*.

Objective 8 Listens to and understands increasingly complex language

Strategies

- Use *parentese* with young infants. Singsong speech and exaggerated facial expressions encourage babies to listen and focus on what is said.

- Talk often with children, using rich language to describe objects, events, and people in the environment.

- Walk over to the child instead of speaking from across the room. The child can attend more easily to what you are saying if you are nearby.

- Have the child's attention when you speak. Place yourself face-to-face at the child's level.

- Be clear and specific when making requests and giving directions.

- Use language that is easy for the child to understand, explaining new vocabulary as you use it.

- Use gestures and concrete objects to clarify what you are saying to a child.

- Use the same words and phrases for common classroom activities. This can help English-language learners associate language with meaning, e.g., say, "Hang your painting on the drying rack."

- Give adequate waiting time, so children can process what they hear and take part in discussions.

- Use precise language because young children are very literal thinkers.

- Learn about and respond appropriately to the conversational styles of the children's families.

- Use same-language and different-language peers as social peer resources. Peers can assist dual language learners in participating in classroom activities and responding appropriately to the teacher's inquiries.

- Alert children when giving complex explanations. Tell them what to listen for. For example say, "This is hard to understand. Listen carefully to each step."

- Positively acknowledge when the child follows directions.

- Use multistep and unrelated directions with kindergarten children. For example, you might say, "First, take the plastic tablecloth and put it on the table. Next, get the paint, droppers, and six containers off the shelf. Put 10 drops of paint into each container. Put a container and piece of paper at each child's place." Also use multiple directions related to different tasks. For example, "Hang your coat up. Take the books back to the library. When you come back, get out your journal."

Uses language to express thoughts and needs

9

Children all over the world follow the same developmental sequence as they learn to speak. They proceed from cooing and babbling in infancy to forming words and sentences as toddlers and 2-year-olds and using more adult-like speech as preschoolers. Children talk to express feelings, make requests, discuss plans, gain information, understand concepts, solve problems, and share ideas and stories. With lots of practice over time, children develop the ability to speak clearly and to use *decontextualized language* to tell personal stories as they describe objects, people, and events that are familiar, but that occurred in another time and place (Nicolopoulou & Richner, 2007; Snow, 1991). This *narrative talk* or storytelling requires more complex language than is needed for daily conversations (Stadler & Ward, 2005).

The use of language is important to children's literacy development. Children's first writing experiences are usually based on what they learned through narrative talk (Beals, 2001; Dickinson & Tabors, 2001; Hart & Risley, 1995). Later literacy development is influenced by *explanatory talk* such as discussion of cause-and-effect relationships and connections between ideas, events, and actions (Beals, 2001; Dickinson & Tabors, 2001; Hart & Risley, 1995). Children's later literacy development also is influenced by their ability to define words and their knowledge of grammar (National Early Literacy Panel, 2008).

Children's language skills vary greatly. There are major differences due to family background and income. Family language patterns affect how much speech children use to express their feelings, needs, and ideas (Rogoff, Mistry, Goncu, & Mosier, 1993). Some children speak in complex sentences. Others make brief statements and must be supported to say more about their ideas. Children's narrative topics may be limited to a single focus with a clear beginning, middle, and end. Narratives of other children may flow from one topic into another (Stadler & Ward, 2005). By kindergarten, some children living in poverty have only one fourth of the vocabulary of their middle-class peers (Berk, 2006).

Some children use other forms of communication besides spoken language. They may use sign language or augmentative communication including pictures, switch activated devices, or other mechanisms that can speak for them (Cook, Klein, & Tessier, 2004). It is important to include children's use of these devices when assessing a child's development.

For some children, English is not their first language. They may speak only a little English or none at all. Every language has its own vocabulary and rules for how sounds, words, and larger units of meaning fit together. Many children use the structure of their home language and apply it as they learn English (August & Hakuta, 1998). English-language learners and children with language delays may find it difficult to use language that goes beyond what is familiar (Weitzman & Greenberg, 2002).

Objective 9 Uses language to express thoughts and needs

Children with language delays or hearing or cognitive impairments often speak in short, ungrammatical sentences. Children with language delays may have difficulty retrieving words from memory and may confuse word meanings (Ratner, 2001). Impairments in social interactions may make it challenging for some children with autism spectrum disorders to learn new words (Parish-Morris, Hennon, Hirsh-Pasek, Golinkoff, & Tager-Flusberg, 2007).

Teachers can influence children's language development (Copple & Bredekamp, 2009). It is important for teachers to engage in conversations with all children, even if they don't yet speak English (Piker & Rex, 2008). Reciprocal, extended conversations with more skilled speakers help children increase their vocabularies, expand their expressive skills, and move toward more conventional grammar. Through participating in extended conversations with adults or mature language users, most children gradually learn adult-like language constructions.

Objective 9 Uses language to express thoughts and needs

a. Uses an expanding expressive vocabulary

Not Yet	1	2	3	4	5	6	7	8	9
		Vocalizes and gestures to communicate • Coos and squeals when happy • Cries after trying several times to get toy just out of reach • Waves hands in front of face to push away spoon during a feeding • Uses hand gestures to sign or indicate "more"		**Names familiar people, animals, and objects** • Says, "Nana," when grandmother comes into the room • Names the cow, horse, chicken, pig, sheep, and goat as she sees them on the trip to the farm		**Describes and tells the use of many familiar items** • When making pancakes, says, "Here is the beater. Let me beat the egg with it." • Responds, "We used the big, red umbrella so we both could get under it."		**Incorporates new, less familiar or technical words in everyday conversations** • Uses a communication device to say, "My bird went to the vet. He has a disease. He's losing his feathers." • Says, "I'm not sure I can put it together. It's complicated."	

b. Speaks clearly

Not Yet	1	2	3	4	5	6	7	8	9
		Babbles strings of single consonant sounds and combines sounds • Says, "M-m-m;" "D-d-d" • Says, "Ba-ba-ba" • Babbles with sentence-like intonation		**Uses some words and word-like sounds and is understood by most familiar people** • Refers to grandma as "Gum-gum" • Asks, "Where bankit?" and a friend brings his blanket to him • Says, "No go!" to indicate she doesn't want to go inside		**Is understood by most people; may mispronounce new, long, or unusual words** • Says, "I saw ants and a hoppergrass" (grasshopper) • Speaks so is understood by the school visitor		**Pronounces multisyllabic or unusual words correctly** • Says, "Oh, that one has layers, it's a *sedimentary* rock." • Says, "What does *ostracize* mean?" after hearing the word read in *Abiyoyo*	

See pages 17–18 of *Child Assessment Portfolio.*

Objective 9 Uses language to express thoughts and needs

c. Uses conventional grammar

Not Yet	1	2	3	4	5	6	7	8	9

Uses one- or two-word sentences or phrases
- Asks, "More?"
- Says, "Daddy go."
- Uses one word, "Juice," to mean, "I want some juice."

Uses three- to four-word sentences; may omit some words or use some words incorrectly
- Says, "Bed no go."
- Says, "Daddy goed to work."
- Responds, "I want banana," when asked what she wants for snack

Uses complete, four- to six-word sentences
- Says, "I chose two books."
- Says, "We are going to the zoo."
- Says, "Momma came and we went home."

Uses long, complex sentences and follows most grammatical rules
- Says, "We are going to the zoo to see the animals. We'll learn where they live and what they eat."
- Notices when sentences do not make sense; tries to correct them

d. Tells about another time or place

Not Yet	1	2	3	4	5	6	7	8	9

Makes simple statements about recent events and familiar people and objects that are not present
- Says, "Got shoes."
- Hears helicopter, stops and says, "'copter."
- Tells, "Gran lives far away."

Tells simple stories about objects, events, and people not present; lacks many details and a conventional beginning, middle, and end
- Dictates a simple story with few connections between characters and events
- Says, "I've got new shoes. I went to the shoe store."

Tells stories about other times and places that have a logical order and that include major details
- Tells about past experiences, reporting the major events in a logical sequence
- Says, "I went to the shoe store with Gran. I got two pairs of new shoes."

Tells elaborate stories that refer to other times and places
- Dictates an elaborate story of her recent visit to the bakery, including details of who, what, when, why, and how
- Tells many details as he acts out his recent trip to the shoe store

See pages 19–20 of *Child Assessment Portfolio.*

Objective 9 Uses language to express thoughts and needs

Strategies

- Serve as a good speech model for children. Speak slowly, and model correct grammar.

- Respect children's communication styles while encouraging them to achieve higher levels of communication. Instead of correcting the child's incorrect pronunciation and grammar, respond by modeling the correct language. Repeat their words with more complete, grammatically accurate, or expanded talk. For example, when the child says, "He goed," say, "Yes, Marcus went to the museum with his aunt and uncle."

- Encourage children to use explanatory talk (explaining and describing) by modeling it. For example explain, "This jar of paint is hard to open. If I put it under hot water, the cover will expand, and it will be much easier to open."

- Ask open-ended questions that encourage multiple responses. For example say, "What would happen if...?", "What do you think?", "What else could you do?". Even if children are preverbal, open-ended questions encourage children's thinking, and they benefit from hearing the rich language.

- Have one-on-one conversations with children who are reluctant to speak in a group. Support them in contributing to small group discussions.

- Provide props that encourage talking, e.g., telephones and puppets.

- Join children's dramatic play to scaffold their storytelling. For example, you might prompt a child by saying, "What did your grandma say after that?"

- Help children connect their everyday experiences and relate the familiar to the unfamiliar. For example, when introducing a new material say, "You can use these new sponge brushes to paint just like you use the big paint brushes. Let me show you."

- Tell children stories without using books. Tell about things that happened in another time and place. For example, you might tell a story about what they did at school earlier in the year. Encourage kindergarten children to tell their own stories about what they did at school earlier in the year.

- Include materials to encourage verbal children to tell stories, e.g. wordless picture books, miniature items from a story, and picture story starters.

- Help children increase the richness and diversity of their vocabulary. Introduce children to less common words through books, songs, conversations, discussions, pretend play, first-hand experiences, and in-depth studies.

- Repeat and reinforce new words. Talk about the meanings of new words by providing familiar words with similar meanings. Use new words in different contexts throughout the day.

- Use simple language and speak slowly. Use gestures, pictures, and objects to help children understand meaning.

- Play language games with kindergarten children. Have them make up sentences (some that make sense and some that don't), and have the other children indicate "sense" or "nonsense." If it's a nonsense sentence, the other children have to try and tell why it's nonsense.

- Make sure each child can respond to questions, participate in story time, make choices, initiate social conversations, and get your attention when needed. Consider a variety of communication techniques, e.g., gestures, picture boards, and recordable communication devices.

- Ask families about the child's successful communication strategies at home.

Uses appropriate conversational and other communication skills

10

Conversations involve back-and-forth exchanges. When an infant coos back at his mother while she talks to him, a 2-year-old adds her thoughts when there is a pause in the conversation, a preschooler initiates a conversation with his teacher about a recent vacation, and a kindergartner takes turns as he engages in a lengthy conversation with several friends, they are all using appropriate communication and conversational skills.

Children acquire vocabulary, other language skills, and background knowledge about many topics by participating in frequent, meaningful conversations with responsive adults. They benefit from conversations that include varied vocabulary and that challenge their thinking (Dickinson & Tabors, 2001). Such conversations contribute to early reading success. In addition, conversations are important to children's cognitive and social–emotional learning (Hart & Risley, 1995). One-to-one, extended, cognitively challenging conversations can be used to engage even reluctant talkers (Snow, Burns, & Griffin, 1998).

Children also must learn the social rules of communicating. This involves being polite, speaking so the listener understands, and turn-taking. The social rules of conversations often vary from culture to culture and from one community to another (Trawick-Smith, 2006).

Social conventions determine how much silent time is expected for thinking and for carefully selecting the right words before making a response (Rowe, 1987). In some families, children may be expected to listen to adult conversations and to speak only when asked to contribute (National Research Council, 2001). The following list describes differences in several social conventions:

- Turn-taking: Some people engage in conversations where equal turn-taking is not valued; others value it highly.

- Personal space: Some people tend to stand very close together during conversations, while others stand farther apart.

- Eye contact: In some communities, eye contact with an adult is a sign of disrespect or rudeness; in others, eye contact is a sign of respect.

- Touch: A touch, e.g., on the arm or shoulder, may be offensive to some people but considered a friendly gesture by others.

- Gestures: Hand gestures, e.g., making a circle with the thumb and forefinger, may carry different meanings in different cultures.

- Politeness and formality: Some people vary formality and other ways of being polite according to the social status of the person being addressed.

Objective 10 Uses appropriate conversational and other communication skills

a. Engages in conversations

Not Yet	1	2	3	4	5	6	7	8	9

Engages in simple back-and-forth exchanges with others
- Coos at adult who says, "Sweet Jeremy is talking." He coos again, and adult imitates the sounds
- Shakes head for *no*; waves bye-bye
- Joins in games such as pat-a-cake and peekaboo

Initiates and attends to brief conversations
- Says, "Doggy." Teacher responds, "You see a doggy." Child says, "Doggy woof."
- Asks teacher, "Home now?" Teacher responds, "Yes, I'm leaving to go home."
- Looks at teacher and points to picture of car. Teacher responds, "No, I'm going to walk home."

Engages in conversations of at least three exchanges
- Stays on topic during conversations
- Maintains the conversation by repeating what the other person says or by asking questions

Engages in complex, lengthy conversations (five or more exchanges)
- Offers interesting comments with communication device
- Extends conversation by moving gradually from one topic to a related topic

b. Uses social rules of language

Not Yet	1	2	3	4	5	6	7	8	9

Responds to speech by looking toward the speaker; watches for signs of being understood when communicating
- Hears siren and goes to adult pointing, "Fire tuck."
- Looks at adult and says, "Ball", repeatedly until adult says, "Ball. You want the ball?"

Uses appropriate eye contact, pauses, and simple verbal prompts when communicating
- Pays attention to speaker during conversation
- Pauses after asking a question to wait for a response
- Says "please" and "thank you" with occasional prompting

Uses acceptable language and social rules while communicating with others; may need reminders
- Takes turns in conversations but may interrupt or direct talk back to self
- Regulates volume of voice when reminded

Uses acceptable language and social rules during communication with others
- Uses a softer voice when talking with peers in the library and a louder voice on the playground
- Says, "Hello," back to the museum curator on a trip

See pages 21–22 of *Child Assessment Portfolio.*

Objective 10 Uses appropriate conversational and other communication skills

Strategies

- Build on the child's language. Rephrase what the child says and then add more.

- Learn as much as you can about the communication styles of the families in the program.

- Plan specific experiences where children will be encouraged to talk and to use their communication skills.

- Model appropriate conversational skills, e.g., taking turns, eye contact, speech volume, and using polite words.

- Provide many opportunities for children to hear and use language. Engage in frequent conversations with each child. Listen carefully to what is being said. Children will talk more when they know teachers listen.

- Provide interesting experiences for children to discuss.

- Try to maintain conversations with children for extended exchanges. Listen carefully to what the child is saying. Respond with related comments and open-ended questions that keep the conversation going. Try to get the child to tell you more about the topic. For preverbal children, model this conversational style using their cues to guide you. For example, when the infant reaches for a rattle and grunts, say, "Do you want your rattle? What are you going to do with your rattle?" Hand the baby the rattle and when he shakes it say, "Oh you are shaking it." When the baby squeals with delight say, "You like shaking your rattle."

- Encourage the use of social words in context, e.g., "please" and "thank you." Provide them as options on a child's communication device.

- Use the same communication system as the child, e.g. point to pictures on her picture board to ask if she wants to go outside.

- Organize kindergarten children into discussion groups of four or more. Begin with topics they want to talk about. Support them as needed to listen to others (including communicating with children using communication devices), take turns, add relevant information, stay on topic, etc. Include less skillful as well as more skilled children in the group. As children become more skillful, increase the number of children in the group.

Cognitive

Cognitive development, also called intellectual development, is influenced by the child's approaches to learning as well as his or her biological makeup and the environment. A child's background knowledge, or knowledge base, also affects the way a child thinks. This background knowledge influences the child's information processing, memory, classification, problem solving, language acquisition, and reading and mathematics learning (Bjorklund, 2005; McAfee & Leong, 1994). What and how children learn often varies considerably from culture to culture, and minor variations exist in the ways children within a cultural group perform specific cognitive tasks (Trawick-Smith, 2006). Some children have disabilities that interfere with the development of their conceptual and reasoning skills (Cook, Klein, & Tessier, 2004).

Children who have positive approaches to learning are more likely to succeed academically and to have more positive interactions with peers (Fantuzzo, Perry, & McDermott, 2004; Hyson, 2005, 2008; McWayne, Fantuzzo, & McDermott, 2004; Yen, Konold, & McDermott, 2004). These dispositions and behaviors must be nurtured by effective curriculum and intentional teaching methods (Hyson, 2005, 2008; Hyson, Buch, Fantuzzo, & Scott-Little, 2006).

COGNITIVE OBJECTIVES

11 Demonstrates positive approaches to learning

12 Remembers and connects experiences

13 Uses classification skills

14 Uses symbols and images to represent something not present

The physical environment of the classroom and the kinds of interactions children have with adults and other children influence the way children approach learning and influence other aspects of their cognitive development.

Play is important for learning; researchers have found many connections between cognitive competence and play, particularly high-quality dramatic play. The benefits of play include self-regulation; memory development; divergent thinking; problem solving; language development; and academic skill development in literacy, math, social studies, and science (Bergen, 2002; Bodrova & Leong, 2004; Charlesworth, 2007; Krafft & Berk, 1998; Fantuzzo & McWayne, 2002; Howes & Matheson, 1992; Klein, Wirth, & Linas, 2004; Newman, 1990; Nourot & Van Hoorn, 1991; O'Reilly & Bornstein, 1993; Smilansky & Shefatya, 1990; Steglin, 2005).

Demonstrates positive approaches to learning

11

When children have a positive approach to learning, they are likely to want to learn more. There are five dimensions to this objective: attention and engagement, persistence, problem solving, curiosity and motivation, and flexibility and inventiveness.

Attention, Engagement, and Persistence

As children mature, they demonstrate an increasing capacity to concentrate, to persist, and therefore, to become deeply involved in what they are doing, despite distractions and interruptions. The ability to resist distractions, remain positively engaged, and persist at learning tasks are related positively to children's academic achievement, cognitive development, and peer interactions (Blair, 2003; Deater-Deckard, Petrill, Thompson, & DeThrone, 2005; Duncan et al., 2007; Fantuzzo, Perry, & McDermott, 2004; Howse, Lange, Farran, & Boyles, 2003; Hyson, 2008; Jablon & Wilkinson, 2006; Ladd, Birch, & Buhs, 1999; Normandeau & Guay, 1998).

There are variations among children's levels of attention, engagement, and persistence. Bilingual children may sometimes be more likely to attend to relevant details during attention-demanding tasks than their monolingual peers because they have had experience attending to one language while ignoring the other language (Bialystok & Martin, 2004). In general, children show greater persistence on tasks that are challenging for them (tasks that are not too easy or too difficult). They are likely to be more attentive, interested, and engaged when they make choices about their learning (Brophy, 2004; Kohn, 1993).

Some children with particular disabilities may be less likely to become engaged in activities or may show engagement in ways that are different from those of typically developing children. Children with attention deficit disorders (ADD, ADHD) may find it difficult to persist with classroom performance tasks. Children with autism spectrum disorders may repeat behaviors, continuing to do the same things again and again. They may do this even if their strategies are not successful. Children living in poverty may find it hard to regulate their attention and persist with challenging tasks if they are hungry, sick, or sleepy (Howse, Lange, Farran, & Boyles, 2003; Hyson, 2008).

Objective 11 Demonstrates positive approaches to learning

Positive evaluative feedback from adults helps children persist with difficult tasks (Berk, 2003; Burhans & Dweck, 1995; Kelly, Brownell, & Campbell, 2000). Children who are distracted easily may need to work with only a few materials and choices at one time. Sometimes a task must be presented in smaller steps so that the child can understand what to do (Gargiulo & Kilgo, 2007; Lewis, 2003).

Problem Solving

Children solve problems by using available information, resources, and materials to overcome obstacles and achieve a goal. An infant cries when hungry. A toddler backs down steps consistently once he has been taught to go down backwards. A preschool child tries several strategies, modifying them as he goes along. A kindergartner works with peers trying various suggestions for attaching new pieces to a sculpture. In order to use relevant information to solve problems, children need to have organized what they know and be able to retrieve it. Very young children independently discover many ways to solve problems as they explore their bodies and interact with materials and people.

Children become increasingly selective in and adept at using problem-solving strategies. With experience, they become better at selecting and monitoring strategies and applying them in new situations (Berk, 2002, 2003; Bjorklund, 2005). Even after using a more efficient strategy, children often return to using a less effective strategy. This switching among strategies aids cognitive development. It allows children to reason about their choices, comparing more and less effective strategies.

Play gives children many opportunities to solve problems. In particular, sociodramatic play fosters children's problem-solving skills (Bergen, 2002; Fisher, 1992). Research shows that there are cultural and individual differences in the ways children approach problem-solving tasks. Some children interact with others to solve problems. Some children watch how others work with materials before beginning to use them. Other children solve problems independently, handling materials to figure out how they work. (Bergen, 2002; Berk, 2002, 2003; Trawick-Smith, 2006). One way is not necessarily better than another.

Curiosity and Motivation

Young children want to know more about themselves and the world around them. An infant explores a block by putting it in his mouth and banging it on the ground. A toddler turns the water handle repeatedly to make the water start and stop. A 2-year-old repeatedly asks, "Why?" A preschooler who is interested in airplanes asks an adult to read a nonfiction book about how jets are made. These children are all demonstrating their curiosity and motivation to learn.

Curiosity promotes cognitive, social–emotional, and physical development throughout life by stimulating exploratory behaviors (Reio, Petrosko, Wiswell, & Thongsukmag, 2006). By responding to children's questions and providing safe environments that encourage active exploration, adults foster children's curiosity and motivation to learn. When children are motivated, they have a desire to continue with challenging tasks. Most children find new learning self-motivating (Hyson, 2008). Giving them rewards, e.g., food items, smiley faces, stickers, may lessen their curiosity and motivation to pursue the activities in the future (Arnone, 2003; Deci, Koestner, & Ryan, 2001; Elliot & Dweck, 2005; Katz & Chard, 1995; Stipek, 2002).

All children do not show their curiosity or motivation to learn in the same ways, and teachers may interpret some children's behaviors as a lack of interest and motivation. Some children are taught not to ask questions of adults, and some watch how others use materials rather than explore them actively. Some children with particular cognitive disabilities demonstrate little apparent curiosity or motivation, and they need a great deal of adult support.

Flexibility and Inventiveness

Cognitive flexibility is important for children's academic achievement (George & Greenfield, 2005; Hyson, 2008). Children who are flexible in their thinking consider alternative possibilities, find their own ways to resolve conflicts, and solve problems with tools and materials. When a 2-year-old tries a block and then uses a broom handle to reach a toy under a bookshelf and when a preschooler makes up new lyrics to a familiar song, they are approaching tasks with flexibility and inventiveness.

Flexible thinking is critical to children's development of sorting and categorization skills, understanding of concepts, problem-solving skills, reasoning skills, divergent thinking, and inventiveness. Children need unhurried time to explore topics in depth and to complete activities; space that inspires them to create; a varied collection of found, recycled, and purchased materials and props; an encouraging classroom atmosphere that supports risk-taking, acceptance of mistakes, and innovation; and opportunities to express their innovative thinking through creative products (Pope & Springate, 1995).

Flexibility requires children to shift focus from one topic to another, recognize relevant information, and change their strategies to match changing task demands. There are age differences in children's cognitive flexibility. Infants become increasingly able to shift attention from one object or person to another (Berk, 2002). A developmental spurt in children's cognitive flexibility occurs between 3–5 years of age (Deak, 2003; Smidts, Jacobs, & Anderson, 2004). Children who are bilingual may show enhanced cognitive flexibility as they switch between languages (Bialystok, McBride-Chang, & Luk, 2005). Some children with particular disabilities, such as autism spectrum disorders, may have difficulty with flexible thinking and may need specific activities to encourage flexibility of thought (Carruthers, 1996; Gould & Sullivan, 1999; Lewis, 2003).

Objective 11 Demonstrates positive approaches to learning

a. Attends and engages

Not Yet	1	2	3	4	5	6	7	8	9

Pays attention to sights and sounds
- Watches the teacher walk across the room
- Turns head toward sound of mother's voice

Sustains interest in working on a task, especially when adults offer suggestions, questions, and comments
- Takes small blocks from adult and continues to drop them into a container
- Continues ring stacking when the teacher says, "You're putting the biggest ones on first."
- Continues the play about going to a restaurant after the teacher offers a menu

Sustains work on age-appropriate, interesting tasks; can ignore most distractions and interruptions
- Makes relevant contributions to group discussion about class pet
- Focuses on making a sign for a building while others are rolling cars down a ramp nearby

Sustains attention to tasks or projects over time (days to weeks); can return to activities after interruptions
- Returns to Lego® construction over several days, adding new features each time
- Pauses to join in problem-solving discussion at adult's request, then returns to art project

b. Persists

Not Yet	1	2	3	4	5	6	7	8	9

Repeats actions to obtain similar results
- Repeatedly shakes a rattle to produce noise
- Hits a toy on a play gym accidentally; then waves arms to hit it again
- Puts objects in a wagon and then dumps them out over and over again

Practices an activity many times until successful
- Stacks blocks again and again until tower no longer falls
- Uses shovel in many ways to fill small bucket with sand
- Chooses the same puzzle every day until he can insert each piece quickly and easily

Plans and pursues a variety of appropriately challenging tasks
- Keeps looking through all of the magnetic letters for those that are in her name
- Works with others to learn how to use a new software program

Plans and pursues own goal until it is reached
- Keeps building a sand structure, trying multiple ways to get the bridge to hold
- Returns from lunch with a different idea about what to add to his story

See pages 23–24 of *Child Assessment Portfolio.*

Objective 11 Demonstrates positive approaches to learning

c. Solves problems

Not Yet	1	2	3	4	5	6	7	8	9

Reacts to a problem; seeks to achieve a specific goal
- Grunts when cube gets stuck in shape sorter
- Reaches for a toy that is just out of reach
- Blows on warm cereal after seeing someone blow on cereal

Observes and imitates how other people solve problems; asks for a solution and uses it
- Seeks help opening a stuck cap; pulls one end as teacher pulls the other
- Asks another child to hold his cup while he pours milk

Solves problems without having to try every possibility
- Looks at an assortment of pegs and selects the size that will fit in the hole
- Tells another child, "Put the big block down first, or the tower will fall down."

Thinks problems through, considering several possibilities and analyzing results
- Considers new information before trying a strategy: "If I put this box on top, I can see if they are the same size."
- Thinks about a book character's problem and suggests solutions

d. Shows curiosity and motivation

Not Yet	1	2	3	4	5	6	7	8	9

Uses senses to explore the immediate environment
- Turns in direction of a sound
- Moves closer to touch an object
- Shakes or bangs a toy to make it work

Explores and investigates ways to make something happen
- Enjoys taking things apart
- Turns faucet on and off
- Tilts a ramp to find out if a car will go down faster

Shows eagerness to learn about a variety of topics and ideas
- Seeks answers to questions about the storm
- Shows interest in learning how the firefighter's clothes protect him

Uses a variety of resources to find answers to questions
- Locates informational book on insects to identify the butterfly seen outside
- Asks visiting musician questions about her instrument

See pages 25–26 of *Child Assessment Portfolio.*

Objective 11 Demonstrates positive approaches to learning

e. Shows flexibility and inventiveness in thinking

Not Yet	1	2	3	4	5	6	7	8	9
		Imitates others in using objects in new and/or unanticipated ways • Notices another child reach a toy with the broom handle; then tries • Imitates a friend, putting a basket on head to use as a hat		**Uses creativity and imagination during play and routine tasks** • Strings wooden beads into a necklace as part of dramatic play • Uses a table, sheets, and towels to build a tent		**Changes plans if a better idea is thought of or proposed** • Accepts idea to use tape instead of glue to fix the tear • Suggests building on a hard surface when structure keeps falling down		**Thinks through possible long-term solutions and takes on more abstract challenges** • Offers ideas on how to make the block area larger for building • Creates board game; thinks of how to play it from start to finish	

See page 27 of *Child Assessment Portfolio.*

Objective 11 Demonstrates positive approaches to learning

Strategies

- Provide one or two toys or materials at a time for young infants, exchanging them when the child's attention diminishes.

- Provide appropriate amounts of visual stimuli, e.g., pictures, mobiles, and signs, so children are neither over- nor understimulated.

- Use the child's name to get his or her attention, e.g., say, "Look, Juan!" as you begin to speak.

- Help the child stay focused by singing about an activity if it is helpful to the child, e.g., sing, "This is the way we stack the blocks, stack the blocks, stack the blocks...."

- Provide children with time, space, and a variety of interesting materials for play.

- Provide recyclable as well as new materials that can be used in a variety of innovative ways, e.g., boxes, tubes, spools, containers.

- Provide many opportunities for children to make choices from among interesting materials that are familiar and challenging, and encourage children to use them in many ways.

- Rotate materials regularly to maintain children's interest. Provide materials that build on those already familiar to the children.

- Interpret and expand on what children do and say. Model deliberate, strategic engagement in activities and self-talk to help children stay engaged and persist with challenging tasks.

- Provide opportunities for children to observe others solving problems and to work with other children and adults to solve problems together.

- Support children's efforts during challenging tasks by providing specific, positive verbal feedback or physical support while encouraging them to come up with solutions, e.g., "Keep turning the puzzle piece to figure out how it fits."

- Describe children's problem-solving strategies, e.g., "You tried reaching into the jar to get the balls out, and then you turned the jar over and dumped them."

- Limit directions to one step at a time for toddlers and two or three steps at a time for preschoolers and kindergartners. Reinforce the directions visually by demonstrating the activity, by using pictures, or by using picture and word cues.

- Encourage children to learn from their mistakes. Encourage them to make and test predictions and to examine their thinking.

- Respond to children's explorations and discoveries with enthusiasm and encouragement rather than by providing rewards like stickers or prizes.

- Support children's spontaneous interests, e.g., their examinations of the locust shells found in the play yard, in addition to offering teacher-directed activities based on the children's interests.

- Encourage children to solve problems for themselves when appropriate. Be available to offer support, encouragement, and new ideas when needed.

- Demonstrate, explain, and engage children in trying different ways of doing things. Discuss whether the strategies worked well.

- Take time to answer *why* questions, offering explanations that the child can understand.

- Encourage children's inclination to ask questions and wonder. Help them refine their questions and support them in finding answers.

- Play games that support children's curiosity and internal motivation, such as "Mystery Bag." Hide an object inside a bag. Give verbal clues about its identity. Let children feel, describe, and guess what it is before looking at it.

Objective 11 Demonstrates positive approaches to learning

Strategies, *continued*

- Encourage children's imaginations by finding images in clouds or puddles. Discuss pictures in which part of an object is hidden.

- Nurture children's curiosity by providing thought-provoking, hands-on, investigatory experiences that motivate them to apply their developing skills and prior knowledge and that challenge them to think.

- Ask children open-ended questions such as, "What do you think would happen if you...? What else could you do with...? Can you think of another way to...?"

- Point out strategies children used successfully in similar situations, e.g., prompt, "Yesterday you used the broom to get the dishes from behind the sink. I wonder if it would work to get the puzzle piece that dropped behind the shelf?"

- Organize the play environment to encourage sociodramatic play, including props, utensils, and tools to support different roles. Create new settings for dramatic play with preschool and older children, e.g., a post office, clinic, grocery store, bakery, or campsite. Serve as a sensitive play tutor, engaging in play while following the children's leads.

- Plan so that children can spend days or weeks investigating interesting objects in their environment, seeking answers to their questions, and finding solutions to problems.

- Provide well-defined boundaries for preschool and kindergarten children who need support in order to focus, e.g., use freestanding cardboard dividers for table activities and colored tape to define workspaces on the floor. Limit the number of choices they are given.

- Model flexibility by changing an activity to incorporate children's interesting ideas. To help children consider different perspectives or solutions, explain why the activity is being changed.

- Emphasize the process children use to come up with possible approaches to tasks instead of focusing on finished products and answers.

- Guide preschool and older children in doing in-depth, long-term, and open-ended studies and explorations.

- Encourage children to think of multiple ways to create something using the same materials. For example, they might see how many different ways they can make a boat using milk cartons, paper, foil, craft sticks, etc.

Remembers and connects experiences

12

Memory involves complex cognitive processes. To remember, children must attend to the important aspects of information so that it can be stored and later retrieved and used. Children store information in long-term memory if the information is meaningful to them, if they are able to connect it to something they already know, and if they sense its importance. When toddlers name common objects, preschoolers talk about something they did yesterday, and kindergartners retell a story in detail, they are remembering and connecting information and experiences.

When children determine whether something is the same as, similar to, or different from what they have encountered before, they are using *recognition memory*, e.g., the child recognizes a book he or she has heard before. *Recall memory* is harder; children must imagine something that is not present, e.g., recalls foods eaten by the hungry caterpillar without looking at the pictures. Cues improve children's free recall memory (Berk, 2002; Bjorklund, 2005).

As children develop their abilities to attend and to use memory strategies, their learning is enhanced. They use their existing knowledge and understanding as the basis for making new experiences, ideas, and concepts meaningful.

Making links between new and known information may be challenging for some children. Children with learning disabilities may find it hard to attend to relevant information or to organize information so it can be retrieved (Trawick-Smith, 2006). English-language learners must remember words and their meanings in more than one language.

Adults play an essential role in helping children improve their memory skills. Adults help children connect new experiences to prior knowledge and revise their previous thinking to fit with new experiences. Adult scaffolding, or support, helps children attend and use memory strategies such as categorizing (Barry, 2006; Larkina, Guler, Kleinknect, & Bauer, 2008; McAfee & Leong, 1994; Mussen, Conger, Kagan, & Huston, 1990).

Children from different families and communities may depend on different senses to help them obtain and retain information. Some children retain information that they hear for a longer time, while other children more easily remember information they obtained from drawings, photographs, or other graphics (Bjorklund, 2005; McAfee & Leong, 1994; Trawick-Smith, 2006).

Objective 12 Remembers and connects experiences

a. Recognizes and recalls

Not Yet	1	2	3	4	5	6	7	8	9

Recognizes familiar people, places, and objects; looks for hidden object where it was last seen

- Looks for food dropped from high chair
- Uncovers bear after adult covers it with a blanket
- Says or signs names of common objects when sees them

Recalls familiar people, places, objects, and actions from the past (a few months before); recalls 1 or 2 items removed from view

- Looks for horse used a few months ago in bin of toy animals
- Identifies one or two objects taken away while playing "What's Missing?"
- Shows fear of a bee after having been stung

Tells about experiences in order, provides details, and evaluates the experience; recalls 3 or 4 items removed from view

- Identifies four objects taken away while playing "What's Missing?"
- Says, "We went to the baseball game. We sat way up high. We ate peanuts and drank lemonade. I really liked it a lot but my sister didn't."

Uses a few deliberate strategies to remember information

- Creates an observational drawing of a fire truck and then refers to it later while building with blocks
- Tells the teacher, "I'm putting my book in my backpack so I'll remember to take it home."

b. Makes connections

Not Yet	1	2	3	4	5	6	7	8	9

Looks for familiar persons when they are named; relates objects to events

- Turns head toward door when her teacher says, "Bethany, Mommy is here."
- Throws paper away when teacher says, "Please put this in the trash."

Remembers the sequence of personal routines and experiences with teacher support

- Goes to attendance chart with parent upon arrival
- Gets a paper towel after teacher says, "What do we do next, after we wash our hands?"

Draws on everyday experiences and applies this knowledge to a similar situation

- After hearing *A Chair for My Mother* read aloud says, "My Nana has a chair like the one Rosa and her family bought."
- Uses traffic-directing signals on the bike track after seeing a police officer demonstrate them
- Divides crayons into "fair share" groups after watching a teacher do it the day before

Generates a rule, strategy, or idea from one learning experience and applies it in a new context

- Proposes a one-way sign for entering and exiting the cubby area after a neighborhood walk where children discussed one-way street signs
- Tallies friends' favorite ice cream flavors after learning how to make tally marks to count how many people wear shoes with buckles

See pages 28–29 of *Child Assessment Portfolio.*

Objective 12 Remembers and connects experiences

Strategies

- Talk about the child's home experiences and use the child's home language (if possible) to help him or her relate old and new experiences.

- Demonstrate and explain how different experiences relate, e.g., "Your sweater goes over your head, just as your T-shirt goes over your head."

- Use gestures and language to draw attention to particular features of objects and people.

- Give cues involving many senses, not just verbal cues, to help children remember and learn particular information.

- Use photos and objects to talk about the child's past experiences.

- Involve children in "Remember when..." games and discussions, e.g., Ask, "Do you remember the elephant we saw at the zoo yesterday?" Talk with toddlers about events in the immediate past, and talk with preschoolers and kindergartners about events that took place in the more distant past.

- Expand on children's fragmented recollections by asking varied questions, adding information to children's statements, and commenting about events.

- Encourage children to represent events in multiple ways. For example, after a trip to the fire station, follow up discussions by making a class book with photos and drawings of the trip. Place photos of the trip in the Block area so children can re-create the fire station or fire truck. Develop a list with children of new props to include for dramatic play. Read books or look on the internet for information about firefighters, and compare the information with what the children experienced on their trip.

- Give children enough time to think and make connections before expecting an answer.

- Play memory games like "What's Missing?" Display a few items, remove one, and invite children to tell which one is missing. Display and remove more items with older children.

- Guide older preschool and kindergarten children to make analogies. Help them to see ways in which things they learned about earlier are similar to other things. For example, after studying turtles, they may notice that crabs, crawfish, and lobsters also have shells that help protect them.

- Play games like, "What do they have in common?" Show children pictures of various animals, people and/or objects and have them communicate ways in which they are alike.

Uses classification skills

13

Classification refers to the grouping and organizing of objects, pictures, words, or ideas on the basis of particular criteria. When a toddler tries to put a key in a doorknob, a 2-year-old puts all of the beads in a container with a bead label, and a preschooler explains why he put the snake and lizard picture cards in one pile and the birds in another, they are using classification skills.

Children initially identify broad categories, e.g. food. Next they develop subcategories, e.g., fruit. They then differentiate further and identify additional subcategories, e.g., apples (Pauen, 2002). Exploration of objects, expanding knowledge of the world, and increased language skills contribute to children's ability to classify (Berk, 2002; Gelman & Coley, 1990). When children classify they organize their experiences and manage enormous amounts of information that can be retrieved later. The ability to classify is important for learning and remembering (Larkina, Guler, Kleinknect, & Bauer, 2008). It supports the development of logical thinking.

Children's earliest classifications are based on their sensory perceptions (Berk, 2003). By the end of the first year their classifications become more conceptual, based on common functions or behaviors. When children are particularly knowledgeable about a topic, they are likely to categorize at a more mature level (Bjorklund, 2005; Gelman, 1998).

Adults help children classify more accurately and think more deeply about categories by naming categories and by talking with children about pictures and objects (Gelman, 1998; Gelman, Chesnick, & Waxman, 2005; Gelman, Coley, Rosengren, Hartman, & Pappas, 1998). When an adult reads a picture book and explains that chickens and ducks are both birds, children begin to understand that particular similarities group them together despite their differences. Teachers can assess children's classification skills during conversations with them and as they observe children sorting and re-sorting spontaneously, e.g., grouping all shades of blue crayons together while drawing or sorting by properties suggested by someone else, e.g., "Give me all of the blue teddy bears."

Cultural unfamiliarity makes it harder for children to classify accurately and at higher levels (Lin, Schwanenflugel, & Wisenbaker, 1990). Without the support of language, some English-language learners may find sorting and classifying tasks more challenging than their English-speaking or bilingual peers. Some children with learning disabilities develop classification skills more slowly than their typically developing peers, and some may not be able to develop high-level classification skills (Trawick-Smith, 2006).

Objective 13 Uses classification skills

Not Yet	1	2	3	4	5	6	7	8	9

Matches similar objects
- Puts one sock with another sock
- Gathers all the vehicles from a shelf
- Picks out and eats only the animal crackers
- Puts only blue pegs in pegboard; leaves red and yellow pegs to the side

Places objects in two or more groups based on differences in a single characteristic, e.g., color, size, or shape
- Puts all the red beads together and all the blue beads together
- Pulls out all the trucks from the vehicle bin
- Identifies fabric pieces as being scratchy or soft
- Puts pictures into piles of babies, older children, and grown-ups

Groups objects by one characteristic; then regroups them using a different characteristic and indicates the reason
- Says, "These buttons are blue, and these are red"; then resorts buttons into big and little
- Points to groups of animals and says, "These are zoo animals and these are farm animals"; then sorts the zoo animals into those with stripes and those without stripes

Groups objects by more than one characteristic at the same time; switches sorting rules when asked, and explains the reasons
- Organizes a sticker collection into groups and subgroups and explains why and how; then creates a new grouping when the teacher makes a suggestion
- Creates four piles of shapes: big red triangles, small red triangles, big blue triangles, small blue triangles. Switches when asked to form two groups of all the big and small triangles

See page 30 of *Child Assessment Portfolio.*

Objective 13 Uses classification skills

Strategies

- Provide materials that are safe for infants and toddlers to explore by using all of their senses. As they explore objects, describe the characteristics, "That fabric is soft and bumpy" and "Your block is hard and smooth."

- Model sorting and classifying, and provide opportunities for children to practice, e.g., prompt and model, "Let's pick up all the toys that are trucks."

- Play simple classification games with toddlers by gathering items that people use together, e.g., sock/shoe, flower/vase, plate/fork, and coat/hat.

- Sing, recite fingerplays, and read books that focus on colors, shapes, machines, animals, or other categories.

- Play sorting and matching games, using materials that are familiar to the child. Think about the child's family background, neighborhood, and community as you choose familiar materials, e.g., toys, clothing, utensils, food labels.

- As preschool and kindergarten children sort objects, name the categories and use gestures and statements to point out the similarities of the items in each group. Ask children about the groups, e.g., ask, "Why do these things belong together?"

- Provide preschool and kindergarten children with opportunities to arrange collections into groups by using various rules that you and the children make together.

- Use "mystery boxes" to help preschool children develop classification skills. Put one item into the box. Have each child ask one "yes" or "no" question about what is in the box, e.g., "Is it an animal? Is it brown? Does it have four legs?" Support children's efforts by periodically summarizing what is known about the object, e.g., "We know it is a brown animal with four legs. What else do we need to know?"

- Record older preschool and kindergarten children's ideas about each of two groups, e.g., cats and dogs. Ask them to find similarities between the two groups. Present their ideas in a Venn diagram.

Objective 14

Uses symbols and images to represent something not present

14

Children engage in symbolic thinking when they use representations of objects, events, or persons that are not present. A toddler points to a picture of a cow when an adult asks, "Where's the cow?" A preschooler builds an elaborate structure with blocks and announces, "The dragon lives in this castle!" Both of these children are engaging in abstract thinking. As children mature, they use substitutes that are increasingly different in form and/or function from what they symbolize. Thinking symbolically is necessary for language development, problem solving, reading, writing, mathematical thinking, and participating fully in society (Deloache, 2004; Younger & Johnson, 2004).

Children younger than age 3 have trouble understanding and maintaining the distinction between a symbol and what it represents (Berk, 2002; DeLoache, 1987; Fletcher & Sabo, 2006). Before children can effectively use symbols such as letters, numbers, or maps, they must understand implicitly that symbols represent other things (DeLoache, 1991). By about 18 months of age, children begin treating pictures symbolically rather than as objects to explore manually by hitting, rubbing, patting, scratching, etc. (Preissler & Carey, 2004). This marks an important point in their development of symbolic thinking (DeLoache, 2004; Fletcher & Sabo, 2006). Tools such as webs, graphs, and concept maps are symbolic representations that help preschool and kindergarten children organize and visually represent what they know and think (Birbili, 2006).

Dramatic play, sometimes called symbolic, pretend, make-believe, fantasy, or imaginative play is an important vehicle for development and learning (Bergen, 2002; Klein, Wirth, & Linas, 2004; Nourot & Van Hoorn, 1991; Similansky & Shefatya, 1990; Steglin, 2005). Dramatic play contributes to children's development of abstract thinking and imagination and supports their school adjustment, memory, language, and self-regulation abilities (Bodrova & Leong, 2004; Fantuzzo & McWayne, 2002; Krafft & Berk, 1998; Newman, 1990).

Sociodramatic play is a complex, abstract type of dramatic play that involves more than one child playing together. Advances in cognition and language allow children to use more involved play themes and story lines. Sociodramatic play has several important elements (Similansky & Shefatya, 1990): *role play* (pretending to be someone else); *props* (use of real or imaginary objects); *verbal make-believe* (substituting speech for actions and situations); *interaction* (agreeing on roles for two or more children and relating to one another from the perspectives of their roles); *verbal communication* (interacting verbally about the play situation and roles); and *persistence* (remaining at play for a sustained period). As children act out their roles, they arrive at a shared understanding of the rules for behavior (Bodrova & Leong, 2004). The type of props influences children's pretend play. Children act out more familiar, everyday roles when realistic props are provided. They engage in more fantasy roles when nonrealistic props are offered (Berk & Winsler, 1995).

There are cultural differences in the ways children play. Children from some family backgrounds do not engage in dramatic play unless the classroom environment resembles their home environment (Heisner, 2005; Levy, Wolfgang, & Koorland, 1992; Trawick-Smith, 1998). English-language learners or children with language delays may find it difficult to engage in elaborate, verbal negotiations and to make their ideas about pretend themes and roles clear (Bergen, 2002; Casby, 1997). Disabilities may also affect children's dramatic play. Children with visual or hearing impairments may seek adults, rather than peers, as play partners. Some children with autism spectrum disorders do not engage readily in sociodramatic play (Trawick-Smith 2006).

Objective 14 Uses symbols and images to represent something not present

a. Thinks symbolically

Not Yet	1	2	3	4	5	6	7	8	9
		Recognizes people, objects, and animals in pictures or photographs • Touches the cow in the illustration when an adult reads, "And the cow jumped...." • Points to photograph and says, "Mommy" • Identifies a duck in a variety of different photos and illustrations		**Draws or constructs, and then identifies what it is** • Draws various shapes and says, "This is my house." • Glues red yarn on paper and says, "I made spaghetti."		**Plans and then uses drawings, constructions, movements, and dramatizations to represent ideas** • Sees a dump truck outside and plans how to draw it • Says, "Let's pretend to be seeds growing like in the book."		**Represents objects, places, and ideas with increasingly abstract symbols** • Makes tally marks • Makes and interprets graphs with teacher's help • Attempts to write words to label a picture	

b. Engages in sociodramatic play

Not Yet	1	2	3	4	5	6	7	8	9
		Imitates actions of others during play; uses real objects as props • Holds a toy phone to ear • Wraps a blanket around a doll and then rocks it		**Acts out familiar or imaginary scenarios; may use props to stand for something else** • Puts beads in a muffin tin, places tin in oven, and asks, "Who wants some cupcakes?" • Uses a short rope as a fire hose • Pretends to be the birthday boy at the party and blows out the candles on the pegboard 'cake' after others sing "Happy Birthday"		**Interacts with two or more children during pretend play, assigning and/or assuming roles and discussing actions; sustains play scenario for up to 10 minutes** • Pretends to be the bus driver. Tells the other children, "You can be the passengers. Give me your tickets, and I will give you change."		**Plans and negotiates complex role play; joins in detailed conversation about roles and actions; play may extend over several days** • Joins in elaborate play about taking a dog to the veterinarian, assigning roles, switching roles, creating props, and returning to the play day after day	

See pages 31–32 of *Child Assessment Portfolio.*

Objective 14 Uses symbols and images to represent something not present

Strategies

- Provide many opportunities for children to learn about diverse symbols and their functions, such as language, gestures, letters, numerals, photographs, drawings, models, maps, graphs, webs, and video images.

- Provide books appropriate for the age and abilities of the child, e.g., chubby, cardboard, and cloth books for infants and toddlers.

- Point to pictures during story reading, calling attention to what the pictures mean.

- Show children common objects and encourage them to think of how to use them to represent something different.

- Collect data about the classroom routines of preschool and kindergarten children, e.g., attendance, transportation to school, or snack choices. Graph or otherwise present the information by first using concrete objects, then pictures, and then abstract symbols.

- Schedule adequate time for pretend play to take place indoors and outdoors.

- Match play props to the family backgrounds and developmental characteristics of the children.

- Model pretending, e.g., pretend to take a bite of a plastic apple or rock a baby doll to sleep.

- Provide familiar household items for children to use during pretend play, e.g., a toy broom for sweeping and empty food boxes representative of the foods children eat at home.

- Arrange the environment and introduce props that will encourage play. Observe children while they are playing to gather information about what props to include and what suggestions to make. Decide whether to sustain play by participating or by not intervening.

- Offer both highly realistic and less realistic props for pretend play to accommodate the range of developmental levels.

- Provide multipurpose, open-ended props that can represent many things, e.g., blocks and boxes. Encourage children to use gestures and descriptive language as they dramatize.

- Encourage children 18-months and older to pretend without props as another way of engaging in dramatic play.

- Describe what children are doing, offer suggestions, and make modifications for children with disabilities.

- Ask open-ended questions to extend children's imaginative play and expressive language.

- Extend children's pretend play by interacting with them. Imitate what they are doing; comment and ask questions; or take a role, using a play voice and gestures.

- Plan specific activities to enhance preschool and kindergarten children's knowledge of the world and the roles of people in various settings, e.g., field trips, book reading, visitors. Talk about people's roles.

- Encourage older preschool and kindergarten children to make their own props to use in play or to support their learning, e.g., number lines, word walls, alphabet books, etc.

Literacy

The early years are critical for literacy development. Children who do not learn to read and write by the end of the primary grades are at risk for school failure. Children who are especially likely to have difficulty learning to read in the primary grades are those who begin school with less prior knowledge, verbal abilities, phonological sensitivity, familiarity with the basic purposes and mechanisms of reading, and letter knowledge (National Early Literacy Panel, 2008; Snow, Burns, & Griffin, 1998). The level to which a child progresses in reading and writing is one of the best predictors of whether the child will function competently in school and in life (Neuman, Copple, & Bredekamp, 2000).

Literacy learning begins at birth. During the early childhood years, children engage in emergent reading and writing behaviors that form the foundation for conventional literacy, but many children do not receive the ongoing experiences that support this learning. By age 3, differences in children's understanding and use of literacy skills are enormous. Reading aloud to children appears to be one of the most important activities for building the understandings and skills needed for reading success (Neuman et al., 2000). Children from middle-class families have been read to for about 1,000 hours before beginning kindergarten. Children from families living in poverty have been read to for about 25 hours (Berk, 2006; Neuman, 2003).

LITERACY OBJECTIVES

15 Demonstrates phonological awareness

16 Demonstrates knowledge of the alphabet

17 Demonstrates knowledge of print and its uses

18 Comprehends and responds to books and other texts

19 Demonstrates emergent writing skills

When children enjoy having books read to them, and when they are excited about what they are hearing and learning, they are motivated to learn to read, and later, to read to learn (Heroman & Jones, 2004).

Listening, speaking, reading, and writing develop interdependently in children, and each contributes to development of the other. Children's literacy development may be negatively affected by factors including poverty; limited English proficiency; visual, hearing, and language impairments; cognitive deficiencies; and parents who have had difficulty reading (National Early Literacy Panel, 2008; Snow et al., 1998).

Effective instruction in the early years can have a large impact on children's literacy development. Children who would otherwise be most at risk for school failure stand to benefit the most from high–quality experiences (Campbell, Ramey, Pungello, Sparling, & Miller-Johnson, 2002). Teachers are critical and can inspire children to read, write, and learn through thoughtful planning and developmentally appropriate literacy instruction (Neuman et al., 2000).

Objective 15

Demonstrates phonological awareness

Phonological awareness, or phonological sensitivity, is the ability to discern the sounds and patterns of spoken language. As this awareness develops, children learn to hear the separate sounds of oral language that are blended in ordinary speech. For some children, distinguishing the parts of spoken language is difficult because it requires them to attend to the sounds of speech separately from meaning.

Phonological awareness is an important skill in learning to read. Children typically begin to demonstrate this awareness by about age 3, and their skills improve gradually over many years (Snow, Burns, & Griffin, 1998). Phonological sensitivity is a strong predictor of later reading, writing, and spelling ability (National Early Literacy Panel, 2004, 2008). Instruction that strengthens children's phonological awareness has been shown to contribute to later reading success (Ehri et al., 2001; National Early Literacy Panel, 2008). Children become phonologically aware through experiences such as reciting poems, singing, and clapping the syllables of chanted words (Adams, 1990, 2001; Carroll, Snowling, Hulme, & Stevenson, 2003; Strickland & Schickedanz, 2004). Phonological awareness skills are typically learned in a particular order (Anthony, Lonigan, Driscoll, Phillips, & Burgess, 2003). However, children acquire these skills in an overlapping sequence rather than by mastering one level before the next (Dickinson & Neuman, 2006).

Children who are learning two or more languages must learn very different sound systems (Gonzalez, 1998). They must distinguish English phonemes that may not be part of their native languages. A child may therefore have difficulty hearing and/or producing the sounds of English.

Objective 15 Demonstrates phonological awareness

a. Notices and discriminates rhyme

Not Yet	1	2	3	4	5	6	7	8	9

Joins in rhyming songs and games (2)
- Hums along and joins in random words in rhyme
- Sings with a group, "One, two, buckle my shoe…"

Fills in the missing rhyming word; generates rhyming words spontaneously (4)
- Completes the rhyme in the phrase, "The fat cat sat on the ____ (mat)."
- Chants spontaneously, "Me, fee, kee, tee, lee, bee."

Decides whether two words rhyme (6)
- "Do bear and chair rhyme? What about bear and goat?"
- Matches rhyming picture cards

Generates a group of rhyming words when given a word (8)
- Says, "Bat, sat, lat," when asked, "What words rhyme with cat?"

b. Notices and discriminates alliteration

Not Yet	1	2	3	4	5	6	7	8	9

Sings songs and recites rhymes and refrains with repeating initial sounds (2)
- Sings, "I'm bringing home a baby bumble bee…"

Shows awareness that some words begin the same way (4)
- Says, "Max and Maya…our names start the same!"

Matches beginning sounds of some words (6)
- Groups objects or pictures that begin with the same sound
- Picks up a toy bear when asked, "What begins the same way as box, baby, and bike?"

Isolates and identifies the beginning sound of a word (8)
- Says, "/m-m-m/," when asked "What is the first sound of the word milk?"
- Responds, "/t/," after being asked, "What's the beginning sound of toy, toe, teeth?"

See pages 33–34 of *Child Assessment Portfolio.*

Objective 15 Demonstrates phonological awareness

c. Notices and discriminates smaller and smaller units of sound

Not Yet	1	2	3	4	5	6	7	8	9
		Hears and shows awareness of separate words in sentences • Joins in clapping each word while chanting, "I like ice cream." • Jumps upon hearing a specified word in a story		**Hears and shows awareness of separate syllables in words** • Claps each syllable of name, *Tri-na* • Puts together *pen* and *cil* to say *pencil* • Puts together *foot* and *ball* to say *football*		**Verbally separates and blends onset and rime** • Says, "Hat," after hearing /h/.../at/ • Points to Jonathan when teacher plays game and asks, "Where's _onathan?"		**Verbally separates and blends individual phonemes in words** • Claps each phoneme of the word *hat*: /h/ /a/ /t/ • Says, "Hat," after hearing /h/ /a/ /t/	

See page 35 of *Child Assessment Portfolio*.

Objective 15 Demonstrates phonological awareness

Strategies

- Know each child's level of phonological awareness and provide appropriate experiences. Plan specific activities to help children attend to rhyme, alliteration, and smaller and smaller units of sound.

- Encourage children to listen to sounds in the environment. Record different sounds for children to identify.

- Use songs, stories, and rhymes that play with language. Informally, but intentionally, draw children's attention to the sounds of language.

- Encourage children to play with words and to make up their own rhymes.

- Have children fill in rhyming words in a verse. For example, "The cat wore a____ (hat). He slept on a ____ (mat). He played with a _____(bat)."

- Play games that focus on alliteration (initial sounds). For example, have children think of words that begin with the same sound as another child's name (Bonito, Betty, baby, bath, buttons, etc.).

- Clap or tap rhythm sticks to mark the syllables of preschool and kindergarten children's names as you say them.

- Draw children's attention to the phonemes in spoken words during daily routines. For example, dismiss children to go to lunch by saying, "If your name begins with the /m/ sound like Matthew, you may go to lunch."

- Plan activities with older preschool and kindergarten children that focus on onset and rime. For example, have children group words by their beginning sounds (*rake, rat, rose*) or create word families that emphasize the ending sounds (*ring, sing, king*).

- Encourage kindergarten children to draw pictures and write their own rhyming words to share with other children.

- Provide opportunities for older kindergarten children to make up their own alliteration sentences, e.g., a "T sentence" might be, "Tommy tells Tyron to tickle Terry."

Demonstrates knowledge of the alphabet

16

Knowledge of letters and words is an important component of literacy. It involves more than reciting the alphabet song or recognizing individual letters. Children must understand that speech can be recorded in print and that words in print can be spoken. Readers must understand that a letter is a symbol that represents one or more sounds. A more complex level of understanding requires knowing that these symbols can be grouped together to form words and that words have meanings. The idea that written words are composed of letters that represent sounds is called the *alphabetic principle*. Children's understanding of the alphabetic principle is a predictor of future reading success.

Young children's alphabet knowledge, especially their ability to rapidly name letters and numerals in random order, is a strong predictor of later reading, writing, and spelling ability (Adams, 1990; National Early Literacy Panel, 2004, 2009; Stevenson & Newman, 1986). In addition, preschool children's letter knowledge is a unique predictor of growth in phonological sensitivity across the year (Burgess & Lonigan, 1998). There is a high correlation between knowing the names of the letters and knowing the letter sounds. These appear to be overlapping skills (Lomax & McGee, 1987; Richgels, 1986; Worden & Boettcher, 1990). Children's knowledge of the alphabet is also closely related to their comprehension skills by the end of second grade (Cats, Fey, Zhang, & Tomblin, 2001).

Objective 16   Demonstrates knowledge of the alphabet

a. Identifies and names letters

Not Yet	1	2	3	4	5	6	7	8	9
		Recognizes and names a few letters in own name		Recognizes and names as many as 10 letters, especially those in own name		Identifies and names 11–20 upper- and 11–20 lowercase letters when presented in random order		Identifies and names all upper- and lowercase letters when presented in random order	

b. Uses letter–sound knowledge

Not Yet	1	2	3	4	5	6	7	8	9
		Identifies the sounds of a few letters		Produces the correct sounds for 10–20 letters		Shows understanding that a sequence of letters represents a sequence of spoken sounds • Asks when writing, "How do you spell *cough*?"		Applies letter–sound correspondence when attempting to read and write • Sees the word *cat*; begins to sound out the word: /k/ /a/ /t/ • Makes an *open* sign for the doctor's office by writing "opn"	

See pages 36–37 of *Child Assessment Portfolio*.

Objective 16 Demonstrates knowledge of the alphabet

Strategies

- Focus on letters as part of meaningful activities. Point out particular letters as you take dictation, compose messages, and read stories. Call attention to the letter-sound relationship. For example you might say, "That word begins just like Tamika. It begins with the letter T."

- Display the alphabet at the child's eye level. Make smaller versions for children to use as references. For example, provide alphabet strips or alphabet cards in the Library area. Children can refer to these as they read or write.

- Use the children's names to help them learn the alphabet letters and their sounds. For example, have children place cards with their photos and names printed on them underneath alphabet letters posted around the room. Talk about whose names are under each letter and the sound the letter makes.

- Sing the alphabet song. Sing each letter slowly so children can hear each letter. Point to each letter on a large alphabet chart as you sing.

- Read alphabet books. For example, *Chicka, Chicka Boom Boom* (Bill Martin, Jr.) and *The Alphabet Tree* (Leo Lionni) are good for group reading. Talk about the letters, their shapes, and the names of the pictured objects that begin with the letter.

- Place alphabet books in the Library area and in other interest areas. Select books that include words with a single letter sound (*snake*), rather than a blend (*ship*) to avoid confusion. Younger children and English-language learners benefit from books that focus on a single letter, word, and picture per page.

- Encourage sensory exploration of the alphabet. Offer children a variety of ways to explore the alphabet: by using sandpaper or felt letters, salt trays, clay, magnetic letters, and by forming letters with their bodies.

- Support kindergarten children as they make their own letter dictionaries. They might illustrate using photographs, drawings, and/or words. Children can add additional words to their books as the year progresses.

- Have kindergarten children assist with creating lists of new vocabulary words they learned at school. They can take the list home and talk with family members about their words and what they mean.

Demonstrates knowledge of print and its uses

17

Long before they learn to read, young children try to make sense of the print around them. Children see print in their homes, in their schools, on street signs, and elsewhere throughout their communities. They see it in books, on grocery lists, and on food containers. Knowledge of print and its uses includes understanding that print carries a message and that print is organized and read in particular ways. Through print-rich environments and scaffolding by adults, children learn about the many functions of print; how books are handled; and features of print, such as punctuation. Children need these skills to be successful readers and writers.

Young children's concepts about print are a good predictor of later reading, writing, and spelling ability (National Early Literacy Panel, 2004, 2008; Clay, 1979a, 1979b; McCormick & Mason, 1986; Wells, 1985). Understanding that print is meaningful is one of the first steps children take in learning to read and write (Mason, 1980). Children learn much about print from what is included in the environment, e.g., signs and labels, and from including print in their play (McGee, Lomax, & Head, 1988; Neuman & Roskos, 1993). They learn the uses of written language before they learn its forms (Gundlach, McLane, Scotte, & McNamee, 1983; Taylor, 1983). Although the first stages of reading and writing are predominately about function, children develop an interest in print conventions. However, children do not systematically progress from one stage to the next (Morrow, 2005).

Objective 17 Demonstrates knowledge of print and its uses

a. Uses and appreciates books

Not Yet	1	2	3	4	5	6	7	8	9
		Shows interest in books • Gazes at the pages of a book • Brings book to adult to read		**Orients book correctly; turns pages from the front of the book to the back; recognizes familiar books by their covers** • Hands teacher book and says, "Let's read *Corduroy!*"		**Knows some features of a book (title, author, illustrator); connects specific books to authors** • Says, "I want to read this Dr. Seuss book today." • Says, "Eric Carle wrote this book. He is the author."		**Uses various types of books for their intended purposes** • Selects the book about insects to identify the butterfly seen on the playground	

b. Uses print concepts

Not Yet	1	2	3	4	5	6	7	8	9
		Shows understanding that text is meaningful and can be read • Points to the words on the sign by the fish bowl and says, "Just one pinch!"		**Indicates where to start reading and the direction to follow** • Points to beginning of text on the page when pretending to read and moves finger left to right as she continues down the page		**Shows awareness of various features of print: letters, words, spaces, upper- and lowercase letters, some punctuation** • Points to the word *hippopotamus* and says, "That's a long word." • Says, "That means stop reading," as he points to a period at the end of a sentence.		**Matches a written word with a spoken word, but it may not be the actual written word; tracks print from the end of a line of text to the beginning of the next line** • Touches each word on the page while reciting the words from *Brown Bear, Brown Bear, What Do You See?* • Picks up finger and returns it to the beginning of the next line when pretend reading	

See pages 39–40 of *Child Assessment Portfolio.*

Strategies

- Create a print-rich environment. Include print that is meaningful, functional, and interesting. Avoid displaying so much print that it clutters the room.

- Display print at the child's eye level. If you place print too high, children will not be able to see it or attend to its features.

- Support children's play with print as they imitate real-life situations. For example, offer books, newspapers, or magazines to add to the doctor's office. Supply paper and markers for making signs, writing checks, or creating appointment books.

- Write signs, charts, recipes, labels, and other classroom materials in the children's presence. Describe the process as children watch you write. Call attention to the features of print such as individual letters, words, spaces, upper- and lowercase letters, and punctuation.

- Distinguish between children's drawing and writing. Use the words *drawing* and *writing* when making comments about their products. For example, you might say, "You *drew* a rainbow. I see you *wrote* your name and Toben's name next to your picture."

- Point out the title, author, and illustrator as you read books with older children.

- Draw children's attention to the conventions of print. For example, when you record a child's dictation, talk about where you are starting to write, why you are beginning the sentence with an uppercase letter, and what the punctuation mark means at the end of the sentence. As you read, move your finger under the words to help children learn directionality.

- Use story and informational books and planned writing experiences to teach about print. Intentionally read books aloud to individuals, small groups, and large groups of children. Place both fiction and non-fiction books in various interest areas so children can find the information they need and discover purposes for print. For example, you might include books about plants in the Discovery area if you have plants there.

- Talk with children about the many ways print is used around them. For example, look on the Internet to check the day's weather. Read the lunch menu. Read aloud a card to be sent to a sick child.

- Talk about concepts about books when you read to children. Talk about where the writing starts on the page and which way to proceed when reading.

Objective 18

Comprehends and responds to books and other texts

18

Comprehension, the process of finding meaning, is the goal of reading instruction. Comprehending text involves connecting what is heard and read with background knowledge and experiences. The more the language and meaning of the text relates to a person's prior knowledge, the easier it is to make sense of what is read. Comprehension of oral language and simple texts is essential to future reading success; children learn to process what they hear and read (Teale & Yokota, 2000). Children who engage in frequent activities with books have larger, more literate vocabularies. These children learn to read better than children who have few book experiences (Dickinson & Tabors, 1991; Wells, 1986). Although most children are not reading before they enter kindergarten, the development of listening comprehension skills is important. Through meaningful language activities, children develop and integrate comprehension skills.

Children follow a typical progression in learning to read storybooks. Initially they point to and label pictures in a book, treating each page as a separate entity. As they pretend to read, the story they tell does not flow from page to page. Next they begin to talk about the pictures and follow the story across the pages. Their language transitions from sounding like "talk" to a more reading-like intonation. Finally, they begin using different strategies (known words, knowledge of letters and sounds, patterns in text, picture and context clues) to make meaning of the text (Sulzby, 1985).

Dramatic play relates to comprehension in powerful, complex ways (Christie, 1983; Pellegrini & Galda, 1982; Saltz, Dixon, & Johnson, 1997; Silvern, Williamson, & Waters, 1983). *Metaplay*, in which children assume a role and negotiate what will happen next, has been shown to increase story comprehension (Trawick-Smith, 1998). Retelling stories also helps children develop a sense of story structure and other understandings about language that contribute to their comprehension of text (Morrow, 1985). Children who speak a dialect or who are English-language learners may retell a story using the grammar of their dialect or home language. Their use of standard English grammar increases over time as they gain more experience with listening and responding to stories (Schickedanz, 1999).

Objective 18 Comprehends and responds to books and other texts

a. Interacts during read-alouds and book conversations

Not Yet	1	2	3	4	5	6	7	8	9
		Contributes particular language from the book at the appropriate time • Says, "You're not big enough," when teacher pauses in *The Grouchy Ladybug*		**Asks and answers questions about the text; refers to pictures** • Responds, "He was mad. He threw his hat down."		**Identifies story-related problems, events, and resolutions during conversations with an adult** • When prompted says, "George got put in jail. He ran out the open door and got out."		**Reconstructs story, using pictures, text, and props; begins to make inferences and draw conclusions** • Joins in story discussion then says, "I think Max was upset that he was sent to bed without his supper."	

b. Uses emergent reading skills

Not Yet	1	2	3	4	5	6	7	8	9
		Pretends to read a familiar book, treating each page as a separate unit; names and describes what is on each page, using pictures as cues		**Pretends to read, using some of the language from the text; describes the action across pages, using pictures to order the events; may need prompts from adult**		**Pretends to read, reciting language that closely matches the text on each page and using reading-like intonation**		**Tries to match oral language to words on page; points to words as reads; uses different strategies (e.g., sounding out words, known words, and patterns in text) to make meaning from print**	

See pages 41–42 of *Child Assessment Portfolio.*

Objective 18 Comprehends and responds to books and other texts

c. Retells stories

Not Yet	1	2	3	4	5	6	7	8	9
		Retells some events from a familiar story with close adult prompting • Says, "The pig builds a house from it" when the teacher asks, "What does the first little pig do with the straw?" Then says, "The wolf blows it down," when the teacher asks, "What does the wolf do to the house?"		**Retells familiar stories using pictures or props as prompts** • Retells the basic events of *The Three Little Pigs* using felt pieces on a felt board		**Retells a familiar story in proper sequence, including major events and characters** • Retells *The Three Little Pigs*, starting with the pigs saying good-bye to their mother, remembering the correct order in which the pigs build their houses, and ending with the wolf climbing down the chimney and falling into the pot of hot water		**Retells stories with many details about characters, events, and storylines** • Retells *The Three Little Pigs*, and includes details about how the mother felt about her children's leaving home, the pigs' personalities, and why building a house from bricks is better than building a house from straw or sticks	

See page 43 of *Child Assessment Portfolio.*

Objective 18 Comprehends and responds to books and other texts

Strategies

- Provide high-quality children's literature from a variety of genres. Include picture books, poetry, and informational books. Call attention to how ideas are presented in different ways in different types of books.

- Prepare children for reading by taking a *picture walk*. Introduce the story by previewing the pictures. Ask children to predict what the story is about by looking at the cover. Turn the pages slowly as you *walk* through the book so children can make predictions about the story.

- Provide opportunities for children to talk about stories before and after they are read. Encourage them to ask questions and to make predictions.

- Support children's use of language from books. Introduce and discuss new words in meaningful contexts.

- Engage children in helping you read repeated phrases in books. For example, from *The Very Busy Spider* (Eric Carle) they might "read" with you as you point to the words, "The spider didn't answer. She was very busy spinning her web."

- Help children connect new information and ideas to what they already know. For example, you might say, "What does this remind you of _____?" "How is _____ like _____?" "Have you ever_____?"

- Facilitate story retellings. Use simple pictures, puppets, costumes, or props to help children recall the story. For example, for the story *Jump Frog, Jump*! (Robert Kalan), you might use a toy fly, frog, fish, snake, turtle, net, and basket as props.

- Support story retellings by taking turns telling parts of the story. Have children tell more of the story as they are able.

- Provide repeated readings of the same book so children can focus on different aspects of the book each time, e.g., story line, details, specific vocabulary words.

- Read chapter books with older preschool and kindergarten children.

- Model using different strategies for making meaning from print. Show children how to use picture cues, context, sounding out words, and known (high frequency) words.

Objective 19

Demonstrates emergent writing skills

19

Writing is an important aspect of emergent literacy. Writing letters or name writing is a predictor of later literacy (National Early Literacy Panel, 2008). Writing begins with making a mark. Then, when children are given the time, opportunities, and materials to practice, their writing skills continue to advance. Children begin to understand that writing is recorded speech. As their phonological awareness advances, children write a few letters that represent sounds in words. Their writing gradually becomes more conventional, typically as they enter the elementary grades.

Writing originates from drawing and is supported by make-believe play. Children learn to associate symbols with meaning (Vygotsky, 1997). To write, children need to understand that letters are symbols. By exploring writing, children learn about letters, sounds, and the meaning of text (Schickedanz & Casbergue, 2004). Understanding the mechanics of the writing system (letter naming and letter–sound correspondences) has a moderate correlation with reading in the primary grades (Stuart, 1995).

Writing letters requires children to know how each letter looks and how to put line segments together to form them. They must also know the orientation of letters and learn the particular order of the letters in each word (Schickedanz, 1999). Reversed letters are very common in preschool and kindergarten

children's writing (Schickedanz & Casbergue, 2005) and are not a cause for concern. Because fine-motor skills are necessary to control writing tools, it is helpful to know that markers are easiest for children to use; followed by chalk; then crayons; and, last, pencils (Charlesworth, 2007). Hand dominance, which usually develops between 1 and 2 years of age, may not develop fully until around age 7.

Objective 19 Demonstrates emergent writing skills

a. Writes name

Not Yet	1	2	3	4	5	6	7
	Scribbles or marks • Scribble writes deliberately • Makes marks that appear to adults to be in random order	**Controlled linear scribbles** • Scribbles lines, circles, or zigzags in rows • Often repeats action and forms	**Mock letters or letter-like forms** • Writes segments of letter forms, e.g., lines, curves • May use too many segments to create a letter, e.g., five horizontal lines on the letter E • May not orient letter segments correctly	**Letter strings** • Writes some letters correctly • Writes letters in unconventional order	**Partially accurate name** • Writes all the letters of own name, although some may not be sequenced correctly • Writes all the letters of own name, but some of the letters are not formed or oriented correctly	**Accurate name** • Writes all the letters of own name in the correct sequence, form, and orientation • Uses uppercase or lowercase letters (or a combination of both) when writing name	
	Carolyn	Lilly	Paula	Emma	Vicky	Brooke	

See page 44 of *Child Assessment Portfolio.*

Objective 19 Demonstrates emergent writing skills

b. Writes to convey meaning

Not Yet	1	2	3	4	5	6	7
	Scribbles or marks • Scribble writes deliberately • Makes marks that appear to adults to be in random order	**Controlled linear scribbles** • Scribbles lines, circles, or zigzags in rows • Often repeats action and forms	**Mock letters or letter-like forms** • Writes segments of letter forms, e.g., lines, curves • May use too many segments to create a letter, e.g., five horizontal lines on the letter E • May not orient letter segments correctly	**Letter strings** • Writes strings of letters • Writes some letters correctly • Writes letters in unconventional order • Begins to separate groups of letters with spaces • May copy environmental print	**Early invented spelling** • Uses first letter of word to represent whole word • Writes initial and/or final sounds of a word to represent the whole word *Note: In Spanish, early invented spelling may consist primarily of vowels.*	**Late invented spelling** • Begins to include beginning, middle, and ending sounds in words • Represents most of the sounds heard in words in the correct order	
	Maya said, "Here Mommy. Read this."	*Carolyn said, "That's my phone number. You can call me."*	*Erica said, "I'm writing my ABCs just like my sister."*	*Jordan said, "Here's a ticket! You're under arrest!"*	*Meir wrote, "Uncle Clay, I love you."*	*Jenna said, "I need to buy some blackberries and grapes at the store."*	

See page 45 of *Child Assessment Portfolio.*

Objective 19 Demonstrates emergent writing skills

Strategies

- Provide ample time, materials, and space for children to write throughout the day. Offer unlined and lined paper of different sizes and shapes, pencils of various sizes, crayons, markers, and white boards, magic slate, and other writing supplies.

- Provide specific opportunities to write outdoors. For example, write letters in the dirt or sand with fingers or small sticks or write on the sidewalk with chalk or water. Encourage older preschool and kindergarten children to make meaningful signs to use during outdoor activities, e.g., "STOP" or "detour" for a puddle of water.

- Include activities that give children reasons to write their names. For example, they may write their names on drawings, letters, greeting cards, sign-up sheets for a popular activity, or attendance sheets upon arrival each day.

- Provide accurate models of children's names. Print clearly using upper- and lowercase letters. Make names available for children to use as resources as they write.

- Plan specific activities that focus on writing. For example, with older children you might write the story of the day on chart paper.

- Model writing with children. Talk about what you are doing as you write. For example, you might say, "I'm making a sign to let people know the toilet is out of order." As you write "Out of order," say each word slowly and spell it. Call attention to each phoneme by saying the sound aloud as you write the letter(s).

- Encourage children to write words that are important to them as they create drawings, messages, greeting cards, lists, signs, menus, or books.

- Support the writing efforts of children. Say words slowly, emphasizing each sound so children can write the sounds they hear. Talk about directionality and letter shapes as you form the letters.

- Encourage kindergarten children to revise their original writings. Use simple word processing software as well as writing utensils and paper. Model the process writers go through to revise their writing. Children might revise their writings by first looking back at a previous writing sample, e.g., done a month before, and revising it based on their new knowledge and skills. They also might write about a topic they wrote about previously and then go back and look at their writing and compare it to their current writing.

Mathematics

Children slowly construct informal mathematical knowledge, beginning in the first few months of life. First-hand exploration is important for learning mathematics. As infants, children begin to use their everyday experiences to construct a variety of fundamental mathematical concepts and strategies. The knowledge children acquire informally provides the foundation for the concepts and skills that they later learn formally in school. Through the essential process skills of problem solving, reasoning, communicating, making connections, and representing, children learn mathematics content (Copley, 2000; Geist, 2009).

Research has made a clear link between early math skills and later school reading and math achievement. An analysis of six longitudinal studies showed that early math skills have the greatest predictive power, followed by reading and then attention skills (Duncan et. al., 2007). Children's knowledge at kindergarten entry is considered predictive of future mathematics success throughout their years in school. Evidence shows that high-quality early childhood education programs can make a difference in children's mathematical learning (Clements & Sarama, 2009).

MATHEMATICS OBJECTIVES

20 Uses number concepts and operations

21 Explores and describes spatial relationships and shapes

22 Compares and measures

23 Demonstrates knowledge of patterns

Regardless of social class, culture, or disability, most children develop mathematical skills. However, there are gaps in some children's informal knowledge that make it difficult for them to understand school mathematics (Benigno & Ellis, 2004; Klein & Starkey, 2004).

Language plays a central role in teaching and learning mathematics. For a child with a disability, the environment or materials may need to be adapted, routines adjusted, or an activity modified. The teacher's role is to determine what special supports a child needs to participate fully (Copley, Jones, & Dighe, 2007).

Adults play a significant role in helping children learn mathematical vocabulary, concepts, and process skills. If children are to develop the knowledge needed for later formal learning, they need frequent practice with materials in play settings and adult-guided activities that include meaningful discussions and applications (Varol & Farran, 2006).

Objective 20

Uses number concepts and operations

20

Children's understanding of counting, number symbols, and number operations are fundamental to their success with more complex mathematics (Ginsburg & Baroody, 2003; Zur & Gelman, 2004). When an infant signs *more* to request another bite of applesauce, a young child proudly announces, "I 2 years old," and a preschooler counts out 18 napkins at snack time, they are using number concepts and operations. Teachers play a critical role in helping children develop an understanding of number concepts and operations through intentional teaching during planned activities and daily routines.

To count well, children must learn: 1) the verbal number sequence; 2) one-to-one correspondence, i.e., that one number name is matched to a single object in a set being counted; and 3) cardinality, i.e., that the last number named when counting objects tells how many. Children can look at a small group of objects and identify the quantity without counting, e.g., counters or domino patterns. This is *subitizing*. From this children explore concepts of more and less, how many, and parts and wholes (Clements & Sarama, 2009). As they learn to discuss mathematical ideas, they learn ordinal counting: how to indicate the position of something in a sequence, e.g., first, second, third, and so forth. Over time children develop strategies such as counting on from a quantity (rather than beginning at one), counting back, or counting by groups (skip counting), e.g., by twos, fives, or tens.

Through everyday experiences and planned learning activities, young children begin to construct understandings about the number operations of separating (subtracting) and combining (adding). Taking away is a common separating operation that makes a collection smaller and answers the question "How many are left?" Children can often solve subtraction problems before they can solve addition problems (Copley & Hawkins, 2005). Addition problems involve combining sets of objects to find out "How many in all?" Young children typically use fingers or other objects to solve problems involving combining or separating, (Baroody, 2004). Physical objects that are directly related to the problems being solved are best (Clements & Sarama, 2009).

Young children also must learn to connect quantities with their written number symbols, or numerals. Displaying numerals with representations of their quantities helps children associate the amount with the numeral (Copley, 2000; Payne & Huinker, 1993). Before children can connect quantities with numerals they must develop a mental image of each numeral and its spoken name. Children sometimes confuse numerals that are similar in appearance, e.g., 2 and 5, and 6 and 9. Numerals that are easily confused should be taught side by side so the teacher can point out how they differ (Baroody, 1987). Some children benefit from handling three-dimensional numerals with textured surfaces (Charlesworth, 2005).

Objective 20 Uses number concepts and operations

a. Counts

Not Yet	1	2	3	4	5	6	7	8	9

Verbally counts (not always in the correct order)
- Says, "One, two, ten," as she pretends to count

Verbally counts to 10; counts up to five objects accurately, using one number name for each object
- Counts to ten when playing "Hide and Seek"
- Counts out four scissors and puts them at the table

Verbally counts to 20; counts 10–20 objects accurately; knows the last number states how many in all; tells what number (1–10) comes next in order by counting
- Counts to twenty while walking across room
- Counts ten plastic worms and says, "I have ten worms."
- When asked, "What comes after six?" says, "One, two, three, four, five, six, seven…seven."

Uses number names while counting to 100; counts 30 objects accurately; tells what number comes before and after a specified number up to 20
- Counts twenty-eight steps to the cafeteria
- When asked what comes after fifteen, says "Sixteen."

b. Quantifies

Not Yet	1	2	3	4	5	6	7	8	9

Demonstrates understanding of the concepts of one, two, and more
- Says, "More apple," to indicate he wants more pieces than given
- Takes two crackers when prompted, "Take two crackers."

Recognizes and names the number of items in a small set (up to five) instantly; combines and separates up to five objects and describes the parts
- Looks at the sand table and says instantly, without counting, "There are three children at the table."
- Says, "I have four cubes. Two are red, and two are blue."
- Puts three bunnies in the box with the two bears. Counts and says, "Now I have five."

Makes sets of 6–10 objects and then describes the parts; identifies which part has more, less, or the same (equal); counts all or counts on to find out how many
- Says, "I have eight big buttons, and you have eight little buttons. We have the same."
- Tosses ten puff balls at the hoop. When three land outside she says, "More went inside."
- Puts two dominoes together, says, "Five dots," and counts on "Six, seven, eight. Eight dots all together."

Uses a variety of strategies (counting objects or fingers, counting on, or counting back) to solve problems with more than 10 objects
- Uses ladybug counters to solve the problem, "You had eight ladybugs. Two flew away. How many ladybugs are left?"
- Says, "I have ten cars. I left two at Grandma's, so now I have ten, nine, eight left."
- Uses two-sided counters to determine different number combinations for fourteen

See pages 46–47 of *Child Assessment Portfolio.*

Objective 20 Uses number concepts and operations

c. Connects numerals with their quantities

Not Yet	1	2	3	4	5	6	7	8	9
		Recognizes and names a few numerals • Points to the *1* when the teacher says, "Where is the numeral *1*?" • Notices numerals around the room and calls some of them by name		**Identifies numerals to *5* by name and connects each to counted objects** • Says, "Five" as she attaches five clothespins to the *5* card • Tells her friend, "That's a *3*, and there are three puppies on this page."		**Identifies numerals to *10* by name and connects each to counted objects** • Shouts, "Seven," and jumps seven times when the teacher holds up the number *7* card • Says, "I put nine buttons in the *9* box."		**Identifies numerals to *20* by name and connects each to counted objects** • Says, "Kaufee put the *12* card and twelve beads on his necklace." • Says, "I drew fifteen flowers to go on page 15 of our number book."	

See page 48 of *Child Assessment Portfolio.*

Objective 20 Uses number concepts and operations

Strategies

- Provide a variety of materials to help children develop an understanding of quantity. Offer buttons, bottle caps, keys, sticks, beans, cubes, counting bears, and other materials for children to count and compare. Model comparison vocabulary. Use words like *more, most, less, fewer, least, same as,* or *equal.*

- Recite fingerplays or rhymes and sing songs about numbers. Read stories that include numerals and items to count.

- Observe children to determine their counting skills. For those just beginning to count, display a few identical items in a straight line. As children gain skills, change the arrangement of objects. Gradually add more and varied objects to count.

- Use everyday activities as opportunities to count. Talk aloud as you count to solve problems. For example, you might say, "I wonder how many glue sticks we need to put out so everyone at the table has one? Let's count the children to find out."

- Model counting strategies. Touch or point to each object as you count slowly, saying the number name. Show how to keep track of the objects counted. For example, you might physically move the objects toward you as you count each one. Count on from an amount, e.g., "How much is four and three more? Four...five, six, seven. Seven."

- Practice counting in ways that involve multiple learning styles and representations. Involve the senses as children touch, hear the spoken number, see the numeral, or physically move their bodies.

- Include materials and activities that associate numerals with sets.

- Use everyday situations to illustrate combining and separating. For example, when a child leaves the dramatic play area you might say, "We had three children in the dramatic play area. Tommy went to play in the blocks area. How many children are left?"

- Encourage older preschool and kindergarten children to tell *how many* stories. For example, they might tell how many children are on the climber or how many markers they have after their friend gave them more or put some away.

- Provide various materials for kindergarten children to make number combinations. For example, use two sided colored beans, e.g., white on one side and blue on the other, to make combinations for the number four. When children shake and spill the beans they will discover different number combinations for four (i.e., 1 blue and 3 white beans; 2 blue and 2 white; 3 blue and 1 white; 4 blue and 0 white beans; or 4 white and 0 blue). Children can record their findings on their Number 4 Combination chart.

Explores and describes spatial relationships and shapes

21

Understanding spatial relationships and shapes helps children build the foundation for understanding geometry. Spatial awareness, how objects are oriented in relation to one another, develops as children begin to explore the relationship between their bodies and the things around them. As they learn to navigate their environment, they learn about direction, perspective, distance, symbolization, and location. The awareness of spatial relationships develops as infants see faces from different positions and perspectives. Toddlers try to fit their bodies into boxes of different sizes. Preschoolers walk around block structures to see which sides they want to draw, and kindergartners attempt to give directions to particular locations. Children who have a strong spatial sense do better in mathematics (Clements, 2004).

Positional words describe spatial relationships and help children deepen their understanding of those relationships. Directional words describe *which way*, e.g., up, down, forward, and backward. Distance words tell *how far*, e.g., near, far, and close. Location words specify *where*, e.g., on, off, under, and over. Children from a variety of cultures generally understand the spatial terms of *in, on*, and *under* before they understand *next to* or *by* (Plumert & Hawkins, 2001).

Young children explore two- and three-dimensional shapes long before they can name and describe them. In addition to square, rectangle, triangle, and circle, preschool children can learn the three-dimensional shapes of cube ("like a box"), rectangular prism ("like a box"), cylinder ("like a can"), and sphere ("like a

ball") (Copley, Jones, & Dighe, 2007). Typically, young children form a visual prototype that they use to classify shapes by their overall appearance (Clements, 2004). For example, they say that a triangle is a triangle because it "looks like one" (Van Hiele, 1986). It is important to provide a wide variety of models of each shape so that children do not perceive that a particular shape looks only one way, e.g. think all triangles must have a point on top in the middle (Clements, Battista, & Sarama, 2001). Many types of squares and rectangles should be presented to help children understand that a square is a special type of rectangle. Double-naming, as in *square-rectangle* may be helpful (Clements & Sarama, 2009). Shapes should be rotated into different positions (e.g., on their sides or upside down), and examples should be provided for comparison (Charlesworth, 2005).

Children do not develop their ideas about shapes by simply looking at them. They need to manipulate, draw, compare, describe, sort, and represent the shapes in a variety of ways (Charlesworth, 2005; Clements, 1999). Infants, toddlers, and twos explore shapes as they fit a circle into the matching hole on a shape sorter; work shape puzzles; and blow bubbles outdoors, saying "Lots of balls!" Older preschool and kindergarten children can combine shapes to produce composite shapes, e.g., using two triangles to produce a square (Clements, Wilson, & Sarama, 2004). This is an important process that helps children understand and analyze shape (Clements, 2004).

Objective 21 Explores and describes spatial relationships and shapes

a. Understands spatial relationships

Not Yet	1	2	3	4	5	6	7	8	9

Follows simple directions related to position (*in, on, under, up, down*)
- Follows teacher's directions to put the trash *in* the can
- Raises hands *up* and *down* as the song directs

Follows simple directions related to proximity (*beside, between, next to*)
- Follows teacher's direction to put the cup *next to* the plate
- Sits beside her friend when he says, "Sit *between* me and Laura."

Uses and responds appropriately to positional words indicating location, direction, and distance
- Says, "Look for the surprise *behind* the tree."
- Moves game piece *backward* when playmate gives directions

Uses and makes simple sketches, models, or pictorial maps to locate objects
- Constructs a map of the play yard using landscape toys
- Uses a map of the classroom to find the hidden treasure

b. Understands shapes

Not Yet	1	2	3	4	5	6	7	8	9

Matches two identical shapes
- Puts a circular puzzle piece in the circular space
- Places shapes in a shape-sorting box

Identifies a few basic shapes (circle, square, triangle)
- Looks at a wheel and says, "A circle."
- Names shape pieces as he puts them on a shape lotto card

Describes basic two- and three-dimensional shapes by using own words; recognizes basic shapes when they are presented in a new orientation
- Says, "It's a ball 'cause it rolls."
- Puts hand in feely box and says, "It has three sides and three points. It's a triangle."

Shows that shapes remain the same when they are turned, flipped, or slid; breaks apart or combines shapes to create different shapes and sizes
- Says, "It's still a triangle no matter how you turn it."
- Cuts apart a rectangle to make two squares

See pages 49–50 of *Child Assessment Portfolio.*

Objective 21 Explores and describes spatial relationships and shapes

Strategies

- Label shapes with correct names as the children use them. For example, when a child says, "I got a round one," when describing a sphere, you might say, "Yes, it is round. It looks like a ball. It's called a sphere."

- Guide children's explorations of shapes. Discuss the features as children explore. Use the word *not* as you talk about a shape. For example, you might say, "This is *not* a circle because it does not have curved lines."

- Present shapes that differ in size and orientation. For example, so that children will not think that all triangles have equal-length sides, present narrow triangles, wide triangles, and triangles rotated in various positions.

- Encourage children to create new shapes from other shapes. Use computer software that allows children to manipulate shapes and see the results as they move and combine pieces.

- Model and encourage the use of positional words as children climb in, out, on, or through objects. For example, you might say, "Lars crawled *over* the box and *under* the rope. Now he is *in* the tunnel."

- Use maps or other representations with older preschool and kindergarten children to help them think spatially. For example, provide a simple map with easily found landmarks and specific clues about the location of the hidden object or photograph classroom materials and activities from different positions. Discuss where in the classroom the materials or activities are located and where you stood to take the photo.

- Encourage older preschool and kindergarten children to represent shapes in various ways. For example, they might draw shapes and then recreate them on the geo board or with tangram pieces.

Compares and measures

22

Young children frequently compare measurement as they interact. They say, "I want so much grapes, not little bit grapes!" "I'm bigger!" or, "Joe has the longest one!" They understand that there are different ways of measuring. They begin to recognize the attributes of *length, height,* and *width* (how long, tall, and wide something is), *capacity* (how much something holds), *weight* (how heavy something is), *area* (how much space is covered), and *time* (sequence and duration). Time is a difficult measurement concept for children to learn because it is not a physical attribute of objects. In fact, telling time does not develop well until after kindergarten, but preschoolers develop an understanding of the passage of time as they go through predictable daily routines (Geist, 2009).

Children's initial ideas about size, quantity, and seriation involve comparisons related to their play materials and books. They know about the differently sized beds and bowls in *The Three Bears*. Young children experiment first by lining up objects, then they can begin to connect number to length as they use nonstandard measurement tools, e.g., links, blocks, rods (Clements & Sarama, 2009). Experimenting with tools that give different results, e.g., sometimes measuring an object with links and later measuring the same object with rods, is an essential step to understanding why standard tools, e.g., rulers, measuring tape, are important for comparing measurements.

In addition to nonstandard measurement tools, children can benefit from exploring and using tools with uniform units, e.g., rulers and centimeter cubes, as their measurement ideas and skills are developing (Clements, 2003; Sarama & Clements, 2006). Actual measurement involves associating a numeral with an attribute of an object, e.g., "This box is 9 inches long." Understanding how to measure accurately is a skill that takes many years to learn (Mix, Huttenlocher, & Levine, 2002).

Objective 22 Compares and measures

Not Yet	1	2	3	4	5	6	7	8	9

Makes simple comparisons between two objects

- Pours sand or water from one container to another
- Indicates which ball is bigger when shown a tennis ball and a beach ball

Compares and orders a small set of objects as appropriate according to size, length, weight, area, or volume; knows usual sequence of basic daily events and a few ordinal numbers

- Puts blocks side by side in order of length
- Says, "We go outside after lunch."
- Lays two short blocks on top of a long block to see if it's the same length
- Responds, "You're second to use the computer."

Uses multiples of the same unit to measure; uses numbers to compare; knows the purpose of standard measuring tools

- Measures by using paper clips, cubes, string, hands, feet or other objects
- Measures block tower with linking cubes and says, "I made mine fifteen cubes high!!"
- Stands on scale while pretending to be in a doctor's office

Uses measurement words and some standard measurement tools accurately; uses ordinal numbers from *first* to *tenth*

- Says, "We need two cups of flour and one cup of salt to make dough."
- Says, "If I add three more tiles to this side of the scale, they'll be the same."
- Looks at the clock and says, "It's 12 o'clock. It's time for lunch."

See page 51 of *Child Assessment Portfolio*.

Objective 22 Compares and measures

Strategies

- Take advantage of daily opportunities to talk about comparing and measuring. Extend children's visual comparisons of length, height, weight, and area. For example, when children debate about who found the longest rope or who has the biggest leaf, encourage them to compare by laying them side by side or placing one on top of the other.

- Provide many opportunities for children to measure using non-standard measures. For example, offer plastic snap cubes, plastic chains, paper clips, blocks, paper strips, straws, plastic cups, or large spoons. Encourage children to think of other materials they can use to measure.

- Plan activities that allow children to compare measuring with non-standard and with standard measures. For example, make a small batch of play dough using cups and spoons from dramatic play. Make another batch using standard measuring cups and spoons. As children compare the products, guide them to discover the advantages of standard measuring tools.

- Encourage children to use measuring tools in their own ways during measurement activities and during dramatic play. Model the conventional use of measuring tools during class activities. Explain tools and methods as you engage in real measurement activities. Use measurement vocabulary to describe the process.

- Offer a variety of standard measuring tools for children to investigate and use. Include rulers, yardsticks, measuring tapes, thermometers, balance scales, measuring cups, and centimeter grid paper.

- Use estimation vocabulary. Use words such as *about*, *approximate*, *nearly*, *almost*, and *close to* in the context of real-life situations. Encourage children to check their estimations by measuring.

- Involve older preschool and kindergarten children in using recipes and measuring tools to make their own snacks independently.

- Provide opportunities for kindergarten children to compare and record how much something will hold (capacity). For example, use a snack-size zip bag and see how many snap cubes, bottle tops, or counting bears it will hold when full. Have children record and compare their results.

Demonstrates knowledge of patterns

23

A pattern is a regular arrangement of something, e.g., numbers, objects, shapes, colors, sounds, or movements. Guiding children to understand patterns is a foundational skill in mathematics. As they learn to label patterns by having one name stand for something else, they are creating an algebraic representation. Children begin to identify patterns in their environment at an early age. An infant waves her arms in anticipation as you arrive with her bottle. A toddler repeats a repetitive phrase from a storybook while you read aloud. A preschooler describes a simple pattern on a shirt, "Green stripe, red stripe, green stripe, red stripe." A kindergartner describes how he counts by using even numbers, "Two, four, six, eight. I skip a number every time."

In *repeating patterns*, the core unit repeats a minimum of five times, e.g., red, blue; red, blue; red, blue; red, blue; red, blue. Children often mistakenly believe that something is a pattern because it is repeated once. Young children can recognize the relationship between repeating patterns that share the same core unit but that are perceptually different, e.g., color and movement, as in a color pattern of red, blue; red, blue; red, blue... and a movement pattern of stomp, clap; stomp, clap; stomp, clap... (Sarama & Clements, 2006).

Growing patterns are more complex than repeating patterns. In growing patterns, the pattern increases by at least plus one and continues to increase. A block staircase is an example of a growing pattern (Copley, 2000). The familiar song, "My Aunt Came Back," also is an example of a growing pattern. Children add one phrase and action to each verse, repeating the previous phrases and actions, until they reach the tenth verse with ten actions and phrases (Copley, Jones, & Dighe, 2007).

The study of patterns is exciting for young children. They first learn to copy simple patterns made with objects. They later learn to extend and create their own patterns (Clements, 2004; Klein & Starkey, 2004). Patterns help children know what comes next and to make predictions about things they cannot yet observe. Exploring patterns helps children understand some basic algebraic ideas. Learning experiences that focus on patterns facilitate children's generalizations about number combinations, counting strategies, and problem solving (Copley, 2000).

Objective 23 Demonstrates knowledge of patterns

Not Yet	1	2	3	4	5	6	7	8	9

Shows interest in simple patterns in everyday life

- Notices that a special song is played whenever it is time to clean up
- Points to the tiles in the bathroom and says, "They go this way, that way, this way, that way."

Copies simple repeating patterns

- Beats a drum as the teacher does, e.g., loud, soft; loud, soft; loud, soft; etc.
- Strings beads as her friend does, e.g., red, blue, blue; red, blue, blue; red, blue, blue; etc.

Extends and creates simple repeating patterns

- Makes a repeating movement pattern, e.g., stomp, stomp, clap, clap; stomp, stomp, clap, clap; stomp, stomp, clap, clap; etc.
- When shown pattern of cubes, e.g., red, blue, blue, red; red, blue, blue, red; etc., adds to it correctly

Recognizes, creates, and explains more complex repeating and simple growing patterns

- Describes even numbers, e.g., 2, 4, 6, 8, etc., as "skipping" every other number on a 100's chart
- Says, "If I add one to three, it's the next number: four. If I add one to four, it's the next number: five."
- Extends a growing pattern by adding one cube like a staircase, e.g., 1 cube, 2 cubes, 3 cubes, 4 cubes, etc.

See page 52 of *Child Assessment Portfolio.*

Objective 23 Demonstrates knowledge of patterns

Strategies

- Identify patterns in daily routines. For example, you might say, "Every day we follow the same pattern. After choice time, we have cleanup, then snack, then story."

- Call attention to patterns in the environment. For example, you might say, "Magnus, you have a pattern in your shirt: blue stripe, red stripe; blue stripe, red stripe; blue strip, red stripe…" or "Sai, you made a pattern with your blocks: up, down; up, down; up, down…"

- Support children as they copy and extend patterns. Begin with simple repeating color patterns. Use objects that are identical except for their color. Progress to shape patterns where objects are the same color, same size, but vary in shape. Continue by using same-colored, same-shaped, but differently sized objects. Encourage children to repeat their patterns at least five times.

- Describe patterns with words, sounds, movements, and objects rather than with letters. Using letters, e.g., ab, abb, abc patterns, can be confusing to children who are learning letters and their sounds.

- Encourage children to talk about and identify patterns. For example, children can become "pattern detectives" as they describe and represent patterns they identify in the environment. Include their discoveries in a class book titled, *Patterns Discovered by Our Class*.

- Read patterning stories and verses. For example, *Mrs. McTats and Her Houseful of Cats* (Alyssa S. Capucilli), *The Napping House* (Audrey Wood), and *The Relatives Came* (Cynthia Rylant) are books that include patterns that can be acted out by children.

- Encourage kindergarten children to compare patterns and to find similarities and differences among them. For example, two patterns may use the same colors, but one is a yellow, green; yellow, green; yellow, green pattern and the other is a yellow, green, green; yellow, green, green; yellow, green, green pattern.

- Have kindergarten children create growing patterns using materials such as small cube blocks, stacking cubes, or linking chains. They can represent their patterns through drawings.

Science and Technology

Science content during early childhood typically focuses on living things (life science), the physical properties of materials and objects (physical science), and Earth's environment and how we care for it (earth science). The best way to learn science is to *do* science through integrated, hands-on, child-centered inquiry (Lind, 1997; 2001). Learning to engage in the process of scientific thinking, gaining understanding, and making connections are more important than learning scientific facts at an early age.

Young children are natural investigators. They are curious about how things work and what will happen next (Mantzicopoulos, Patrick, & Samarapungavan, 2008). Hands-on science learning begins in infancy with sensory stimulation that sharpens the infant's observation and discrimination skills. With adults' help and encouragement, this leads to more detailed exploration and discovery (Desouza & Czerniak, 2002). During the preschool and kindergarten years, scientific exploration should focus on naturalistic and informal learning that promotes exploration and discovery through everyday experiences. As children become more systematic in their explorations, their understanding deepens and their ideas come closer to current scientific understanding (Chalufour & Worth, 2004).

Young children have many scientific understandings, although they may be incomplete or inaccurate (Eshach & Fried, 2005; Hannust & Kikas, 2007; Nobes et al., 2003; Tenenbaum, Rappolt-Schlichtmann, & Zanger 2004).

SCIENCE AND TECHNOLOGY OBJECTIVES

24 Uses scientific inquiry skills

25 Demonstrates knowledge of the characteristics of living things

26 Demonstrates knowledge of the physical properties of objects and materials

27 Demonstrates knowledge of Earth's environment

28 Uses tools and other technology to perform tasks

They can think and talk in complex ways about science topics when they have related knowledge and experience (Gelman & Brenneman, 2004; Peterson & French, 2008). Adult-child conversations can support children's evolving theories of science (Tenenbaum & Callanan, 2008). When children have frequent opportunities to hear and use scientific vocabulary in meaningful contexts, they begin to use scientific words accurately (Gelman & Brenneman, 2004).

Science topics should be appropriate for children's developmental levels so that they do not develop scientific misconceptions or become disinterested. Appropriate, integrated scientific-inquiry activities can help children enjoy and feel competent about learning science (Mantzicopoulos, Patrick, & Samarapungavan, 2008). Some language can hinder children's scientific understanding. For example, saying *dead battery* or *lively music* may cloud children's understanding of living and nonliving things. Exploring which items sink or float is more appropriate than discussing the abstract concepts of buoyancy and density, that is, why things sink and float (Eshach & Fried, 2005; Tenenbaum, Rappolt-Schlichtmann, & Zanger, 2004). Some topics, such as astronomy, are difficult for young children to understand because they involve concepts that cannot be explored firsthand and objects that cannot be touched (Hannust & Kikas, 2007).

Young children need many opportunities to explore science concepts firsthand over time so they can connect new understandings to related experiences. Hurried exposure to disconnected science topics does not provide opportunities for rich conceptual growth (Gelman & Brenneman, 2004). In-depth investigations are an appropriate way for children to learn science content, the basic skills needed to use tools and other technology, and such process skills as observing, comparing, classifying, measuring, and communicating. Collaboration with peers and the guidance of a supportive teacher help children acquire basic science concepts and fundamental inquiry skills.

Objective 24

Uses scientific inquiry skills

24

Scientific inquiry is the *doing* of science (Epstein, 2007). Children use a variety of inquiry skills as they connect what they know to new experiences. Inquiry skills include making focused observations, posing meaningful questions, determining what is already known by examining books and other resources, making predictions, selecting appropriate techniques and tools, conducting investigations, reflecting on experiences, and communicating their findings (Chalufour & Worth, 2004; National Committee on Science Education Standards and Assessment, National Research Council, 1996). Adults can help children develop scientific inquiry skills through everyday experiences, such as observing worms, and helping them represent their observations in various ways, such as recording in science journals (Brenneman & Louro, 2008).

As you create exploratory opportunities and plan experiences for children, think about how each child uses the skills of scientific inquiry. Focus your observations on

HOW AND WHEN THE CHILD

- observes and explores things in the environment

- reacts to changes

- manipulates objects to understand their properties

- connects new observations to what he or she already knows

- identifies problems, makes predictions, thinks of ways to solve problems, and tries possible solutions

- organizes information

- makes comparisons and classifies

- communicates with others about discoveries

- represents his or her thinking through drawing, dramatizing, graphing, or making models

See page 53 of *Child Assessment Portfolio.*

Objective 24 Uses scientific inquiry skills

Strategies

- Model focused observation by showing curiosity about things in the environment, observing intently, using multiple senses, and calling attention to details. For example, when children wonder in what part of the tank a fish usually stays, encourage them to observe to find out. Involve the children in making a chart to record their observations.

- Support children as they practice scientific inquiry. Use scientific terms like *observe*, *hypothesize*, *predict*, and *estimate*. Guide children as they revisit and extend their investigations. For example, you might document their inquiry with photographs taken with a digital camera. Help children to think about their experiences, talk about the strategies they used, and analyze and synthesize the information they collected.

- Help children connect new discoveries to what they already know. For example, compare children's drawings before and after a field trip. Ask open-ended questions such as, "How is this magnet like/ different from the magnet we used last week?"

- Conduct in-depth investigations with preschool and kindergarten children, using living things, objects, and materials from the local environment. Encourage children to communicate their discoveries in multiple ways. For example, they might draw, dictate, write, take photos, dramatize, make models, or graph their findings. Support children's use of explanatory language as they talk about their discoveries.

- Support kindergarten children as they record their scientific predictions and observations in their science notebooks or journals. For example, they might predict what will happen over time to the pumpkin they picked from their garden, how tall the tomato plant will grow, or what will dissolve in water. Children can record their observations using a digital camera, drawings, and/or writing and then report and discuss their findings.

Objective 25

Demonstrates knowledge of the characteristics of living things

25

Young children are interested in living things. They are especially interested in the plants and animals in their immediate environment. They want to learn about their habitats and how they grow and change. For example, children in Louisiana may want to learn more about the crawfish they see in the bayous, while children in New Mexico may want to explore the different cactus plants they see growing around them (Dodge, Colker, & Heroman, 2002). No matter what topic of the life sciences children study, they can learn the major concepts as they interact with living things. Through regular contact with nature, children expand their curiosity and observation skills, practice nurturing behaviors as they care for living things, and gain knowledge in other academic areas (Rosenow, 2008; Russo, 2008).

As you create exploratory opportunities and plan experiences for children related to living things, think about how each child is beginning to understand concepts about living things. Focus your observations on

HOW AND WHEN THE CHILD

- shows a growing ability to classify living and nonliving things
- communicates about the characteristics of living things
- demonstrates understanding that living things grow, change, and reproduce
- shows awareness of life in different environments or habitats
- groups or categorizes living things, e.g., appearance, behavior, plant, or animal
- demonstrates awareness that living things go through a growth cycle

See page 53 of *Child Assessment Portfolio.*

Objective 25 Demonstrates knowledge of the characteristics of living things

Strategies

- Include opportunities for children to care for living things. For example, they might care for a pet fish or grow a small garden in the play yard. Discuss what living things need to grow and stay healthy.

- Provide opportunities for children to observe the life cycle of living things. For example, they might observe the life cycle of a frog and record changes that occur by drawing pictures or taking photographs.

- Sing, recite fingerplays, and read stories about how living things grow and change.

- Go on nature walks to look for worms, ladybugs, roly-polies (pill bugs), grasshoppers, or other living things to observe. Use magnifying glasses to get a better look.

- Use correct terminology when discussing living things. Use words like *germinate*, *sprout*, *bud*, or *stalk* when talking about plants. Use words like *habitat*, *camouflage*, *herbivore*, *antennae*, or *predator* when talking about animals.

- Help children understand animal behavior. After observing and talking about specific behaviors, encourage children to act like their favorite animals. For example, they might dramatize how cats stalk, preen themselves, or play.

- Encourage children to categorize living things. They might group according to appearance, behavior, or whether things are plants or animals. Have children explain their classifications.

- Guide kindergarten children to look up information on the Internet about the habitats or environments of different animals and to record findings in their science journals.

Objective 26

Demonstrates knowledge of the physical properties of objects and materials

26

By preschool, children have already begun building scientific knowledge about the physical properties of objects and materials (Gelman & Brenneman, 2004). They learn about physical properties by observing and manipulating common objects and materials. As they use their senses to explore things, they learn about shape, color, texture, weight, temperature, and how things move and change. As teachers talk with children about the properties of objects and materials, children develop vocabulary and important background knowledge. This background knowledge helps children observe their environment more closely. For example, the child who has been exposed to ramps at school may notice the ramps they see elsewhere in the community and talk about them at home and school. Without this exposure, the ramps may have gone unnoticed by the child (Eshach & Fried, 2005).

As you create exploratory opportunities and plan experiences for children, think about how each child explores and learns about objects and materials. Focus your observations on

HOW AND WHEN THE CHILD

- examines, describes, and measures the observable features of objects

- demonstrates understanding that objects are made from one or more materials, e.g., metal, wood, plastic, or paper

- communicates that the physical properties of objects and materials can change, e.g., when solid ice becomes a liquid

- displays awareness of natural forces that affect objects and materials, e.g., wind and gravity

- explores and describes ways that objects can be moved in space, e.g., pushing, pulling, rising, or sinking

See page 53 of *Child Assessment Portfolio.*

Objective 26 Demonstrates knowledge of the physical properties of objects and materials

Strategies

- Use everyday activities as opportunities for children to learn about the physical properties of objects and materials and the natural forces that affect them. Talk about what children observe throughout the day. For example, when children paint with water they learn about evaporation. When they cook, they learn about changes that occur in matter. When they push trucks up a ramp or move boats in water, they learn about how objects can be moved in space.

- Use appropriate vocabulary to describe phenomena. Use words like *sink*, *float*, *dissolve*, *melt*, *absorb*, *adhere*, *attract*, *repel*.

- Offer a variety of substances for children to explore and learn their characteristics. Include objects made from metal, wood, plastic, and paper.

- Plan experiences where children can observe changes in the physical properties of objects and materials. For example, leave an ice cube outside in the sun and observe as it becomes a liquid. Mix different materials in water to see if they dissolve.

- Repeat experiences often so children can extend their understandings. For example, use different bubble solution recipes. Offer different materials for children to use as bubble wands. Encourage them to compare their new experiences with what they learned from previous experiences.

- Make charts and/or graphs about the physical properties of objects and materials. For example, children might explore concepts such as absorb/repel, sink/float, hot/cold, or rough/smooth.

Objective 27

Demonstrates knowledge of Earth's environment

27

When children learn about Earth's environment, they learn about the composition of the Earth: rocks, sand, dirt, mud, and water. They learn about the weather, day and night, shadows, and recycling. Children learn about Earth's environment best by exploring their own natural surroundings. As children explore the properties of the world around them, they notice changes and make predictions. They begin to understand their environment, learn important ideas, and develop respect for their natural surroundings (Dodge, Colker, & Heroman, 2002).

As you create exploratory opportunities and plan experiences for children, think about how each child is learning concepts about the Earth and the environment. Focus your observations on

HOW AND WHEN THE CHILD

- demonstrates understanding that there are different kinds of weather and that weather changes

- describes and measures weather

- communicates awareness that the environment changes, e.g., season to season, sometimes slowly and sometimes suddenly

- communicates that the Earth's surface is made of different materials, e.g., rocks, sand, dirt, and water, and each material has properties that can be described

- shows awareness that different objects can be seen in the sky

- demonstrates understanding that people can affect the environment in positive and negative ways

See page 53 of *Child Assessment Portfolio.*

Strategies

- Investigate properties of rocks, soil, and water. For example, children may dig in the dirt, explore puddles, or examine rocks of different hardnesses and talk about their discoveries.

- Point out changes you notice in the environment. For example, you might look out the window during diaper changing and say, "It's snowing outside. Soon the ground will be covered with white snow."

- Use collections of natural objects to help children learn more about the environment. For example, children might collect rocks, shells, leaves, or pinecones and group them by characteristics such as size, color, shape, or texture.

- Observe the Earth's environment during different times of the day and different times of the year. For example, observe the sky at different hours. Talk about what the children see. Go on nature walks at different times of the year. Document and discuss how things are the same and different during each visit.

- Use words such as *evaporation*, *condensation*, *atmosphere*, *windy*, *overcast*, *partly cloudy*, *environment*, *recycling*, *pollution*, and *litter* when talking about the Earth's environment.

- Recite fingerplays, sing, and read seasonal or weather-related books. Compare and contrast the information in books with the current season and weather.

- Go on a litter hunt. Talk about the appropriate place for various kinds of litter (recycling bin or trash can) and how children can help to keep the Earth's environment clean.

- Observe shadows during different times of the day. Measure and compare how they are alike and different.

- Involve older children in making their own recycled paper. Tear scraps of construction paper and put them in a blender with water. Blend and then pour the solution through a rectangular mesh screen. Spread so that the liquid drains and the pulp is left on the screen. During the process, talk about changes that occur. Let the pulp dry for several days, and then use the recycled paper for writing or drawing.

Objective 28

Uses tools and other technology to perform tasks

28

Tools and technology make work easier and help people solve problems (Dodge, Colker, & Heroman, 2002). Technology enables children to respond and represent their learning in individual ways (Northwest Educational Technology Consortium, Northwest Regional Educational Laboratory, 2002). Technology can increase participation for English-language learners and children with disabilities (Murphy, DePasquale, & McNamara, 2003). As children use a variety of tools, such as thermometers, funnels, magnifying lenses, balances, hammers, tape measures, measuring cups, cameras, and computers, they learn to select the most appropriate tools for the job.

As you create exploratory opportunities and plan experiences for children, think about how each child develops important concepts related to tools and technology. Focus your observations on

HOW AND WHEN THE CHILD

- shows understanding that different tools and technology are used in different places for different purposes, e.g., finding information, communicating, and designing

- demonstrates the appropriate use of various tools and other technology

See page 53 of *Child Assessment Portfolio.*

Objective 28 Uses tools and other technology to perform tasks

Strategies

- Offer a variety of tools and other technology for children to use during explorations. For example, you might offer ramps, pulleys, water wheels, egg beaters, and magnets for children to explore their physical world. Include magnifying glasses, tape recorders, and a digital camera as children study living things. Offer sifters, balance scales, plastic thermometers, or rain gauges as they explore the Earth's environment.

- Encourage children to try different tools to accomplish a task. Have them evaluate and compare the results.

- Talk with children about how tools and other technology are used in daily living. For example, you might say, "The hearing aid helps Benny hear what others are saying," or "The mixer helps Mrs. Horton stir the ingredients together to make bread."

- Model technology applications in daily activities. For example, check the weather forecast for the day or look up information about ants on the Internet.

- Demonstrate the appropriate use of tools and other technology, emphasizing safety and proper care. For example, show children how to navigate a software program or operate a digital camera.

- Provide discarded items for children to take apart and find out what is inside or how they work. For example, offer record players, radios, clocks, or telephones. Remove the electrical cord and other unsafe parts before children explore. Offer different sizes and kinds of screwdrivers, pliers, and other tools. As they take these and other things apart, they discover pulleys, magnets, levers, springs, and circuit boards. Remind children not to take things at home apart unless they are given permission.

- Support older children as they write and illustrate stories using simple word processing programs, computer art programs, and digital cameras.

- When children find an interesting object outdoors, e.g., rock, fur, pine needles, dandelion helicopters, get them to observe it carefully with their naked eye and then draw what they see. Provide magnifying tools, e.g., magnifying glass, scope on a rope, microscope, jeweler's loupe, for closer study, and discuss how the magnifying devices made their observation better. Have children draw the object again and compare and discuss their drawings.

Social Studies

Social studies is the study of people and the ways they relate to others. As a discipline, social studies incorporates concepts and ideas from the fields of history, geography, anthropology, sociology, civics, and economics (Seefeldt, 1995). When young children explore social studies, they learn how to be researchers, critical thinkers, and active members of a classroom community.

Everyday experiences provide the foundation for learning social studies. Teachers can build upon children's interests and use them to introduce children to other places, traditions, and cultures. Many children today are immigrants or come from immigrant-headed households. These children face particular challenges, such as being different or learning a new language (Baghban, 2007). Issues of human diversity can be addressed through social studies as children learn how people live, work, get along with others, solve problems, and are shaped by their surroundings.

The focus of social studies during infancy and toddlerhood is on self-development within social settings (Mindes, 2005b). Young children begin with an egocentric perspective, showing interest first in themselves and then in their families. Adults enhance this self-development by providing safe, secure environments and materials that foster curiosity and exploration (Epstein, 2007). During the preschool years, children become interested in other people and their community.

SOCIAL STUDIES OBJECTIVES

29 Demonstrates knowledge about self

30 Shows basic understanding of people and how they live

31 Explores change related to familiar people or places

32 Demonstrates simple geographic knowledge

As they become more aware of the larger world through their understanding of themselves and their individual experiences, preschool and kindergarten children can engage in long-term studies of meaningful topics. Their interests lead children to ask questions, actively investigate issues, and make connections between what they are learning in their daily lives. In the process of their investigations, children learn how to be researchers, and they become experts on topics related to everyday life.

Objective 29

Demonstrates knowledge about self

29

Young children describe themselves in terms of age, gender, physical traits, material possessions, behavior, preferences, skills, experiences, role in the family, family routines, and environment. During the preschool years children begin to develop their racial identities and notice differences in social class (Feeney & Moravcik, 2005; Ramsey, 2003). The child's culture, family, and social settings (child care, school, and neighborhood) play an important role in determining what features of the self are incorporated into the child's concept of self. Personal storytelling involving family members serves as a rich source of self-knowledge and helps to instill a child's cultural values (Burger & Miller, 1999; Miller, Fung, & Mintz, 1996).

As you create exploratory opportunities and plan experiences for children, think about how each child demonstrates knowledge of him- or herself. Focus your observations on

HOW AND WHEN THE CHILD

- demonstrates understanding that each person has unique characteristics, ways of communicating, and ways of solving problems
- communicates that each person is part of a family that has unique characteristics
- shows awareness that each person has basic needs that must be met to stay healthy, e.g., food, clothing, shelter

See page 54 of *Child Assessment Portfolio.*

Objective 29 Demonstrates knowledge about self

Strategies

- Offer multiple ways for children to express their individuality and preferences. For example, they might communicate their ideas and feelings through painting, drawing, storytelling, song, or dance.

- Encourage children to recognize their unique characteristics as well as characteristics they share with others. For example, use transition times to call attention to similarities and differences by saying, "If you have curly hair, you may go to the rug."

- Use photographs of children involved in classroom activities. Display photos in accessible places so children can refer to them throughout the day. For example, place individual photos in a basket or on rings for children to use during art or writing activities. Create charts or graphs showing children's likenesses and differences (eye color, hair, favorite class activity). Make puzzles using different class pictures.

- Create short stories about children in the class. Take photographs of each child involved in daily activities. Write a short sentence or two about what the child is doing. Make the books accessible during the day. Send them home so children can share them with family members. Encourage kindergarten children to create their own short stories about their daily school activities.

- Encourage families to share traditions, songs, games, or special stories they read at home with their children.

- Include materials that demonstrate awareness of differences among children in the program. For example, include various shades of skin tone paint, crayons, markers, and construction paper. Offer dolls that represent different ethnicities, props, musical instruments, puzzles, books, and other materials that recognize diversity.

- Support the home languages of children in your program. For example, learn a few words in the home languages of the children. Write children's names, *hello* and *goodbye*, or names of familiar objects in English and in the home languages. Involve children and families in the process.

- Help older preschool and kindergarten children to learn their full names, addresses, and phone numbers.

- Guide older children to illustrate and write books about themselves. Topics might include "My Family," "Things I Like to Do," "Foods I Like to Eat," or "Places in My Neighborhood." Teachers can take dictation for younger children or children who cannot write.

Objective 30

Shows basic understanding of people and how they live

30

Young children are eager to learn about other people and how they live. They are interested in the physical characteristics of people; similarities and differences in habits, homes, and work; family structures and roles; and the exchange of goods and services. It is important for them to learn to respect others and to understand how people rely on each other. Reading appropriate books to children can be an effective way to help them develop positive attitudes about others and to better understand how people live throughout the world (Feeney & Moravcik, 2005).

As you create exploratory opportunities and plan experiences for children, think about how each child demonstrates understandings related to people and how they live. Focus your observations on

HOW AND WHEN THE CHILD

- shows awareness that there are similarities and differences among people and families

- demonstrates understanding of the various jobs of people in the community

- shows understanding that people buy, sell, and trade to get goods and services that they do not raise, make, or find themselves

- communicates about the various means of transportation that people use to move goods and go from place to place

- shows increasing awareness that respect for others, cooperation, and fairness help us get along in communities

- demonstrates increasing understanding that there are rules in our homes, schools, and community and that each rule has a purpose

- communicates understanding that people have various rights and responsibilities

See page 54 of *Child Assessment Portfolio*.

Objective 30 Shows basic understanding of people and how they live

Strategies

- Include puzzles, block people, props, and other materials representing a range of jobs and cultures. As children play, comment on the tools people use in their jobs.

- Take frequent walks in the neighborhood. Help children notice the patterns of life and work as they see people going about their daily activities. For example, they might see street vendors selling their wares, roofers repairing a roof, a delivery person delivering a package, sanitation workers collecting trash, or a bus driver picking up passengers.

- Take trips to visit workplaces in the community. Before the trip read books, introduce new vocabulary words, and discuss what children might see. During the trip ask workers to demonstrate and talk about what they do. Point out how people work together. Follow up trips by talking about the experience, adding new materials to support play, or documenting through art, writing, or making maps.

- Support older preschool and kindergarten children in interviewing people in the school, program, and community to learn more about their jobs. Guide children as they generate questions. For example, they might ask, "Why do you wear a uniform?" or "What tools do you use to do your job?"

- Help children expand their understanding of how children and families in other places are alike and different from themselves. For example, create e-mail partners with children in another part of the country or world. Guide children as they share information about themselves and generate questions to ask.

- Develop a "pen-pal" relationship with a kindergarten class in another part of the country. Share information through photographs, drawings, and writings about the activities in which the children in the class are involved or community activities that are particularly meaningful to them.

- Include books that show people from other cultures or people in unfamiliar jobs dealing with issues or doing things that are similar to the issues and activities of people with whom the children are familiar.

Objective 31

Explores change related to familiar people or places

31

To gain a sense of history, children must first understand that people and places change over time. Change is difficult for young children to understand because they focus on the here and now (Seefeldt, 1997). Children can learn about time and change in relation to themselves, including their daily schedule, what they did yesterday, and what they will do tomorrow. The calendar, when used appropriately, can help preschool and kindergarten children understand the passage of time. When children use the calendar to count the days until a special event, they are learning about the future. When they count the number of days since they lost their first tooth, they are learning to think about the past. Preschool children love to think about what they can do now that they could not do when they were babies. They can appreciate stories about other times and places that are relevant to their own experiences (Dodge, Colker, & Heroman, 2002).

As you create exploratory opportunities and plan experiences for children, think about how each child explores the concept of change. Focus your observations on

HOW AND WHEN THE CHILD

- demonstrates understanding that people and things change over time
- shows that time can be measured
- communicates about time, e.g., uses words such as *yesterday, today, tomorrow, day, week, month, minute, hour*

See page 54 of *Child Assessment Portfolio*.

Strategies

- Use children in the class to demonstrate change over time. For example, have children place photos of themselves and their friends at different ages in a series from youngest to oldest. Create scrapbooks of each child's life. Include photographs, art, dictations, notes, or other artifacts about important events and accomplishments. Talk about changes over time.

- Take photos of children engaged in the same activity or in the same location during different times of the year. Discuss changes the children notice.

- Provide opportunities for children to recall family memories or events in the community. For example, children might tell a story about something that happened when they were babies or make collages that illustrate a recent visit to grandparents.

- Involve grandparents or other senior citizens in the program. For example, ask them to tell simple stories of what life was like when they were young. Support children to generate interview questions as they talk with elders. They might ask, "What did you like to play when you were little?" or "What was your favorite fruit when you were little?" or "What is your favorite fruit now?"

- Display photographs of buildings in the community. As the year progresses, look for changes that occur. For example, children might notice that a building was painted or another had a "Going out of business" sign in the window. Talk about the changes and about what may have contributed to the changes.

- Avoid spending long periods on "calendar time" activities. Use calendars with preschool and kindergarten children in ways that are meaningful and functional. For example, you might mark special upcoming events at the beginning of the week or month. Indicate special recurring events such as, every other Thursday an elder volunteer reads a story. Indicate daily jobs such as who feeds the pet. Show what group project was completed. Involve children in determining what should be marked on the calendar and ways to do it.

Objective 32

Demonstrates simple geographic knowledge

32

Geography is the study of the earth's physical environment and the relationship of this environment to the people who live in it. The study of geography for young children needs to be relevant to their experiences. They can learn about the characteristics of the places where they live and the relationship between that place and other places (Dodge, Colker, & Heroman, 2002).

Preschool and kindergarten children often make simple maps to show their understanding of familiar places, e.g., classroom, play yard, neighborhood. Their first attempts at mapmaking may be with three-dimensional constructions in the block, sand, or art areas. Children's experiences with mapmaking help them to develop the concepts of representation, symbolization, perspective, and scale (Lenhoff & Huber, 2000).

As you create exploratory opportunities and plan experiences for children, think about how they demonstrate simple geographic knowledge. Focus your observations on

HOW AND WHEN THE CHILD

- demonstrates understanding that we are surrounded by geographical features, e.g., mountain, hill, desert, lake, river, creek, bayou, and there is specific information that identifies a location, e.g., address

- communicates that we depend on people who live far away for many necessities and information

- shows increasing understanding that maps are tools with symbols that help us locate objects, find where we are, and where we are going

See page 54 of *Child Assessment Portfolio.*

Strategies

- Invite children to build, construct, or create various geographic landscapes. Provide materials to support their ideas. For example, you might offer sea shells, large rocks, or grasses for children to use in the sand and water table as they create mountains, the sea shore, or rivers and levees.

- Take walks in the neighborhood. Take photos of landmarks that children can use to create representations of their immediate environment. For example, you might take a picture of a nearby bridge or a hill or large mountain seen from the play yard. Attach photos with laminating paper onto blocks for children to use in block play.

- Support children as they create maps of familiar places. For example, provide chalk and encourage children to make a map of the play yard on the concrete. Offer blocks and landscape toys for children to make a map of the classroom.

- Read books and plan activities that focus on a variety of geographical regions. For example, after reading *Make Way for Ducklings* (Robert McCloskey), support children to work together to create a mural or diorama of the pond and island where the ducklings went to live.

- Use children's personal travels as a springboard for discussion of other places. With younger children, talk about possible landmarks such as a lake or tall mountain. With older preschool and kindergarten children, refer to the city and state, and locate children's travels on a map or globe.

- Assist older children in creating a "Where does it come from?" web or diagram. For example, kindergarten children might study how the milk they have a school gets to the cafeteria. They might use observation, books, the Internet, and interviews to help them get the needed information.

The Arts

Children express themselves creatively through the visual arts, music, dance and movement, and drama. In addition to using the arts to create, children can also develop an awareness and appreciation of the art of others. The arts are intrinsically rewarding as an avenue for expressing feelings and ideas that may be difficult to share verbally. Other areas of learning and development are supported when children are involved in the arts (Epstein, 2007). As children draw, paint, construct, mold, weave, dramatize, sing, dance, and move, they make new discoveries and integrate what they are learning.

The early childhood years are very important to children's realizing their creative potential (Kemple & Nissenberg, 2000). Their creative expressions and continued interest in the arts vary greatly according to the quantity and quality of their early experiences (Denac, 2008; Kemple & Nissenberg, 2000; Szechter & Liben, 2007; Zimmerman & Zimmerman, 2000). Children need time, space, supportive adults, opportunities to explore various media, and a variety of world experiences to enhance their creativity. When adults demonstrate techniques, children develop greater skill in expressing their creative ideas, but too much or too little structure can hinder the development of creative expression (Bae, 2004; Epstein, 2007; Jalongo & Isenberg, 2006). Activities such as coloring within the lines, imitating a model, competitions, and highly scripted performances do not further young children's creative expression (Jalongo & Isenberg, 2006).

THE ARTS OBJECTIVES

33 Explores the visual arts

34 Explores musical concepts and expression

35 Explores dance and movement concepts

36 Explores drama through actions and language

For children, the arts involve active exploration and inquiry. Infants respond to musical sounds by babbling and moving (Kenney, 1997). These experimentations satisfy the infants. They gain more control over vocalizations and movements during toddlerhood. During the preschool and kindergarten years, children perform, create, listen to, and describe music (Andress, 1995). Building on their early play behaviors, preschool and kindergarten children enact stories and dramatize a variety of increasingly complex, familiar, and imaginary scenarios.

Children's drawings, paintings, and other visual art creations change dramatically during early childhood (Thompson, 1995). Artwork begins almost by accident as the toddler experiments with materials. Children's creations evolve from what appear to adults to be random, unplanned expressions to more elaborate representations, during preschool and kindergarten, of people, objects, and events. During this time, the arts provide opportunities for collaboration with peers. Children engage in studies and demonstrate what they know through music, drama, dance and movement, and visual arts.

Objective 33

Explores the visual arts

33

Visual art experiences include painting, drawing, making collages, modeling and sculpting, building, making puppets, weaving and stitching, and printmaking. Children benefit from working with many different kinds of materials and having conversations about their artwork and the work of others (Bae, 2004; Colbert, 1997; Johnson, 2008). The more they are able to experiment with various media and to discuss different ways to use materials, the more children are able to express their ideas through the visual arts (Dodge, Colker, & Heroman, 2002).

As you create exploratory opportunities and plan experiences for children, think about how each child creates and responds to the visual arts. Focus your observations on

HOW AND WHEN THE CHILD

- shows appreciation for various forms of visual art
- shows appreciation for the artwork of peers
- communicates what he or she sees and how it makes him or her feel
- uses and cares for art materials
- explores different materials, tools, and processes
- shows increasing awareness of color, line, form, texture, space, and design in his or her artwork or the work of others
- communicates about his or her artwork, e.g., what it is made of, what he or she was thinking, and from where the idea comes

See page 55 of *Child Assessment Portfolio*.

Strategies

- Offer diverse, open-ended materials for children to explore. Include materials with different patterns, textures, and colors.

- Encourage children to explore various art media, tools, and processes. Provide opportunities to draw, paint, print, stitch, sculpt, photograph, and make collages.

- Encourage children to use various media to express their ideas. For example, they may represent the ideas expressed in a drawing by using blocks or collage materials.

- Incorporate technology. For example, offer drawing and painting software. Provide a camera. Invite children to paint while listening to different types of music.

- Encourage close observation as part of creative work. Model the examination of objects from different angles before drawing. Show children how to look from time to time to compare their drawings with the object, and to check when finished to see if anything else needs to be added.

- Demonstrate manipulative skills and how to use and care for art materials. For example, model how to cut and how to wipe a paintbrush on the edge of the cup.

- Display children's art creations attractively and prominently in the room, as much as possible at children's eye level. Show collaborative as well as individual work. Remove displays before the room becomes cluttered or when children lose interest.

- Talk about art techniques used by illustrators. For example, after reading books by Leo Lionni, discuss how he uses torn paper collage in his illustrations. Offer materials for children to experiment with and encourage them to try new techniques.

- Invite family members or local artists to share their work with the children. Get them to talk about the materials, tools, and techniques they use to create their work; how their work has changed over time; and if and where they display or sell their art.

- Ask open-ended questions that invite children to think about their creations and why they made particular choices. Take photos of their work, and record or audiotape their explanations.

- After exploring various art media, provide kindergarten children with opportunities to classify photographs of art by its medium. For example, they might sort photographs of clay sculptures, wood sculptures, fabric collages, mixed media collages, line drawings, and paintings into piles.

Objective 34

Explores musical concepts and expression

34

Music is combining voice, instrumental or mechanical sounds to create melody, rhythm, or harmony (Dodge, Colker, & Heroman, 2002). Children learn to appreciate different kinds of music and become comfortable with different forms of musical expression when they listen to recordings, create melodies, learn songs as a group, talk about sounds, and explore musical instruments. The teacher's expression of interest and choice of musical activities influence children's interest and musical development (Denac, 2008; Kenney, 1997). Music can affect children's literacy development and academic performance (Shore & Strasser, 2006; Wiggins, 2007). Musical activities that relate to story reading can focus children's attention and enhance their social interactions (deVries, 2008).

As you create exploratory opportunities and plan experiences for children, think about how each child relates to musical concepts and expression. Focus your observations on

HOW AND WHEN THE CHILD

- shows awareness and appreciation of different kinds of music

- expresses thoughts, feelings, and energy through music

- shows increasing awareness of various components of music: melody (tune), pitch (high and low sounds), rhythm (the beat), tempo (speed), dynamics (changes in volume), and timbre (sound quality distinguishing one instrument or voice from another)

See page 55 of *Child Assessment Portfolio.*

Objective 34 Explores musical concepts and expression

Strategies

- Include music and movement experiences and activities throughout the day. Use musical activities as you transition children from one activity to another. Include songs or movement activities as part of most large-group activities. Sing or use musical instruments during outdoor activities.

- Encourage children to make up new lyrics and actions to familiar tunes or to create their own songs. Include software that enables children to create tunes.

- Personalize songs. For example, sing the child's name or the name of a favorite food.

- Create songbooks or song charts with pictures to illustrate songs children frequently sing.

- Play a variety of music. Offer different genres, such as jazz, country, classical, or rock and roll. Include music that inspires children to move quickly (polka) or slowly (lullaby). Discuss differences and how each type of music makes them feel.

- Include songs and lullabies from many cultures. Teach children songs that are familiar to their families so they can sing them together.

- Encourage children to focus on particular musical elements through your comments and questions. Use words such as *pitch* (*high, low, up, down*); *rhythm* or *beat* (*steady, fast, slow*); *volume* (*loud, soft*); and *duration* (*long, short*).

- Provide a variety of musical instruments from various cultures for children to explore.

- Involve children in making their own musical instruments. Encourage them to explore sounds by modifying their instruments. For example, compare the sounds of empty coffee can drums to those of drums with water in them.

- Invite musicians to bring instruments. Have them play and talk about their instruments.

- Transform the Dramatic Play area into a musical stage or recording studio. Include musical instruments, a toy microphone, an audio recorder, and other appropriate props.

- Make printed music available to children. Support older preschool and kindergarten children's experimentation with musical symbols and notations. For example, provide staff paper for beginners and encourage children to "write" music. Encourage children to "read" their music and to perform by singing or playing an instrument. Audiotape their creations.

Objective 35

Explores dance and movement concepts

35

One of the first ways that children express themselves is through movement. Each new movement gives children more information about the capabilities of their bodies (Lutz & Kuhlman, 2000). Dance involves using one's body to express ideas and feelings and to response to music. Preschool children demonstrate knowledge of dance and movement in many ways when they imitate animals or use scarves and streamers as they respond to music. Movement, taught with pretend imagery, is beneficial to children's learning and enjoyment of dance (Sacha & Russ, 2006). Teachers can help children learn *how* their bodies can move, *where* their bodies can move, and the *relationships* among parts of their own bodies, relationships with other persons, and relationships among persons in space (Sanders, 2002).

As you create exploratory opportunities and plan experiences for children, think about how each child relates to dance and movement. Focus your observations on

HOW AND WHEN THE CHILD

- communicates feelings and ideas through dance and movement

- demonstrates spatial awareness (*where* the body moves): location (separate or shared space); directions (up or down, forward or backward); levels (low, middle, high); and pathways (straight, curved, zigzag)

- demonstrates effort awareness (*how* the body moves): speed (fast or slow); force (strong or light); and control (bound or free)

- demonstrates relational awareness (*relationships* the body creates): with the physical self (body parts); with body shapes and size (big, small, straight); roles with other people (leading or following, mirroring, alternating); and in space (near or far, over/ or under, around or through)

See page 55 of *Child Assessment Portfolio.*

Objective 35 Explores dance and movement concepts

Strategies

- Encourage children to participate in various creative movement activities. For example, they might move like an elephant, a swan, falling leaves, a kite, a windstorm, or growing plants.

- Model movements and invite children to join you. Suggest new movements and techniques or ways to combine different actions.

- Use pretend imagery. Have children first imagine the movement and then carry it out. For example, they might close their eyes and imagine reaching for a small bird in a tree, and then they carry out the movements they envisioned.

- Use objects and props to help children focus. For example, use a blue mat as a pond and have children leap over the pond as if they were deer, rabbits, or frogs.

- Provide space and materials for dance and movement activities indoors and outdoors. Use large open spaces to support their exploration of movement and direction. Use small spaces for isolated movement and specific patterns. Offer streamers, ribbons, scarves, balloons, blankets, or parachutes.

- Use vocabulary that supports children's understanding of movement concepts. Describe *how* their bodies move in space (*fast, slow, heavy, light*). Tell *where* their bodies can move (*forward, backward, low, middle, high, straight, curved, zigzag*). Describe the *relationship* of their bodies to other people or objects (*near, far, leading, following, mirroring, together, apart*).

- Ask movement experts to visit. For example, invite a member of a dance troupe to demonstrate dance techniques and how to control body movements.

- Watch videos that show examples of a wide variety of dances in other cultures. Take children to see a children's ballet or other dance performance.

- Involve children in designing and making scenery or stage sets for performances.

Objective 36

Explores drama through actions and language

36

Drama is portraying characters and telling stories though action, dialogue, or both (Dodge, Colker, & Heroman, 2002). Drama is an important part of development and learning for young children. It positively affects children's language development and literacy, self-awareness, social–emotional reasoning, and problem solving (Brown, 1990; Pinciotti, 1993; Wright, et al., 2008). As children participate with others in drama-related play, they develop basic skills and knowledge in the use of props, movement, pantomime, sound, speech, character, and story making (Pinciotti, 1993). Children learn to tell stories through repeated exchanges with people who are important to them. Experiences and cultural traditions influence what stories children tell and how they tell stories (Curenton & Ryan, 2006; Wright et al., 2008). Adult guidance is important in helping children develop the skills they need act out scenarios and stories. When teachers read stories for later dramatization or provide children with puppets to act out a story, clothing they can use for dress up, and props that can transform blocks into an imaginary city, they are teaching children drama. As children play with materials such as these, they express their feelings and process their experiences.

As you create exploratory opportunities and plan experiences for children, think about how each child explores drama. Focus your observations on

HOW AND WHEN THE CHILD

- shows that real-life roles can be enacted
- communicates a message or story through action and dialogue
- represents ideas through drama, e.g., pretends to be the big bad wolf
- shows appreciation of the dramatizations of others

Note: See Objective 14 for related information about sociodramatic play.

See page 55 of *Child Assessment Portfolio*.

Objective 36 Explores drama through actions and language

Strategies

- Extend the play of children by encouraging additional scenarios. Provide a variety of props for the exploration of different roles.

- Extend children's play by helping them to see a range of actions, solutions, and possibilities. Provide opportunities to act out different characters and feelings. For example, have children make angry, fierce, sad, joyful, kind, and brooding faces. Provide an imaginary bag with imaginary costumes and have children use them in their play.

- Provide verbal prompts to support children's dramatizations. For example, to help children get started you might say, "Act as though...," "Imagine you are...," or "Once there was a..." To help them continue, say, "Then what happened?" or "What happened next?" To help them close, you might prompt, "How did it end?" or "What happened last?"

- Invite children to dramatize stories you read. Read the story, calling attention to the setting, mood, characters, and plot. Provide puppets or other props for children to use to enact the story. Read the story a second time, pausing so children can act out the various parts.

- Invite children to act out familiar stories such as *Caps for Sale*.

- Encourage children to build scenery and props for dramatization. For example, they might create houses to act out *The Three Little Pigs* or make masks to dramatize *The Three Billy Goats Gruff*.

- Encourage children to dictate stories to act out later. Send copies of stories home for children to enact with their families.

- Attend a children's theater performance or arrange for a mime, actor, or storyteller to visit.

- Provide opportunities for children to try different theater roles. For example, they might be the writer, actor, director, designer, or audience member. Support them as they develop knowledge and skills in the use of props, movement, pantomime, sound, speech, character, and storytelling.

English Language Acquisition

Language learning is a basic feature of the early development of all children. If a child is raised in a family in which English is spoken, she will learn to speak English. If a child is raised in a family in which Spanish is spoken, he will learn to speak Spanish. If a child is raised in a family in which both English and Spanish are spoken, she will become bilingual as she learns both languages. If a child is raised in a family in which Spanish is spoken and the child attends an early childhood classroom in which English is spoken, he will be a second-language learner, adding English to his home language of Spanish. Bilingual children, who are also called *simultaneous* language learners, and second-language-learning children, who are also called *sequential* language learners, are both presented with a challenging cognitive task: They must learn and maintain two languages, rather than just one. Therefore children in both of these groups are dual-language learners.

The language-learning process for simultaneous language learners closely resembles the process for monolingual children. However, because of simultaneous language learners' need to know twice as many words, their vocabulary development may be less extensive in each language in comparison to monolingual children (Oller & Eilers, 2002).

Young sequential language learners follow a slightly different developmental sequence. At first these children may continue to use their home language in a second-language setting. Later, when they realize that their home language is not being understood, they enter a nonverbal period during which they gain receptive abilities in the new language and may experiment with language sounds.

ENGLISH LANGUAGE ACQUISITION

37 Demonstrates progress in listening to and understanding English

38 Demonstrates progress in speaking English

Next, they begin to use memorized words and phrases in their new language, and some of the phrases might be quite long. Finally they develop productive use of the new language, constructing original sentences with the words and phrases they already know (Tabors, 2008). This sequence is not specific to a particular language, so Objectives 37 and 38 may be adapted to assess progress in acquiring any second language. The language in the examples must be modified to reflect the new language the child is learning.

Learning a second language is cumulative and often uneven. Children may sound very sophisticated in situations where they know the vocabulary and the grammar that they need in order to be understood. In other situations, however, they might be unable to communicate because of emotional or linguistic constraints (Tabors, 2008).

One of the major concerns about young children who are learning a second language in a society where that is the dominant language is that the first language may no longer be developed. The loss of the first language can be detrimental for personal, familial, religious, and cultural reasons (Wong Fillmore, 1991). Furthermore, research shows that the second-language learners who do best in school are those who have a strong grounding in their home language (Collier, 1987).

There are considerable individual differences in how young children take on the task of learning a second language. Highly motivated children, children with more exposure to the new language, children who are older when they begin the process, and children who have more outgoing personalities may make more rapid progress. Some children may spend an entire year in the nonverbal period, while others may start to use social words right away. Second-language learners may be socially isolated because of their inability to communicate. Effective teachers use strategies to integrate these children into classroom activities, and they develop techniques for helping children begin to understand and use their new language.

Demonstrates progress in listening to and understanding English

37

The first task for second-language learners is to gain receptive understanding of the new language. Once they have learned that they are in an environment where a new language is being used and that they will need to use that language if they want to be understood, they must begin to hear the sounds of the new language and begin the process of connecting those sounds to the objects and activities around them. Children take on this task at different rates (Saville-Troike, 1988; Wong Fillmore, 1979; Itoh & Hatch, 1978). If it is possible to communicate in their home language with adults and children in the classroom, they may choose to do so without making the effort to learn the new language (Meyer, 1989). If they find that nonverbal communication is effective, they may use that for a considerable period of time.

However, once motivated to begin to understand the new language—because they want to play with peers or want to understand the teachers who are using the new language—they begin to observe and listen closely. At this time children use *spectating* behaviors, focusing their attention on how words are formed, and *rehearsing* behaviors, mouthing words or practicing by saying words to themselves (Tabors, 2008). As they acquire the phonology of the new language, children may also play with the sounds of the language by inventing new words (Saville-Troike, 1988).

Classroom routines and the language used in those contexts help children begin to understand the new language. However, assessing children's receptive abilities can be complicated by the fact that young learners are extremely good at guessing meaning from context. In order to check receptive comprehension, teachers must be careful that they are assessing understanding without providing contextual cues like gestures or eye gaze.

Objective 37 Demonstrates progress in listening to and understanding English

1	2 Beginning	3	4 Progressing	5	6 Increasing	7	8 Advancing	9
	Observes others as they converse in English during play or other small-group experiences; may engage in similar activities by imitating behavior; attends to oral use of English		**Responds to common English words and phrases when they are accompanied by gestures or other visual aids**		**Responds to words and phrases in English when they are not accompanied by gestures or other visual aids**		**Understands increasingly complex English phrases used by adults and children**	
	• Moves closer to the dramatic play area to watch a small group of children		• Joins a group in the block area when one child motions with a hand to come, and says, "Come play."		• Goes to table when teacher says, "It's lunchtime. Take your seats at the tables."		• Responds by putting the correct block where directed when another child says, "Hey, put that square block over there by the horse to make the fence."	
	• Sits across from two children who are stringing beads and talking, and begins stringing beads, too		• Goes to the sink when the teacher says it is time to brush teeth and pantomimes toothbrushing		• Puts the caps on the markers and then puts the markers on the shelf when reminded		• Points to the correct piece when the teacher asks, "Which circle is the biggest?"	
	• Watches another child hold up a cup to request milk and does the same		• Nods when classmate says, "Hello."		• Points to ear when asked, "Where's your ear?"		• Touches the car at the top of the tallest ramp when the teacher asks, "Which car do you think will roll the fastest?"	
	• Participates by doing hand movements while other children and the teacher sing in the new language		• Sits by the teacher when she holds up a book and asks, "Would you like to read a book?"		• Picks up a car from a group of toys when asked, "Where's the car?"			
					• Picks up the puzzle with the puppy on it when another child says, "Let's do the puppy puzzle together."			

See page 56 of *Child Assessment Portfolio.*

Objective 37 Demonstrates progress in listening to and understanding English

Strategies

- Gather personal information from each family, including what language or languages are spoken at home and which family members speak them. In-depth information includes an estimate of how much time each person in the home spends using a particular language with the child, and what language or languages the child uses when speaking with each family member.

- If the child is using a language other than English at home, ask whether or not a parent feels the child is making appropriate progress in that language.

- If you do not share the home language with an English-language learner, ask the parents for a few words in the home language that can be used to welcome the child to the classroom. If parents agree, make a tape recording of these words to use in the classroom to comfort their child or to help other children hear the sounds of the child's home language.

- Set up classroom routines and use consistent language when referring to activities (clean-up time) and objects (cubby, block area) throughout the day in the classroom.

- Make sure English-language learners are included in situations in the classroom where they can hear English. Assign seating so that English-language learners are near English-speaking children during activities, or snack, group time, and rest time.

- Pair an English-language learner with an outgoing English-speaking child for certain periods during the day, so that the English-speaking child may help to integrate the English-language learner into classroom activities.

- When speaking English with an English-language learner, use these guidelines:

  - Speak slowly. This helps children hear and learn the individual words.

  - Use repetition. When children hear the same word used multiple times for an object, they are more likely to make the connection between the spoken word and the name of the object.

  - Simplify your message.

  - Place important words at the end of a sentence and emphasize those words. For example, "This is your *hand*. Do you want to trace your hand?"

  - Double the message with gestures, actions, visual aids, or directed gaze while you are talking. For example, when asking children to put on their coats, model putting on your own coat. These visual aids help children understand what is being said.

  - Use *running commentary* by telling English-language learners what you are doing as you are doing it. For example say, "Now I will put the milk in the batter."

  - Use parallel talk, describing the actions of the child, "You are stacking the blue block on top of the red block."

- Be alert to an English-language learner's use of non-verbal communication, such as pointing silently to a paint brush. Supply the words in English for what the child is trying to communicate. For example, "You want the paint brush? Here is the paint brush."

- Talk about what is right in front of the English-language-learning child, so the context will be obvious.

- Provide pictures to accompany the daily schedule, classroom rules, and other print in the classroom. This helps children know the expectations even though they may not yet understand the language.

Objective 37 Demonstrates progress in listening to and understanding English

Strategies, *continued*

- Use repetitive songs and games during group times. Children who are English-language learners often say their first words in English when singing familiar songs and fingerplays.

- Read books in children's home languages if possible prior to reading the book in English to them. This helps them become familiar with the words and the story line before hearing it in English. Reading it in the home language should not happen immediately prior to reading it in English, but rather earlier in the day or the week.

- Choose books with repetitive refrains when reading aloud with English-language learners. Read the same books over and over again so that the words become very familiar to them.

- Supply English words for any object that an English-language learner shows interest in (often they will bring objects to you to identify). Then see if you can elicit what the name for that object is in the child's home language.

- Plan small-group activities so that there are times when an activity is done with only English-language-learning children and all language can be tailored to their needs, and there are times when the group has both English-language-learning children and English-speaking children and the language can be more complex.

- Keep talking. English-language-learning children will need lots and lots of input to hear the sounds of English and to begin to understand what they mean.

Demonstrates progress in speaking English

38

The second task for second-language learners is to begin the process of using their new language. Most children begin by repeating words or phrases, either in one-on-one interactions with adults or in group situations when all of the children are using the same words, for instance, during a group sing-along.

A distinct feature of young children's second-language acquisition is their memorization and use of social interactive terms (Wong Fillmore, 1976, 1979) to help them enter play situations and to have their needs met. Once children have acquired a number of words and socially useful phrases, they can begin to construct original sentences. Eventually second-language learners use the input from speakers of the new language to develop their ability to use questions, negatives, and past and future tenses. Second-language learners make many of the same mistakes made by young children learning their home language. Throughout this process, second-language learners continue to acquire vocabulary so they will have the words they need in order to communicate verbally with other speakers of the new language.

Objective 38 Demonstrates progress in speaking English

1	2	3	4	5	6	7	8	9
	Beginning		Progressing		Increasing		Advancing	

	Repeats sounds and words in English, sometimes very quietly		**Uses a few socially interactive terms in English appropriately; uses one or two words in English to represent a whole idea**		**Develops multiword phrases by using socially interactive terms in English; adds new words to the phrase**		**Uses increasingly complex grammar in English; makes some mistakes typical of young children**	
	• Mouths the words of a song during circle time • Echoes a word or phrase, e.g., says, "Monkey," while group chants "Five Little Monkeys Jumping on the Bed" • After teacher says, "Up," child repeats, "Up." • Repeats, "Mil, mil, mil," after the teacher asks, "Would you like more milk?"		• Says , "Hi"; "Lookit"; "My turn"; and "Stopit." • Hears someone nearby say, "Be careful!" and repeats phrase as a warning in a similar situation later • Points at snack basket and says, "More crackers." • Looks out the window and says, "Go outside." • Says, "No, mine," when another child takes her toy truck		• Says, "I do a ice cream"; "I want my mommy"; and "Lookit this, Teacher." • Says, "How you do this flower?" • Says, "Big. I gotta big." • Says, "How do you gonna make dese?"		• Develops entire sentences, e.g., "The door is a square," and "The house has a lot of windows." • Uses questions and negatives, e.g., "Your name is what?" and "You no my mommy." • Uses past and future tenses, e.g., "I goed to the park," and "I'll get it." • Interacts in elaborate play schemes, "I be the mommy and you be the baby. Here's your bottle, Baby."	

See page 57 of *Child Assessment Portfolio.*

Objective 38 Demonstrates progress in speaking English

Strategies

- Spend time one-on-one with English-language learners; they may be more likely to start using English if they are not in a group situation.

- Be alert to children beginning to use English very softly, perhaps rehearsing what they want to say.

- Use repetitive songs, games and fingerplays during group times. Children who are English-language learners often say their first words in English when singing familiar songs and fingerplays. Singing in a group helps give children a secure environment in which to try out their emerging English skills.

- Try to have English-language-learning children repeat words as you demonstrate what objects or illustrations they refer to.

- Validate children's language attempts in either language. If English-language-learners use their home language, acknowledge their effort, and if you can guess what they are talking about, respond in English.

- Give English-language-learners lots of time to think about what they want to say. If you ask a question ("what would you like to do?") wait longer than you would normally. It may take longer for the children to think of the words they want to say in English.

- For children who are at the beginning stages of learning English, ask close-ended questions and offer some options for response ("Would you like to paint or would you like to build?")

- When reading books with repetitive refrains, pause and let the children fill in the next word. For example, "Brown bear, brown bear, what do you_____?" This helps children feel successful and builds confidence when they know what comes next and are able to fill in the missing word.

- Intentionally introduce new vocabulary words. Use those words frequently in different contexts throughout the day. Provide visual aids and gestures to illustrate the meaning of the words.

- Give English-language-learners a chance to respond in English in group situations when they can answer in chorus with all of the children.

- Encourage families to bring pictures and objects from home. Children are more likely to talk about things they know and that are familiar to them. Children are also more likely to engage in dramatic play if objects similar to what they see used at home are included in the classroom.

- Engage children in conversations on interesting topics that connect to their daily lives. This provides children opportunities to express ideas and thoughts about things that are relevant and important to them.

- Expand and extend any effort that a child makes to use English. For example, when a child says, "car", you might say, "Yes! That's a racing car."

- Notice which phrases a child uses ("Hey," "OK," "Mine," "Stopit") and help the child build from those phrases ("Hey you," "I'm okay," "That's mine," "Stopit, please.")

- Make learning new vocabulary words in English a primary goal of instruction and all communication. Choose words you want all of the children to know and use them repeatedly in the classroom. Introduce the words using objects or illustrations and develop activities during which the children will need to use these words.

- Help children move from nonverbal responses to productive responses by prompting them with questions. For example, when a child points to her untied shoe ask, "What do you need?" If the child does not respond ask, "Do you need me to tie your shoe?" When the child responds, "Tie...shoe," recognize her effort and say, "Okay! I will tie your shoe."

- Encourage interactions between English-language-learners and English-speaking children by modeling initiations. For example, you might say to a child, "Ask Sally, 'May I play with you?'"

- Model correct English versions of phrases used by English-language learners. For example, if a child says, "I goed to the store," you respond, "You went to the store? What did you get?"

Glossary

/ /: surrounding a letter, diagonal lines indicate the sound (rather than the name) of that letter, e.g., /k/ for the initial consonant sound in *cat* or /s/ for the initial consonant sound in *cell*

abstract symbol: a sign, figure, mark, image, or numeral that is used to represent an object, person, concept, idea, or number

alliteration: the repetition of initial consonant sounds in two or more neighboring words, e.g., *big blue balloons*

alphabetic principle: the fact that written words are composed of letters that represent sounds

areas of development and learning: the broadest domains of development and learning, e.g., *Social–Emotional*

attend: pay attention to an activity or experience

colored bands: in *Objectives for Development & Learning* and the *Child Assessment Portfolio*, the colored bands or lines (red, orange, yellow, green, blue, and purple) that show the age or the class/grade ranges for widely held developmental and learning expectations

compare and contrast: examine the relationship between two items or groups of items to determine how they are alike and how they are different

count on: a strategy by which a child figures out a quantity by beginning with the sum of a small number of objects and then counting the remaining objects until he counts them all. For example, with a group of five objects, the child might say, "Three," and then point to the remaining objects, saying, "Four, five. I have five." *Counting on* is a more advanced strategy than *counting all*, in which a child would count "One, two, three, four, five. I have five."

decontextualized language: language that is not tied to the immediate context, e.g., that refers to past events, future events, or imaginary scenarios

dimension: a specific aspect or subskill of an objective, e.g., *Manages feelings* or *Follows limits and expectations*

direction: related to where a person or thing is going or from where a person or thing has come

distance: how near or far away a person or object is located

dual-language learners: children who acquire two or more languages simultaneously, as well as those who learn a second language while continuing to develop their first language

engaged in learning: when children are focused, deeply interested, and involved in experiences through which they learn knowledge and skills. When they are engaged, they exhibit attention, persistence, flexibility, and self-regulation.

engage: interact or become deeply involved with a person or activity

examples: in *Objectives for Development & Learning*, different ways that children show what they know and can do, e.g., *Moves to the sand table at the suggestion of an adult when there are too many at the art table*

explanatory talk: talk that consists of explaining and describing, including definitions of words; discussion of cause-and-effect relationships; and discussion of connections between ideas, events, and actions

"fair share" groups: the result of dividing objects, food, etc. into groups so that each person gets an equal or approximately equal amount

fine-motor skills: small movements that involve the small muscles of the fingers and wrists, such as grasping something with one's thumb and index finger

gallop: a traveling movement that involves leaping (taking a big step forward), keeping the same foot in front of the body at all times, and bringing the rear foot to meet the front foot

genre: a kind or type of art (e.g., folk art and modern art), literature (e.g., picture books and poetry), or music (e.g., classical music and pop music)

gross-motor skills: large movements that involve the large muscles in the arms, legs, torso, and feet, such as running and jumping

growing pattern: a pattern that increases by at least plus one and continues to increase, e.g., a block staircase

home language: a language spoken in the home that is different from the main language spoken in the community

indicators: knowledge, skills, or behaviors that children demonstrate at four levels of each developmental progression. In *Objectives for Development & Learning* and the *Child Assessment Portfolio*, these statements are in bold print for levels 2, 4, 6, and 8, e.g., *Accepts redirection from adults.*

invented spelling: (also called *sound spelling* or *developmental spelling*) a child's attempt to spell words by writing a letter for each sound he or she notices. This is an important step toward conventional spelling.

large ball: a beach ball or playground ball

lowercase letters: the letters of the alphabet that are not uppercase (capital) letters, e.g., *a*, *b*, and *c*. Although children often refer to these as "small" letters, adults should use the term *lowercase* when referring to them because their actual size varies from text to text

levels: in *Objectives for Development & Learning* and the *Child Assessment Portfolio*, the rating scale that describes specific points along the progression for each objective

listen (vs. hear): to pay attention to sound, to hear something with thoughtful attention, or to be alert to catch an expected sound

location: relates to positional language that indicates where a person or thing is situated

nonstandard measuring tools: tools that are not formal measuring tools. These may have units of equal length (e.g., same-sized cubes, links, or paper clips) or units of unequal length (e.g., children's strides).

numeral: the symbol that represents a number, e.g., the number *four* is shown as the numeral *4*

objective: a statement of expectations of knowledge, skills, and behaviors, e.g., *Regulates own emotions and behaviors*

onset: the first consonant sound(s) before the vowel in a one-syllable word, e.g., /k/ in *cat* and /th/ in *think*

parentese: singsong speech and exaggerated facial expressions. This type of communication encourages young infants to listen and focus on what is said.

persist: remain focused on an activity for an adequate length of time

phoneme: the smallest unit of sound in a word

pictorial map: a map that uses drawings or pictures to represent objects in the environment

phonological awareness: the understanding that spoken language can be divided into smaller and smaller units that can be manipulated

position: an indication of where a person or object is located in relation to someone or something else

progress checkpoints: three or four points during the year when teachers determine the progress a child is making toward an objective

progressions of development and learning: paths, or trajectories, that children typically follow when acquiring a skill or behavior

proximity: the closeness or nearness of something, often described as *beside, next to, touching*, or *alongside*

redirection: guiding children's behavior by restating or providing an attractive alternative

repeating pattern: a pattern in which the core unit repeats a minimum of five times, e.g., red, blue; red, blue; red, blue; red, blue; red, blue

rhyme: words with the same ending sounds but not necessarily the same ending letters

rime: the vowel sound and all the sounds that follow the vowel in a syllable or one-syllable word, e.g., /at/ in *cat* and /ink/ in *think*

scenario: a series of real or imagined events

secure attachment: the strong emotional bond or trusting relationship between a child and an important person in his or her life

secure base: a familiar, trusted adult to whom a child returns for protection when the child becomes frightened or uneasy while exploring his or her world

self-talk: (sometimes referred to as *private speech*) the language an adult uses with children to describe his or her actions at the time they are being performed, e.g., "Now I am putting milk in the refrigerator."

skip: a traveling movement involving a step and a hop, using alternating feet

sociodramatic play: dramatic play, e.g., role-playing or fantasy play, with the additional component of social interaction with either a peer or an adult

standard measuring tools: formal tools that mark units of measurement with numerals, e.g., rulers, measuring tapes, and meter sticks

story-related problems: in sophisticated picture books, the difficulties characters face that the reader must infer from the information provided. These problems require the reader to analyze information and make predictions.

subitize: to quickly glance at a small group of objects and identify the quantity without counting the objects one at a time

tally: use marks to keep a record of whatever has been counted

tally marks: one-to-one representations of counted items, usually vertical and diagonal lines arranged in groups of five with four vertical lines in a row "crossed" by one diagonal line

teaching strategies: what teachers can do to support and scaffold children's learning as it relates to a particular objective

three-dimensional shape: a figure that has width, height, and depth (thickness), e.g., a sphere, cube, triangular prism, cone, cylinder, or pyramid

two-dimensional shape: a figure that has width and height only, e.g., a circle, square, rectangle, triangle, or pentagon

uppercase letters: the capital letters of the alphabet, e.g., *A*, *B*, and *C*. Although children often refer to these as "big" letters, adults should use the term *uppercase* when referring to them because their actual size varies from text to text

References

Adams, M. J. (1990). *Beginning to read: Thinking and learning about print.* Urbana, IL: University of Illinois Center for the Study of Reading.

Adams, M. J. (2001). Alphabetic anxiety and explicit systematic phonics instruction: A cognitive science perspective. In S. B. Neuman & D. K. Dickinson (Eds.), *Handbook of early literacy research* (pp. 66–80). New York: Guilford Press.

American Academy of Pediatrics (2003). *Baby & Child Health.* Jennifer Shu, M.D., Editor-in-Chief, New York: DK Publishing.

Andress, B. (1991). From research to practice: Preschool children and their movement responses to music. *Young Children, 47*(1), 22–27.

Andress, B. (1995). Transforming curriculum in music. In S. Bredekamp & T. Rosegrant (Eds.), *Reaching potentials: Transforming early childhood curriculum and assessment,* Vol. 2 (pp. 99–108). Washington, DC: National Association for the Education of Young Children.

Anthony, J. L., Lonigan, C., Driscoll, K., Phillips, B. M., & Burgess, S. R. (2003).Preschool phonological sensitivity: A quasi-parallel progression of word structure units and cognitive operations. *Reading Research Quarterly, 38,* 470–487.

Araujo, N., & Aghayan, C. (2006). *Easy songs for smooth transitions in the classroom.* St. Paul, MN: Redleaf Press.

Arnone, M. P. (2003). *Using instructional design strategies to foster curiosity.* Retrieved July 9, 2007, from http://www.marilynarnone.com/ERICDigestonCuriosityand1D.pdf

Arste, J. C., Woodward, V. A. & Burcke, C. I. (1984). *Language stories and literacy lessons.* Portsmouth: Heinemann.

Aubrey, C. (2001). Early mathematics. In T. David (Ed.), *Promoting evidenced-based practice in early childhood education: Research and its implications, Vol. 1,* (pp. 185–210). Amsterdam: Elsevier Science.

August, D., & Hakuta, K. (1998). *Educating language minority children.* New York: National Academy Press.

Ayoub, C. C. & Fischer, K. W. (2006). Developmental pathways and intersections among domains of development. In K. McCartney & D. Phillips (Eds.), *Blackwell handbook of early childhood development* (pp. 62–81).

Bae, J. (2004). Learning to teach visual arts in an early childhood classroom: The teacher's role as a guide. *Early Childhood Education Journal, 31*(1), 247–254.

Baghban, M. (2007). Immigration in childhood: Using picture books to cope. *The Social Studies, 98*(2), 71–76.

Bailey, A. (2008). Assessing the language of young learners. In N. H. Hornberger, P. Clapham, & C. Corson (Eds.), *Encyclopedia of language and education,* Vol. 7., *Language testing and assessment* (2nd ed.), (pp. 379–400). New York: Springer Science Business Media.

Baker, B. L., & Brightman, A. J. (2004). *Steps to independence: Teaching everyday skills to children with special needs* (4th ed.). Baltimore, MD: Paul H. Brookes.

Barbour, A. C. (1999). The impact of playground design on the play behaviors of children with differing levels of physical competence. *Early Childhood Research Quarterly, 14,* 75–98.

Barkley, R. A. (1997). *ADHD and the nature of self-control.* New York: Guilford Press.

Baron-Cohen, S. (1995). *Mindblindness: An essay on autism and theory of mind.* London: MIT Press.

Baroody, A. J. (1987). *Children's mathematical thinking: A developmental framework for preschool, primary, and special education teachers.* New York: Teachers College, Columbia University.

Baroody, A. J. (2000). Research in Review: Does mathematics instruction for three-to five-year-olds really make sense? *Young Children, 55*(4), 61–67.

Baroody, A .J. (2004). The developmental bases for early childhood number and operations standards. In D. H. Clements, J. Sarama, & A. Diabiase (Eds.), *Engaging young children in mathematics: Standards for early childhood mathematics education* (pp. 173–220). Mahway, NJ: Lawrence Erlbaum Associates.

Baroody, A. J., & Wilkins, J. L. M. (1999). The development of informal counting, number, and arithmetic skills and concepts. In J. V. Copley (Ed.), *Mathematics in the early years* (pp. 48–65). Reston, VA: National Council of Teachers of Mathematics.

Barry, E. S. (2006). Children's memory: A primer for understanding behavior. *Early Childhood Education Journal, 33*, 405–411.

Beals, D. E. (2001). Eating and reading: Links between family conversations with preschoolers and later language and literacy. In D. K. Dickenson & P. O. Tabors (Eds.), *Beginning literacy with language: Young children learning at home and school* (pp. 75–92). Baltimore: Paul H. Brookes.

Beckman, M., & Edwards, J. (2000). The ontogeny of phonological categories and the primacy of lexical learning in linguistic development. *Child Development, 71*, 240–249.

Beland, K. R. (1996). A school wide approach to violence prevention. In R. L. Hampton, P. Jenkins, & T. P. Gulatta (Eds.), *Preventing violence in America* (pp. 209–231). Thousand Oaks, CA: Sage Publications.

Benigno, J. P., & Ellis, S. (2004). Two is greater than three: Effects of older siblings on parental support of preschoolers' counting in middle-income families. *Early Childhood Research Quarterly, 19*, 4–20.

Benoit, L., Lehalle, H., & Jouen, F. (2004). Do young children acquire number words through subitizing or counting? *Cognitive development, 19*(3), 291–307.

Bergen, D. (2002). The role of pretend play in children's cognitive development. *Early Childhood Research and Practice, 4*(1). Retrieved May 27, 2007, from http://www.ecrp.uiuc.edu/v4n1/bergen.html.

Berger, S. E., Adolph, K. E., & Lobo, S. A. (2005). Out of the toolbox: Toddlers differentiate wobbly and wooden handrails. *Child Development, 76*, 1294–1307.

Berk, L. E. (2002). *Infants, children, & adolescents* (4th ed.). Boston: Allyn & Bacon.

Berk, L. E. (2003). *Child development* (6th ed.). Boston: Allyn & Bacon.

Berk, L. E. (2005). *Child development* (7th ed.). Boston: Allyn & Bacon.

Berk, L. E. (2006). Looking at kindergarten children. In D. F. Gullo (Ed.), *K today: Teaching and learning in the kindergarten year* (pp. 11–25). Washington, DC: National Association for the Education of Young Children.

Berk, L. E., & Winsler, A. (1995). *Scaffolding children's learning: Vygotsky and early childhood education.* Washington, DC: National Association for the Education of Young Children.

Bernstein, B. (1971). *Class codes and control. Vol. 1.* London: Routledge and Kegan Paul.

Bialystok, E., & Martin, M. M. (2004). Attention and inhibition in bilingual children: Evidence from the dimensional change card sort task. *Developmental Science, 7*, 325–339.

Bialystok, E., McBride-Chang, C., & Luk, G. (2005). Bilingualism, language proficiency, and learning to read in two writing systems. *Journal of Educational Psychology, 97*, 580–590.

Bialystok, E., & Senman, L. (2004). Executive processes in appearance-reality tasks: The role of inhibition of attention and symbolic representation. *Child Development, 75*, 562–579.

Bilmes, J. (2004). *Beyond behavior management: The six life skills children need to thrive in today's society.* St. Paul, MN: Redleaf Press.

Bilmes, J. (2006). *Common psychological disorders in young children: A handbook for childcare professionals.* St. Paul, MN: Redleaf Press.

Birbili, M. (2006). Mapping knowledge: Concept maps in early childhood education. *Early Childhood Research and Practice. 8*(2). Retrieved June 20, 2007, from http://www.ecrp.uiuc.edu/v8n2/birbili.html

Birch, S., & Ladd, G. (1997). The teacher-child relationship and children's early school adjustment. *Journal of School Psychology, 35*, 61–69.

Bisgaier, C. S., Samaras, T., & Russo, M. J. (2004). Young children try, try again: Using wood, glue, and words to enhance learning. *Young Children, 59*(4), 22–29.

Bjorklund, D. F. (2005). *Children's thinking: Cognitive development and individual differences.* Belmont, CA: Wadsworth Thomson Learning.

Black, B., & Hazen, N. L. (1990). Social status and patterns of communication in acquainted and unacquainted preschool children. *Developmental Psychology, 26*, 379–387.

Blair, C. (2002). School readiness: Integrating cognition and emotion in a neurobiological conceptualization of children's functioning at school entry. *American Psychologist, 57*(2), 111–127.

Blair, C. (2003). *Self-regulation and school readiness.* Retrieved May 24, 2007, from http://www.ericdigests.org/2004-1/self.htm

Blair, C., & Razza, R. P. (2007). Relating effortful control, executive function, and false belief understanding to emerging math and literacy ability in kindergarten. *Child Development, 78,* 647–663.

Blaut, J. M., & Stea, D. (1974). Mapping at the age of three. *Journal of Geography, 73*(7), 5–9.

Bloodgood, J. W. (1999). What's in a name? Children's name writing and literacy acquisition. *Reading Research Quarterly, 34,* 342–367.

Bodrova, E., & Leong, D.J. (2001). *The tools of the mind project: A case study of implementing the Vygotskyian approach in American early childhood and primary classrooms.* Geneva, Switzerland: International Bureau of Education, UNESCO.

Bodrova, E., & Leong, D. J. (2004). Chopsticks and counting chips: Do play and foundational skills need to compete for the teacher's attention in an early childhood classroom? In D. Koralek (Ed.), *Spotlight on young children and play* (pp. 4–11). Washington, DC: National Association for the Education of Young Children.

Bodrova E., & Leong, D. J. (2005). Self-regulation as a key to school readiness: How can early childhood teachers promote this critical competency? In M. Zaslow & I. Martinez-Beck (Eds.), *Critical issues in early childhood professional development* (pp. 223–270). Baltimore: Paul H. Brookes.

Bodrova, E., & Leong, D. J. (2008). Developing self-regulation in kindergarten: Can we keep all the crickets in the basket? *Young Children, 63*(2), 56–58.

Bosma, A. Domka, A., & Peterson, J. (2000). Improving motor skills in kindergartners. St. Xavier University (ERIC Document Reproduction Service No. ED453913). Retrieved August 10, 2008 from http://www.eric.ed.gov/contentdelivery/servlet/ERICServlet?accno=ED453913

Bowey, J. A., & Francis, J. (1991). Phonological analysis as a function of age and exposure to reading instruction. *Applied Psycholinguistics, 12*(1), 91–121.

Bowman, B., Donovan, M. S., & Burns, M. S. (Eds.). (2001). *Eager to learn: Educating our preschoolers.* Washington, DC: National Academy Press.

Bowman, B., & Moore, E. K. (2006). *School readiness and social-emotional development: Perspectives on cultural diversity.* Washington, DC: National Black Child Development Institute.

Bowman, B., & Stott, F. (1994). Understanding development in a cultural context: The challenge for teachers. In B. L. Mallory & R. S. New (Eds.), *Diversity and developmentally appropriate practices: Challenges for early childhood education* (pp. 119–133). New York: Teachers College Press.

Bredekamp, S., & Copple, C. (1997). *Developmentally appropriate practice in early childhood programs.* Washington, DC: National Association for the Education of Young Children.

Bredekamp, S., & Rosegrant, T. (1992). *Reaching potentials: Appropriate curriculum and assessment for young children,* Vol. 1. Washington, DC: National Association for the Education of Young Children.

Brenneman, K., & Louro, I. F. (2008). Science journals in the preschool classroom. *Early Childhood Education Journal, 36*(2), 113–119.

Breslin, C. M., Morton, J. R., & Rudisill, M. E. (2008). Implementing a physical activity curriculum into the school day: Helping early childhood teachers meet the challenge. *Early Childhood Education Journal, 35,* 429–437.

Briody, J., & McGarry, K. (2005). Using social studies to ease children's transitions. *Young Children, 60*(5), 38–42.

Bronson, M. B. (2000). *Self-regulation in early childhood.* New York: Guildford Press.

Bronson, M. B. (2006). Developing social and emotional competence. In D. F. Gullo, (Ed.), *K today: Teaching and learning in the kindergarten year* (pp. 47–56). Washington, DC: National Association for the Education of Young Children.

Brophy, J.E. (2004). *Motivating students to learn* (2nd ed.). Mahwah, NJ: Erlbaum.

Brown, V. (1990). Drama as an integral part of the early childhood curriculum. *Design for Arts in Education, 91*(6), 26–33.

Burger, L. K., & Miller, P. J. (1999). Early talk about the past revisited: Affect in working-class and middle-class children's co-narrations. *Journal of Child Language, 26*(1), 133–162.

Burgess, S. R., & Lonigan, C. J. (1998). Bidirectional relations of phonological sensitivity and prereading abilities: Evidence from a preschool sample. *Journal of Experimental Child Psychology, 70*(2), 117–141.

Burhans, K. K., & Dweck, C. S. (1995). Helplessness in early childhood: The role of contingent worth. *Child Development, 66*, 1719–1738.

Burton, R. A., & Denham, S. A. (1998). Are you my friend?: How two young children learned to get along with others. *Journal of Research in Childhood Education, 12*, 210–224.

Bus, A. G., & van IJzendoorn, M. H. (1988). Mother-child interactions, attachment, and emergent literacy: A cross-sectional study. *Child Development, 50*, 1262–1273.

Buysse, V. (1993). Friendships of preschoolers with disabilities in community-based child care settings. *Journal of Early Intervention, 17*, 380–395.

Buysse, V., Goldman, B. D., & Skinner, M. L. (2003). Friendship formation in inclusive early childhood classrooms: What is the teacher's role? *Early Childhood Research Quarterly, 18*, 485–501.

Campbell, F. A., Ramey, C. T., Pungello, E., Sparling, J., & Miller-Johnson, S. (2002). Early childhood education: Young adult outcomes from the Abecedarian project. *Applied Developmental Science, 6*, 42–57.

Campbell, N. E., & Foster, J. E. (1993). Play centers that encourage literacy development. *Early Childhood Education Journal, 21*(2), 22–26.

Campbell, S. B. (1995). Behavior problems in preschool children: A review of recent research. *Journal of Child Psychology and Psychiatry and Allied Disciplines, 36*, 113–149.

Campbell, S. B., Pierce, E. W., March, C. L., Ewing, I. J., & Szumowski, E. K. (1994). Hard-to-manage preschool boys: Symptomatic behavior across contexts and time. *Child Development, 65*, 836–851.

Carroll, J. M., Snowling, J. J., Hulme, C., & Stevenson, J. (2003). The development of phonological awareness in preschool children. *Developmental Psychology, 39*(5), 913–923.

Carruthers, P. (1996). *Autism as mind-blindness: An elaboration and partial defense*. Retrieved July 18, 2007, from http://cogprints.org/1193/00/autism.htm

Casby, M. W. (1997). Symbolic play of children with language impairment: A critical review. *Journal of Speech, Language, and Hearing Research, 40*(3), 468–479.

Cats, H. W., Fey, M. E., Zhang, X., & Tomblin, J. B. (2001). Estimating the risk of future reading difficulties in kindergarten children: A research-based model and clinical implications. *Language, Speech and Hearing Services in School, 32*, 38–50.

Chalufour, I., & Worth, K. (2004). *Building structures with young children: The Young Scientist Series*. St. Paul, MN: Redleaf Press.

Chalufour, I., & Worth, K. (2006). Science in Kindergarten. In D. F. Gullo (Ed.), *K today: Teaching and learning in the kindergarten year* (pp. 95–106). Washington, DC: National Association for the Education of Young Children.

Chaney, C. (1992). Language development, metalinguistic skills, and print awareness in 3-year-old children. *Applied Psycholinguistics, 13*, 485–514.

Chapin, J. R. (2006). The achievement gap in social studies and science starts early: Evidence from the Early Childhood Longitudinal Study (Survey). *The Social Studies, 97*(6), 231–238.

Charlesworth, R. (2005a). *Experiences in math for young children* (5th ed.). Clifton Park, NY: Thomson Delmar Learning.

Charlesworth, R. (2005b). Prekindergarten mathematics: Connecting with national standards. *Early Childhood Education Journal, 32,* 229–236.

Charlesworth, R. (2007). *Understanding child development* (7th ed.). New York: Thomson Delmar Learning.

Charlesworth, R., & Lind, K. K. (2009). *Math and science for young children* (6th ed.). Albany, NY: Delmar.

Chen, S. (1996). Are Japanese young children among the gods? In D. W. Shwalb & B. J. Shwalb (Eds.), *Japanese child rearing: Two generations of scholarship* (pp. 31–43). New York: Guilford Press.

Chen, Z., Sanchez, R. P., & Cambell, T. (1997). From beyond to within their grasp: The rudiments of analogical problem solving in 10- and 13-month-olds. *Developmental Psychology, 33,* 790–801.

Christie, J. F. (1983). The effects of play tutoring on young children's cognitive performance. *Journal of Educational Research, 76,* 326–330.

Cillessen, A. H. N., & Bellmore, A. D. (2002). Social skills and interpersonal perception. In P. K. Smith & C. H. Hart (Eds.), *Blackwell handbook of childhood social development* (pp. 355–374). Oxford: Blackwell.

Clay, M. M. (1979a). *The early detection of reading difficulties* (2nd ed.). Auckland, New Zealand: Heinemann.

Clay, M. M. (1979b). *Reading recovery: A guidebook for teachers in training.* Auckland, New Zealand: Heinemann.

Clements, D. H. (1999). Geometry and spatial thinking in young children. In J.V. Copley (Ed.), *Mathematics in the early years* (pp. 66–79). Reston, VA: National Council of Teachers of Mathematics.

Clements, D. H. (2001). Mathematics in the preschool. *Teaching Children Mathematics, 7*(5), 270–275.

Clements, D. H. (2003, September). *Good beginnings in mathematics: Linking a national vision to state action.* New York: Carnegie Corporation.

Clements, D. H. (2004). Geometric and spatial thinking in early childhood education. In D. H. Clements, J. Sarama, & A. Di Biase, (Eds.), *Engaging young children in mathematics* (pp. 267–298). Mahwah, NJ: Lawrence Erlbaum Associates.

Clements, D. H., Battista, M. T., & Sarama, J. (2001). Logo and geometry. *Journal for Research in Mathematics Education, Monograph Series, 10.*

Clements, D. H., Battista, M. T., Sarama, J., & Swaminathan, S. (1997). Development of students' spatial thinking in a unit on geometric motions and area. *Elementary School Journal, 98*(2), 171–186.

Clements, D. H., & Sarama, J. (2000). Young children's ideas about geometric shapes. *Teaching Children Mathematics, 6*(8), 482–488.

Clements, D. H., & Sarama, J. (2003). Young children and technology: What does the research say? *Young Children, 58*(6), 34–40.

Clements, D. H., Sarama, J., & DiBiase, A. (Eds.). (2004). *Engaging young children in mathematics: Standards for early childhood mathematics education.* Mahwah, NJ: Lawrence Erlbaum Associates.

Clements, D. H., & Sarama, J. (2009). *Learning and teaching early math: The learning trajectories approach.* New York: Routledge.

Clements, D. H., Wilson, D. C., & Sarama, J. (2004). Young children's composition of geometric figures: A learning trajectory. *Mathematical thinking and learning, 6*(2), 163–184.

Cohen, L., & Uhry, J. (2007). Young children's discourse strategies during block play: A Bakhtinian approach. *Journal of Research in Childhood Education, 21,* 302–315.

Colbert, C. (1997). Visual arts in the developmentally appropriate integrated curriculum. In C. H. Hart, D. C. Burts, & R. Charlesworth (Eds.), *Integrated curriculum and developmentally appropriate practice: Birth to age eight* (pp. 201–223). Albany, NY: SUNY Press.

Collier, V. (1987). Age and rate of acquisition of second language for academic purposes. *TESOL Quarterly, 21*(4), 617–641.

Collier, V. (1989, September). How long? A synthesis of research on academic achievement in second language. *TESOL Quarterly, 23*(3), 509–531.

Committee for Children. (2002). *Second Step: A violence-prevention curriculum.* Seattle: Author.

Conezio, K., & French, L. (2002). Science in the preschool classroom: Capitalizing on children's fascination with the everyday world to foster language and literacy development. *Young Children, 57*(5), 12–18.

Cook, R. E., Klein, M. D., & Tessier, A. (2004). *Adapting early childhood curricula for children in inclusive settings* (6th ed.). Upper Saddle River, NJ: Pearson Merrill Prentice Hall.

Coplan, R. J., Findlay, L. C., & Nelson, L. J. (2004). Characteristics of preschoolers with lower perceived competence. *Journal of Abnormal Child Psychology, 32*, 399–408.

Coplan, R. J., & Prakash, K. (2003). Spending time with teacher: Characteristics of preschoolers who frequently elicit versus initiate interactions with teachers. *Early Childhood Research Quarterly, 18,* 143–158.

Copley, J. V. (Ed.). (1999). *Mathematics in the early years.* Washington, DC and Reston, VA: National Association for the Education of Young Children and National Council of Teachers of Mathematics.

Copley, J. V. (2000). *The young child and mathematics.* Washington, DC: National Association for the Education of Young Children.

Copley, J. V. (2005). *Measuring with young children.* Paper presented at the International Conference for the Education of the Young Child, Madrid, Spain.

Copley. J. V., & Hawkins, J. (2005). *Interim report of C3 coaching grant: Mathematics professional development.*

Copley, J. V., Jones, C., & Dighe, J. (2007). *Mathematics: The Creative Curriculum® approach.* Washington, DC: Teaching Strategies, Inc.

Copple, C., & Bredekamp, S. (2006). *Basics of developmentally appropriate practice: An introduction for teachers of children 3 to 6.* Washington, DC: National Association for the Education of Young Children.

Copple, C., & Bredekamp, S. (Eds.). (2009). *Developmentally appropriate practice in early childhood programs serving children from birth to age 8* (3rd ed.). Washington, DC: National Association for the Education of Young Children.

Cummins, J. (1984). *Bilingualism and special education: Issues in assessment and pedagogy.* San Diego: College-Hill Press.

Curenton, S. M., & Ryan, S. K. (2006). Oral storytelling: A cultural art that promotes school readiness. *Young Children, 61*(5), 78–89.

Curry, N. E., & Johnson, C. N. (1990). *Beyond self-esteem: Developing a genuine sense of human value.* Washington, DC: National Association for the Education of Young Children.

Curtis, D., & Carter, M. (2003). *Designs for living and learning: Transforming early childhood environments.* St. Paul, MN: Redleaf Press.

Cutler, K. M., Gilderson, D., Parrott, S., & Browne, M. T. (2003). Developing math games based on children's literature. In D. Koralek (Ed.), *Spotlight on young children and math* (pp. 14–18). Washington, DC: National Association for the Education of Young Children.

D'Addesio, J., Grob, B., Furman, L., Hayes, K., & David, J. (2005). Social Studies: Learning about the world around us. *Young Children, 60*(5), 50–57.

Danoff-Burg, J. A. (2002). Be a bee and other approaches to introducing young children to entomology. *Young Children, 57*(5), 42–47.

Day, C. B. (2006). Leveraging diversity to benefit children's social-emotional development and school readiness. In B. Bowman & E. K. Moore (Eds.), *School readiness and social-emotional development: Perspectives on cultural diversity* (pp. 23–32). Washington, DC: National Black Child Development Institute, Inc.

Deak, G. O. (2003). *The development of cognitive flexibility and language abilities.* Retrieved May 25, 2007, from http://cogsci.ucsd.edu/~deak/publications/Deak_Advances03pdf

Deater-Deckard, K., Petrill, S. A., Thompson, L. A., & DeThorne, L. S. (2005). A cross-sectional behavioral genetic analysis of task persistence in the transition to middle childhood. *Developmental Science, 8*(3), F21–F26.

Deci, E. L., Koestner, R., & Ryan, R. M. (2001). Extrinsic rewards and intrinsic motivation in education: Reconsidered once again. *Review of Educational Research, 71*(1), 1–27.

Deli, E., Bakle, I., & Zachopoulou, E. (2006). Implementing intervention movement programs for kindergarten children. *Journal of Early Childhood Research, 4*(1), 5–18.

DeLoache, J. S. (1987). Rapid change in the symbolic functioning of very young children. *Science, 238*(4833), 1556–1557.

DeLoache, J. S. (1991). Symbolic functioning in very young children. Understanding of pictures and models. *Child Development, 62,* 736–752.

DeLoache, J. S. (2000). Dual representation and young children's use of scale models. *Child Development, 71,* 329–338.

DeLoache, J. S. (2004). Becoming symbol-minded. *Trends in Cognitive Sciences, 8*(2), 66–70.

Denac, O. (2008). A case study of preschool children's musical interests at home and at school. *Early Childhood Education Journal, 35*(5), 439–444.

Denham, S. A., Blair, K., Schmidt, M., & DeMulder, E. (2002). Compromised emotional competence: Seeds of violence sown early? *American Journal of Orthopsychiatry. 72*(1), 70–82.

Denham, S. A., & Burton, R. (1996). A social-emotional intervention for at-risk 4-year-olds. *Journal of School Psychology, 34*(3), 225–245.

Denham, S. A., & Burton, R. (2003). *Social and emotional prevention and intervention programming for preschoolers.* New York: Springer.

Denham, S. A., Caverly, S., Schmidt, M., Blair, K., DeMulder, E., Caal, S., et al. (2002). Preschool understanding of emotions: contributions to classroom anger and aggression. *Journal of Child Psychology and Psychiatry, 43*(7), 901–916.

Denham, S. A., & Kochanoff, A. T. (2002). Parental contributions to preschoolers' understanding of emotion. *Marriage and Family Review, 34,* 311–343.

Denham, S. A., McKinley, M., Couchoud, E. A., & Holt, R. (1990). Emotional and behavioral predictors of preschool peer ratings. *Child Development, 61,* 1145–1152.

Denham, S., von Salisch, M., Olthof, T., Kochanoff, A., & Caverly, S. (2002). Emotional and social development in childhood. In P. K. Smith & C. H. Hart (Eds.), *Blackwell handbook of childhood social development* (pp. 307–328). Oxford: Blackwell.

Desouza, J. M. S., & Czerniak, C. M. (2002). Social behaviors and gender differences among preschoolers: Implications for science activities. *Journal of Research in Childhood Education, 16*(2), 175–188.

de Vries, P. A. (2008). Parental perceptions of music in storytelling sessions in a public library. *Early Childhood Education Journal, 35*(5), 473–478.

DeVries, R., Haney, J., & Zan, B. (1991). Sociomoral atmosphere in direct-instruction, eclectic, and constructivist kindergartens: A study of teachers' enacted interpersonal understanding. *Early Childhood Research Quarterly, 6*(4), 449–471.

Diamond, K. E. (2002). Social competence in children with disabilities. In P. K. Smith & C. H. Hart (Eds.), *Blackwell handbook of childhood social development* (pp. 571–587). Oxford: Blackwell.

Diamond, K. E., & Hestenes, L. L. (1996). Preschool children's conceptions of disabilities: The salience of disabilities in children's ideas about others. *Topics in Early Childhood Special Education, 16*(4), 458–475.

Dickinson, D., & Neuman, S., Eds. (2002). *Handbook of Early Literacy Research.* New York: Guildford Press.

Dickinson, D., & Neuman, S., Eds. (2006). *Handbook of Early Literacy Research,* Volume 2. New York: Guildford Press.

Dickinson, D. K., & Tabors, P. O. (1991). Early literacy: Linkages between home, school, and literacy achievement at age five. *Journal of Research in Childhood Education, 6,* 30–46.

Dickinson, D. K., & Tabors, P. O. (Eds.). (2001). *Building literacy with language: Young children learning at home and school.* Baltimore: Paul H. Brookes.

Dinwiddle, S. A. (1994). The saga of Sally, Sammy, and the red pen: Facilitating children's social problem solving. *Young Children, 49,* 13–19.

Dodd, J. (1992). *Preventing American Indian children from overidentification with learning disabilities: Cultural considerations during the pre-referral process.* Paper presented at the Council for Exceptional Children, Division for Early Childhood, Topical Conference on Culturally and Linguistically Diverse Exceptional Children (Minneapolis, MN, November 12–14, 1992).

Dodge, D. T., Colker, L. J., & Heroman, C. (2002). *The Creative Curriculum° for preschool* (4th ed.). Washington, DC: Teaching Strategies.

Dodge, D. T, Rudick, S., & Berke, K. (2006). *The Creative Curriculum° for infants, toddlers & twos* (2nd ed.). Washington, DC: Teaching Strategies.

Dodge, K. A., Schlundt, D. C., Schocken, I., & Delugach, J. D. (1983). Social competence in children's sociometric status: The role of peer group strategies. *Merrill-Palmer Quarterly, 29,* 309–336.

Downey, G. & Walker, E. (1989). Social cognition and adjustment in children at risk for psychopathology. *Developmental Psychology, 25,* 835–845.

Drew, W. F., & Rankin, B. (2004). Promoting creativity for life using open-ended materials. *Young Children, 59*(4), 38–45.

Duncan, G. J., Dowsett, C. J., Claessens, A., Magnuson, K., Huston, A. C., Klebanov, P., et al. (2007). School readiness and later achievement. *Developmental Psychology, 43*(6), 1428–1446.

Dunn, J., & Brown, J. (1991). Relationships, talk about feelings, and the development of affect regulation in early childhood. In J. Garber & K. A. Dodge (Eds.), *The development of emotional regulation and dysregulation* (pp. 89–108). New York: Cambridge University Press.

Ehri, L. C., Nunes, S. R., Willows, D. M., Schuster, B. V., Yaghoub-Zadeh, Z., & Shanahan, T. (2001). Phonemic awareness instruction helps children learn to read: Evidence from the national reading panel's meta-analysis. *Reading Research Quarterly, 36,* 250–297.

Eisenberg, A. R. (1985). Learning to describe past experiences in conversation. *Discourse Processes, 8,* 177–204.

Eisenberg, A. R. (1999). Emotion talk among Mexican-American and Anglo-American mothers and children from two social classes. *Merrill-Palmer Quarterly, 45*(2), 267–284.

Eisenberg, N., Fabes, R. A., Shepard, S. A., Murphy, B. C., Guthrie, I. K., Jones, S., et. al. (1997). Contemporaneous and longitudinal predictors of child's social function from regulation and emotionality. *Child Development, 68,* 642–664.

Elbro, C. I., Borstrom, D. K. & Peterson, P. (1998). Predicting dyslexia from kindergarten: The importance of directness of phonological representations of lexical items. *Reading Research Quarterly, 3,* 36–60.

Elias, C. L., & Berk, L. E. (2002). Self-regulation in young children: Is there a role for sociodramatic play? *Early Childhood Research Quarterly, 17,* 216–238.

Elliot, A. J., & Dweck, C. S. (Eds.). (2005). *Handbook of competence and motivation.* New York: Guilford Press.

Ellis, R. (2000). *Second language acquisition.* New York: Oxford University Press.

Engel, B. S. (1995). *Considering children's art: Why and how to value their works.* Washington, DC: National Association for the Education of Young Children.

Epstein, A. S. (2007). *The intentional teacher: Choosing the best strategies for young children's learning.* Washington, DC: National Association for the Education of Young Children.

Epstein, A. S. (2009). *Me, you, us: Social-emotional learning in preschool.* Ypsilanti, MI: HighScope Press.

Eshach, H., & Fried, N. N. (2005). Should science be taught in early childhood? *Journal of Science Education and Technology, 14*(3), 315–336.

Erdley, C. A., & Asher, S. R. (1999). A social goals perspective on children's social competence. *Journal of Emotional and Behavioral Disorders, 7,* 156–167.

Espinosa, L. (2005). Curriculum and assessment considerations for young children from culturally, linguistically, and economically diverse backgrounds. *Psychology in the Schools, 42*(8), 837–853.

Fabes, R. A., Eisenberg, N., Karbon, M., Bernzweig, J., Speer, A. L., & Carlo, G. (1994). Socialization of children's vicarious emotional responding and prosocial behavior: Relations with mothers' perceptions of children's emotional reactivity. *Developmental Psychology, 30,* 44–55.

Fantini, A. (1985). *Language acquisition of a bilingual child.* San Diego: College-Hill Press.

Fantuzzo, J., & McWayne, C. (2002). The relationship between peer-play interactions in the family context and dimensions of school readiness for low-income preschool children. *Journal of Educational Psychology, 94*(1), 79–87.

Fantuzzo, J., Perry, M. A., & McDermott, P. (2004). Preschool approaches to learning and their relationship to other relevant classroom competencies for low-income children. *School Psychology Quarterly, 19*(3), 212–230.

Farver, J. A. M. (1992). Communicating shared meaning in social pretend play. *Early Childhood Research Quarterly, 7,* 501–516.

Feeney, S., & Moravcik, E. (2005). Children's literature: A window to understanding self and others. *Young Children 60*(5), 20–28.

Feldman, R. S., McGee, G., Mann, L. & Strain, P. S. (1993). Nonverbal affective decoding ability in children with autism and in typical preschoolers. *Journal of Early Intervention, 17*(4), 341–350.

Fenson, L., Dale, P. S., Reznick, J. S., Bates, E., Thal, D. J., & Pethick, S. J. (1994). Variability in early communicative development. *Monographs of the Society for Research in Child Development, 59* (5, Serial No. 242).

Ferreiro, E., & Teberosky, A. (1982). Children's metalinguistic knowledge of syntactical constituents: Effects of age and schooling. *Developmental Psychology, 30,* 663–674.

Fisher, E. P. (1992). The impact of play on development: A meta-analysis. *Play and Culture, 5*(2), 159–181.

Fletcher, K. L., & Sabo, J. (2006). Picture book reading experience and toddler's behaviors with photographs and books. *Early Childhood Research and Practice, 8*(1). Retrieved June 20, 2007, from http://ecrp.uiuc.edu/v8n1/fletcher.html

Flynn, L. L., & Kieff, J. (2002). Including everyone in outdoor play. *Young Children, 57*(3), 20–26.

Friedman, S. (2005). Social studies in action. *Young Children, 60*(5), 44–47.

Friel, S. N., Curcio, F. R., & Bright, G. W. (2001). Making sense of graphs: Critical factors influencing comprehension and instructional implications. *Journal for Research in Mathematics Education, 32,* 124–158.

Gabbard, C. (1998). Windows of opportunity for early brain and motor development. *Journal of Physical Education, Recreation & Dance, 69*(8), 54–56.

Gallahue, D. A. (1995). Transforming physical education curriculum. In S. Bredekamp & T. Rosegrant (Eds.), *Reaching potentials: Transforming early childhood curriculum and assessment,* Vol. 2 (pp. 125–144). Washington, DC: National Association for the Education of Young Children.

Gallahue, D.A. (2008). Developmental physical education for all. Champaign, IL: Human Kinetics Publishers.

Gargiulo, R., & Kilgo, J. (2007). *Young children with special needs* (2nd ed). Albany, NY: Thomson Delmar Learning.

Gartrell, D., & Gartrell, J. J. (2008). Guidance matters: Understand bullying. *Young Children, 63*(3), 54–57.

Geist, E. (2001). Children are born mathematicians: Promoting the construction of early mathematical concepts in children under five. *Young Children, 56*(4), 12–19.

Geist, E. (2003). Infants and toddler exploring mathematics. In D. Koralek (Ed.), *Spotlight on young children and math* (pp. 4–6). Washington, DC: National Association for the Education of Young Children.

Geist, E. (2009). *Children are born mathematicians: Supporting mathematical development, birth to age 8.* Upper Saddle River, NJ: Pearson.

Gelman, R., & Brenneman, K. (2004). Science learning pathways for young children. *Early Childhood Research Quarterly, 19*(1), 150–158.

Gelman, R., & Gallistel, C.R. (1978). *The Child's Understanding of Number.* Cambridge, MA: Harvard University Press.

Gelman, S. A. (1998). Categories in young children's thinking. *Young Children, 53*(1), 20–26.

Gelman, S. A., Chesnick, R., & Waxman, S. (2005). Mother-child conversations about pictures and objects: Referring to categories and individuals. *Child Development, 76*, 1129–1143.

Gelman, S. A., & Coley, J. D. (1990). The importance of knowing a dodo is a bird: Categories and inferences in 2-year-old children. *Developmental Psychology, 26*, 796–804.

Gelman, S. A., Coley, J. D., Rosengren, K. S., Hartman, E., & Pappas, A. (1998). Beyond labeling: The role of maternal input in the acquisition of richly structured categories. *Monographs of the Society for Research in Child Development, 63* (1, Serial No. 253).

Genishi, C., & Brainard, M. (1995). Assessment of bilingual children: A dilemma seeking solutions. In E. E. García & B. McLaughlin (Eds.), *Meeting the challenge of linguistic and cultural diversity in early childhood education* (pp. 49–63). New York: Teachers College Press.

George, J., & Greenfield, D. B. (2005). Examination of a structured problem-solving flexibility task for assessing approaches to learning on young children: Relation to teacher ratings and children's achievement. *Applied Developmental Psychology, 26*(1), 69–84.

Ginsburg, H. P., & Baroody, A. J. (2003). *Test of early mathematics ability: Examiner's manual* (3rd ed.). Austin, TX: Pro-Ed.

Ginsburg, H. P. & Golbeck, S. L. (2004). Thoughts on the future of research on mathematics and science learning and education. *Early Childhood Research Quarterly 19*, 190–200.

Ginsburg, H. P., Inoue, N., & Seo, K. (1999). Young children doing mathematics. In J. V. Copley (Ed.), *Mathematics in the early years* (pp. 88–91). Washington, DC and Reston, VA: National Association for the Education of Young Children and National Council of Teachers of Mathematics.

Gober, S. Y. (2002). *Six simple ways to assess young children*. Albany, NY: Delmar Thomson Learning.

Golbeck, S. L. (2005). Research in review: Building foundations for spatial literacy in early childhood. *Young Children, 60*(6), 72–83.

Goldstein, P. (2004). Helping young children with special needs develop vocabulary. *Early Childhood Education Journal, 32*, 1–43.

Gonzalez, V. (1998). *Language and cognitive development in second language learners*. Boston: Allyn & Bacon.

Gonzalez, V., Bauerle, P., & Felix-Holt, M. (1996). Theoretical and practical implications of assessing cognitive and language development in bilingual children with qualitative methods. *Bilingual Research Journal, 20*(1), 93–131.

Gonzalez-Mena, J. (2002). *The child in the family and the community* (3rd ed.). Upper Saddle River, NJ: Merrill Prentice Hall.

Gopnik, A., & Choi, S. (1995). *Beyond names for things: Children's acquisition of verbs*. Hillsdale, NJ: Erlbaum.

Gordon, A. M., & Williams-Brown, K. (1996). *Beginnings and beyond* (4th ed.). Albany, NY: Delmar.

Gould, P., & Sullivan, J. (1999). *The inclusive early childhood classroom: Easy ways to adapt learning centers for all children*. Beltsville, MD: Gryphon House.

Gowen, J. W. (1995). Research in review: The early development of symbolic play. *Young Children, 50*(3), 75–84.

Gullo, D. F. (Ed.). (2006). *K today: Teaching and learning in the kindergarten year*. Washington, DC: National Association for the Education of Young Children.

Gundlach, R., McLane, J., Stott, F. M., & McNamee, G. D. (1985). The social foundations of early writing development. In M. Farr (Ed.), *Advances in writing research: Vol. 1: Studies in children's early writing development*. Norwood, NJ: Ablex.

Hair, E., Halle, T., Terry-Humen, E., Lavelle, B., & Calkins, J. (2006). Children's school readiness in the ECLS-K: Predictions to academic, health, and social outcomes in first grade. *Early Childhood Research Quarterly, 21*(4), 431–454.

Hakuta, K. (1978). A report on the development of grammatical morphemes in a Japanese girl learning English as a second language. In E. M. Hatch (Ed.), *Second language acquisition: A book of readings* (pp. 132–147). Rowley, MA: Newbury House Publishers.

Hakuta, K. (1986). *Mirror of language: The debate on bilingualism.* New York: Basic Books.

Halliday, M. A. K. (2002). Relevant models of language. In B. M. Power & R. S. Hubbard (Eds.), *Language development: A reader for teachers* (2nd ed., pp. 49–53). Upper Saddle River, NJ: Merrill.

Hamre, B. K., & Pianta, R. C. (2001). Early teacher-child relationships and the trajectory of children's school outcomes through eighth grade. *Child Development, 72,* 625–638.

Hannust, T., & Kikas, E. (2007). Children's knowledge of astronomy and its change in the course of learning. *Early Childhood Research Quarterly, 22*(1), 89–104.

Harper, L. V., & McCluskey, K. S. (2002). Caregiver and peer responses to children with language and motor disabilities in inclusive preschool programs. *Early Childhood Research Quarterly, 17,* 148–166.

Hart, B., & Risley, T. R. (1995). *Meaningful differences in the everyday experience of young American children.* Baltimore: Paul H. Brookes.

Hart, B., & Risley, T. R., (2003). The early catastrophe. *Education Review, 17*(1), 110–118.

Hart, C. H., McGee, L. M., & Hernandez, S. (1993). Themes in the peer relations literature: Correspondence to outdoor peer interactions portrayed in children's storybooks. In C. H. Hart (Ed.), *Children on playgrounds: Research perspectives and applications* (pp. 371–416). Albany, NY: SUNY Press.

Harter, S. (1998). The development of self-representations. In W. Damon & N. Eisenberg (Eds.), *Handbook of child psychology,* Vol. 3: *Social, emotional, and personality development* (pp. 553–617). New York: John Wiley & Sons.

Harter, S. (1999). *The construction of the self: A developmental perspective.* New York: Guilford Press.

Hartup, W. W., & Abecassis, M. (2002). Friends and enemies. In P. K. Smith & C. H. Hart (Eds.), *Blackwell handbook of childhood social development* (pp. 285–306). Oxford: Blackwell.

Harwood, R. L., Miller, J. G., & Irizarry, N. L. (1995). *Culture and attachment: Perceptions of the child in context.* New York: Guilford.

Haugland, S. W. (2000). What role should technology play in young children's learning? Part 2: Early childhood classrooms in the 21st century: Using computers to maximize learning. *Young Children, 55*(1), 12–18.

Head Start Bureau. (2002). *Identifying strategies to support English language learners in Head Start and Early Head Start programs.* (English Language Learners Focus Group Report.) Washington, DC: Author.

Heath, S. M., & Hogben, J. H. (2004). Cost-effective prediction of reading difficulties. *Journal of Speech, Language, and Hearing Research, 47*(4), 751–765.

Heise-Baigorria, C. & Tabors, P. O. (2004). *Bilingual early language and literacy assessment (BELA).* Cambridge, MA: Cambridge 0–8 Council/Cambridge Public Schools. Retrieved July 2, 2007, from http://www.cpsd.us/bela

Heisner, J. (2005). Telling stories with blocks: Encouraging language in the block center. *Early Childhood Research and Practice, 7*(2). Retrieved September 23, 2008, from http://ecrp.uiuc.edu/v7n2/heisner.html

Henniger, M. L. (1991). Play revisited: A critical element of the kindergarten curriculum. *Early Child Development and Care, 70,* 63–71.

Henrich, C. C., Wheeler, C. M., & Zigler, E. F. (2005). Motivation as a facet of school readiness in a Head Start sample. *NHSA Dialog, 8*(1), 72–87. Retrieved July 17, 2007, from https://webftp.gsu.edu/~wwwcch/Henrich,Wheeler,&Zigler(2005).pdf

Hensen, R. (2005). Real super-hero play. *Young Children, 60*(5), 37.

Herbert, J., Gross, J., & Hayne, H. (2007). Crawling is associated with more flexible memory retrieval by 9-month old infants. *Developmental Science, 10*(2), 183–189.

Heroman, C., & Jones, C. (2004). *Literacy: The Creative Curriculum® Approach.* Washington, DC: Teaching Strategies, Inc.

Hesse, P., & Lane, F. (2003). Media literacy starts young: An integrated curriculum approach. *Young Children, 58*(6), 20–26.

Hildreth, G. (1936). Developmental sequences in name writing. *Child Development, 7,* 291–302.

Hirschler, J. A. (1994, Winter). Preschool children's help to second language learners. *Journal of Educational Issues of Language Minority Students, 14,* 227–240.

Hirsch-Pasek, K., Golinkoff, R. M., & Naigles, L. (1996). *The origins of grammar: Evidence from early language comprehension.* Cambridge, MA: MIT Press.

Hoisington, C. (2002). Using photographs to support children's science inquiry. *Young Children, 57*(5), 26–32.

Holowka, S., & Petitto, L.A. (2002, August). Left hemisphere cerebral specialization for babies while babbling. *Science, 297,* 1515.

Honig, A. S. (2005). The language of lullabies. *Young Children, 60*(5), 36, 30–36.

Hooper, S. R., Roberts, J. E., Zeisel, S.A., & Poe, M. (2003). Core language predictors of behavioral functioning in early elementary school children: Concurrent and longitudinal findings. *Behavioral Disorders, 29,* 10–24.

Howes, C. (2000). Social-emotional classroom climate in child care: Child-teacher relationships and children's second grade peer relations. *Social Development, 9*(2), 191–204.

Howes, C., Burchinal, M., Pianta, R., Bryant, D., Early, D., Clifford, R., et al. (2008). Ready to learn? Children's pre-academic achievements in pre-kindergarten programs. *Early Childhood Research Quarterly, 23,* 27–50.

Howes, C., Hamilton, C. E., & Matheson, C. C., (1994). Children's relationships with peers: Differential associations with aspects of the teacher-child relationship. *Child Development, 65,* 253–263.

Howes, C., & James, J. (2002). Children's social development within the socialization context of childcare and early childhood education. . In P. K. Smith & C. H. Hart (Eds.), *Blackwell handbook of childhood social development* (pp. 137–155). Oxford: Blackwell.

Howes, C. & Matheson, C. C. (1992). Sequences in the development of competent play with peers: Social and social pretend play. *Developmental Psychology, 94*(1), 79–87.

Howes, C., & Ritchie, S. (1998). Changes in teacher-child relationships in a therapeutic preschool. *Early Education and Development, 4,* 411–422.

Howse, R. B., Lange, G., Farran, D. C., & Boyles, C. D. (2003). Motivation and self-regulation as predictors of achievement in economically disadvantaged young children. *The Journal of Experimental Education, 71*(2), 151–174.

Huang, J., & Hatch, E. M. (1978). A Chinese child's acquisition of English. In E. M. Hatch (Ed.), *Second language acquisition: A book of readings* (pp. 118–131). Rowley, MA: Newbury House Publishers.

Hubbard, J. A., & Coie, J. D. (1994). Emotional correlates of social competence in children's peer relationships. *Merrill-Palmer Quarterly, 20,* 1–20.

Humphryes, J. (2000). Exploring nature with children. *Young Children, 55*(2), 16–20.

Hurley, D. S. (2000). *Developing fine and gross motor skills: Birth to three.* Austin, TX: PRO-ED.

Hyson, M. (2005). Professional Development. Enthusiastic and engaged: Strengthening young children's positive approaches to learning. *Young Children, 60*(6), 68–70.

Hyson, M. (2008). *Enthusiastic and engaged learners: Approaches to learning in the early childhood classroom.* New York: Teachers College Press.

Hyson, M. C. (2004). *The emotional development of young children: Building an emotion-centered curriculum* (2nd ed.). New York: Teachers College Press.

Hyson, M., Buch, L., Fantuzzo, J., & Scott-Little, C. (2006). *Enthusiastic and engaged: Why are positive approaches to learning so important, and how can we support their development in young children?* Paper presented at the Annual Conference of the National Association for the Education of Young Children, Atlanta, GA.

Itoh, H., & Hatch, E. M. (1978). Second language acquisition: A case study. In E. M. Hatch (Ed.), *Second language acquisition: A book of readings* (pp. 76–88). Rowley, MA: Newbury House Publishers.

Izard, C. E., Fine, S. E., Schultz, D., Mostow, A. J., Acerman, B. P., & Younstrom, E. (2001). Emotion knowledge as a predictor of social behavior and academic competence in children at risk. *Psychological Science, 12,* 18–23.

Jablon, J. R., Dombro, A. L., & Dichtelmiller, M. L. (2007). *The power of observation.* (2nd ed.). Washington, DC: Teaching Strategies, Inc. and National Association for the Education of Young Children.

Jablon, J. R., & Wilkinson, M. (2006). Using engagement strategies to facilitate children's learning and success. *Young Children, 61*(2), 12–16.

Jalongo, M. R. (2008). *Learning to listen, listening to learn: Building essential skills in young children.* Washington, DC: National Association for the Education of Young Children.

Jalongo, M. R., & Isenberg, J. P. (2006). Creative expression and thought in kindergarten. In D. F. Gullo (Ed.), *K today: Teaching and learning in the kindergarten year* (pp. 116–126). Washington, DC: National Association for the Education of Young Children.

Jambunathan, S., Burts, D. C., & Pierce, S. H. (1999). Developmentally appropriate practice as predictors of self-competence among preschoolers. *Journal of Research in Childhood Education, 13,* 167–174.

Jipson, J. L., & Gelman, S. A. (2007). Robots and rodents: Children's inferences about living and nonliving kinds. *Child Development, 78*(6), 1675–1688.

Johnson, M. H. (2008). Developing verbal and visual literacy through experiences in the visual arts. *Young Children, 63*(1), 74–79.

Jones, N. P. (2005). Big jobs: Planning for competence. *Young Children, 60*(2), 86–93.

Jordan, N. C., Kaplan, D., Olah, L. N., & Locuniak, M. N. (2006). Number sense growth in kindergarten: A longitudinal investigation of children at risk for mathematics difficulties. *Child Development, 77,* 153–175.

Jung, M., Kloosterman, P., & McMullen, M.B. (2007). Research in review. Young children's intuition for solving problems in mathematics. *Young Children, 62*(5), 50–57.

Kagan, S. L., Britto, P. R., Kauerz, K., & Tarrant, K. (2005). *Washington state early learning and development benchmarks: A guide to young children's learning and development: From birth to kindergarten entry.* Retrieved March 23, 2009, from http://www.k12.WA.US/ Earlylearning/pubdocs/earlylearningbenchmarks.pdf

Kaiser, B., & Rasminsky, S. (2003). *Challenging behavior in young children: Understanding, preventing, and responding effectively.* Boston: Allyn & Bacon.

Kalmar, K. (2008). Let's give children something to talk about! Oral language and preschool literacy. *Young Children, 63*(1), 88–92.

Kantor, R., Elgas, P. M., & Fernie D. (1993). Cultural knowledge and social competence within a preschool peer-culture group. *Early Childhood Research Quarterly, 8,* 125–148.

Katz, L. F., Kramer, L., & Gottman, J. M. (1992). Conflict and emotions in marital, sibling, and peer relationships. In C. U. Shantz & W. W. Hartup (Eds.), *Conflict in child and adolescent development* (pp. 122–149). New York: Cambridge University Press.

Katz, L. G. (1999). *Another look at what young children should be learning.* Retrieved June 16, 2007, from http://ecap.crc.uiuc.edu/eecearchive/digests/1999/ katzle99.pdf

Katz, L. G., & Chard, S. C. (1995). *Engaging children's minds: The project approach.* Norwood, NJ: Ablex.

Kelley, S. A., Brownell, C. A., & Campbell, S. B. (2000). Mastery motivation and self-evaluative affect in toddlers: Longitudinal relations with maternal behavior. *Child Development, 71,* 1061–1071.

Kemple, K. M., Batey, J. J., & Hartle, L. C. (2004). Music play: Creating centers for musical play and exploration. *Young Children, 59*(4), 30–37.

Kemple, K. M., & Nissenberg, S. A. (2000). Nurturing creativity in early childhood education: Families are part of it. *Early Childhood Education Journal, 28*(1), 67–71.

Kenney, S. H. (1997). Music in the developmentally appropriate integrated curriculum. In C. H. Hart, D. C. Burts, & R. Charlesworth (Eds.), *Integrated curriculum and developmentally appropriate practice: Birth to age eight* (pp. 103–144). Albany, NY: SUNY Press.

Kerem, E. A., Kamaraj, I., & Yelland, N. (2001). An analysis of Turkish pre-school teachers' ideas about the concept of creativity and the activities that can foster creativity in young children. *Contemporary Issues in Early Childhood, 2*(2), 248–252.

Kilmer, S. J., & Hofman, H. (1995). Transforming science curriculum. In S. Bredekamp & T. Rosegrant (Eds.), *Reaching potentials: Transforming early childhood curriculum and assessment,* Vol. 2 (pp. 43–64). Washington, DC: National Association for the Education of Young Children.

Kilpatrick, J., Swafford, J., & Findell, B. (2001). *Adding it up: Helping children learn mathematics.* Washington, DC: National Academy Press.

Kim, H., Park, E., & Lee, J. (2001). "All done! Take it home." Then into a trashcan?: Displaying and using children's art projects. *Early Childhood Education Journal, 29*(1), 41–50.

Kim, S. D. G. (2005). Kevin: "I gotta get to the market": The development of peer relationships in inclusive early childhood settings. *Early Childhood Education Journal, 33*(3), 163–169.

Kimple, K. M. (1991). Research in Review: Preschool children's peer acceptance and social interaction. *Young Children, 46*(5), 47–54.

Klein, A., & Starkey, P. (2004). Fostering preschool children's mathematical knowledge: Findings from the Berkeley math readiness project. In D. H. Clements, J. Sarama, & A. M. DiBiase (Eds.), *Engaging young children in mathematics: Standards for early childhood mathematics education* (pp. 343–360). Mahwah, NJ: Lawrence Erlbaum Associates.

Klein, M. D., & Chen, D. (2001). *Working with children from diverse backgrounds.* Albany, NY: Delmar.

Klein, T. P., Wirth, D., & Linas, K. (2004). Play: Children's context for development. In D. Koralek (Ed.), *Spotlight on young children and play* (pp. 28–34). Washington, DC: National Association for the Education of Young Children.

Kohn, A. (1993). Choices for children: Why and how to let students decide. *Phi Delta Kappan, 75*, 8–20.

Kopp, C. B. (1982). Antecedent of self-regulation: A developmental perspective. *Developmental Psychology, 18*, 199–214.

Koralek, D. (Ed.). (2003). *Spotlight on young children and math.* Washington, DC: National Association for the Education of Young Children.

Koralek, D. (Ed.). (2004). *Spotlight on young children and play.* Washington, DC: National Association for the Education of Young Children.

Krafft, K. C., & Berk, L. E. (1998). Private speech in two preschools: Significance of open-ended activities and make-believe play for verbal self-regulation. *Early Childhood Research Quarterly, 13*, 637–658.

Kreidler, W. J., & Whittall, S. T. (2003). Resolving conflict. In C. Copple (Ed.), *A world of difference: Readings on teaching young children in a diverse society* (pp. 52–56). Washington, DC: National Association for the Education of Young Children.

Ladd, G. W. (1990). Having friends, keeping friends, making friends, and being liked by peers in the classroom: Predictors of children's early school adjustment? *Child Development, 61*, 1081–1100.

Ladd, G. W. (1999). Peer relationships and social competence during early and middle childhood. *Annual Review of Psychology 50*, 333–359.

Ladd, G. W., Birch, S. H., & Buhs, E .S. (1999). Children's social and scholastic lives in kindergarten: Related spheres of influence? *Child Development, 70*, 1373–1400.

Ladd, G. W., Buhs, E. S., & Seid, M. (2000). Children's initial sentiments about kindergarten: Is school liking an antecedent of early classroom participation and achievement? *Merrill-Palmer Quarterly, 46*, 255–279.

Lamb, M. E., Bornstein, M. H., & Teti, D.M. (2002). *Development in infancy: An introduction.* Mahwah, NJ: Lawrence Erlbaum Associates.

Lanvers, U. (1999). Lexical growth patterns in a bilingual infant: The occurrence of significance of equivalents in the bilingual lexicon. *International Journal of Bilingual Education and Bilingualism, 2.* 30–32.

Larkina, M., Guler, O. E., Kleinknect, E., & Bauer, P. J. (2008). Maternal provision of structure in a deliberate memory task in relation to their preschool children's recall. *Journal of Experimental Child Psychology, 100,* 235–251.

Lenhoff, R., & Huber, L. (2000). Young children make maps. *Young Children, 55*(3), 6–11.

Levin, D. E. (2003). Teaching young children in violent times: Building a peaceable classroom (2nd ed.). Washington, DC: National Association for the Education of Young Children.

Levy, A. K., Wolfgang, C. H., & Koorland, M. A. (1992). Sociodramatic play as a method for enhancing the language performance of kindergarten age students. *Early Childhood Research Quarterly, 7,* 245–262.

Lewis, M., & Michalson, L. (1993). Children's emotions and moods: developmental theory and measurement. New York: Plenum Press.

Lewis, V. (2003). *Development and disability.* (2nd ed.). Malden, MA: Blackwell.

Lin, P., Schwanenflugel, P. J., & Wisenbaker, J. M. (1990). Category typicality, cultural familiarity, and the development of category knowledge. *Developmental Psychology, 26,* 805–813.

Lind, K. K. (1997). Science in the developmentally appropriate integrated curriculum. In C. H. Hart, D. C. Burts, & R. Charlesworth (Eds.), *Integrated curriculum and developmentally appropriate practice: Birth to age eight* (pp. 75–101). Albany, NY: SUNY Press.

Lind, K. K. (2001). *Science in early childhood: Developing and acquiring fundamental concepts and skills.* Presentation handout retrieved October 21, 2008 from www.hsnrc.org/CDI/pdfs/klind1.pdf

Lomax, R. G., & McGee, L. M. (1987). Young children's concepts of print and reading: Toward a model of word reading acquisition. *Reading Research Quarterly, 22,* 237–256.

Lonigan, C. J., Burgess, S. R., & Anthony, J. L. (2000). Development of emergent literacy and early reading skills in preschool children: Evidence from a latent-variable longitudinal study. *Developmental Psychology, 36,* 596–613.

Lonigan, C. J., Burgess, S. R., Anthony, J. L., & Barker, T. A. (1998). Development of phonological sensitivity in 2- to 5-year-old children. *Journal of Educational Psychology, 90*(2), 294–311.

Lorenzo-Lasa, R., Ideishi, R. I., & Ideishi, S. K. (2007). Facilitating preschool learning and movement through dance. *Early Childhood Education Journal, 35*(1), 25–31.

Lu, M. (2000). *Language development in the early years.* Bloomington, IN: ERIC Clearinghouse on Reading, English, and Communication.

Lutz, T. & Kuhlman, W. D. (2000). Learning about culture through dance in kindergarten classrooms. *Early Childhood Education Journal, 28*(1), 35–40.

Macrina, M., Hoover, D., & Becker, C. (1999). The challenge of working with dual language learners: Three perspectives: Supervisor, mentor, and teacher. *Young Children 64*(2), 27–34.

Mallory, B. L., & New, R. S. (Eds.). (1994). *Diversity and developmentally appropriate practices: Challenges for early childhood education.* New York: Teachers College Press.

Manross, M. A. (2000). Learning to throw in physical education class: Part 3. *Teaching Elementary Physical Education, 11*(3), 26–29.

Mantzicopoulos, P., Patrick, H., & Samarapungavan, A. (2008). Young children's motivational beliefs about learning science. *Early Childhood Research Quarterly, 23*(3), 378–394.

Marcus, G. F. (1995). Children's overregularization of English plurals: A quantitative analysis. *Journal of Child Language, 22,* 447–460.

Marcus, G. F., Pinker, S., Ullman, M., Hollander, M., Rosen, T. J., & Xu, F. (1992). Overregularization in language acquisition. *Monographs of the Society for Research in Child Development, 57* (Serial No. 228).

Mason, J. (1980). When do children begin to read? An exploration of four-year-old children's letter and word reading competencies. *Reading Research Quarterly, 15,* 203–227.

Matlock, R., & Hornstein, J. (2004). Sometimes a smudge is just a smudge, and sometimes it's a saber-toothed tiger: Learning and the arts through the ages. *Young Children, 59*(4), 12–17.

McAfee, O., & Leong, D.J. (1994). *Assessing and guiding young children's development and learning*. Boston: Allyn & Bacon.

McAfee, O., & Leong, D.J. (2007). *Assessing and guiding young children's development and learning* (4th ed). Boston: Allyn & Bacon.

McAfee, O., Leong, D. J., & Bodrova, E. (2004). *Basics of assessment: A primer for early childhood educators*. Washington, DC: National Association for the Education of Young Children.

McCabe, A. (1997). Developmental and cross-cultural aspects of children's narration. In M. Bamberg (Ed.), *Narrative development: Six approaches* (pp. 137–174). Mahwah, NJ: Erlbaum.

McClelland, M. M., Morrison, F. J., & Holmes, D. L. (2000). Children at risk for early academic problems: The role of learning-related social skills. *Early Childhood Research Quarterly, 15*(3), 307–329.

McCormick, C. E., & Mason, J. M. (1986). Intervention procedures for increasing preschool children's interest in and knowledge about reading. In W. H. Teale & E. Sulzby (Eds.), *Emergent literacy: Writing and reading* (pp. 90–115). Norwood, NJ: Ablex.

McGee, L., Lomax, R., & Head, M. (1988). Young children's written language knowledge: What environmental and functional print reading reveals. *Journal of Reading Behavior, 20*, 99–118.

McGee, L., & Richgels, D. J. (1996). *Literacy's beginnings: Supporting young readers and writers*. Boston: Allyn & Bacon.

McGee, L., & Richgels, D. J. (2003). *Designing early literacy programs: Strategies for at-risk preschool and kindergarten children*. New York: Guilford Press.

McHenry, J. D., & Buerk, K. J. (2008). Infants and toddlers meet the natural world. *Young Children, 63*(1), 40–41.

McKay, P. (2006). *Assessing young language learners*. New York: Cambridge University Press.

McKenzie, T. L., Sallis, J. F., Elder, J. P., Berry, C. C., Hoy, P. L., Nader, P. R., et al. (1997). Physical activity levels and prompts in young children at recess: A two-year study of a bi-ethnic sample. *Research Quarterly for Exercise and Sport, 68*(3), 195–202.

McLaughlin, B., Blanchard, A., & Osanai, Y. (1995, June). *Assessing language development in bilingual preschool children* [National Clearinghouse for Bilingual Education Rep. No. 22]. Washington, DC: George Washington University. Retrieved August 16, 2007, from http://www.ncela.gwu.edu/pubs/pigs/pig22.htm

McWayne, C. M., Fantuzzo, J. W., & McDermott, P. A. (2004). Preschool competency in context: An investigation of the unique contribution of child competencies to early academic success. *Developmental Psychology, 40*(4), 633-645. doi:10.1037/0012-1649.40.4.633

McWilliams, R. A., Scarborough, A. A., & Kim, H. (2003). Adult interactions and child engagement. *Early Education and Development, 14*(1), 7–28.

Meisel, J. (1989). Early differentiation of languages in bilingual children. In K. Hylterstam & L. Obler (Eds.), *Bilingualism across the lifespan: Aspects of acquisition, maturity, and loss* (pp. 13–54). Cambridge, England: Cambridge University Press.

Meisels, S. (1994). Designing meaningful measurements for early childhood. In B. L. Mallory & R. S. New (Eds.), *Diversity and developmentally appropriate practices: Challenges for early childhood education* (pp. 202–222). New York: Teachers College Press.

Menn, L., & Stoel-Gammon, C. (2001). Phonological development: Learning sounds and sound patterns. In J. B. Gleason (Ed.), *The development of language* (pp. 39–100). Boston: Allyn & Bacon.

Metsala, J. L., & Walley, A. C. (1998). Spoken vocabulary growth and the segmental restructuring of lexical representations: Precursors to phonemic awareness and early reading ability. In J. L. Metsala & L. C. Ehri (Eds.), *Recognition in beginning literacy* (pp. 89–120). Mahwah, NJ: Lawrence Erlbaum Associates.

Meyer, C. (1989). *The role of peer relationships in the socialization of children to preschool: A Korean example*. Unpublished doctoral dissertation, Ohio State University, Columbus.

Miller, P. J., Fung, H., & Mintz, J. (1996). Self-construction through narrative practices: A Chinese and American comparison of early socialization. *Ethos, 24*(2), 237–280.

Miller, S. E. (1999). Balloons, blankets, and balls: Gross-motor activities to use indoors. *Young Children, 54*(5), 58–63.

Mindes, G. (2005a). Resources for teaching and learning about social studies. *Young Children 60*(5), 58–60.

Mindes, G. (2005b). Social studies in today's early childhood curricula. *Young Children, 60*(5), 12–18.

Mindes, G. (2006). Social studies in kindergarten. In D. F. Gullo (Ed.), *K today: Teaching and learning in the kindergarten year* (pp. 107–115). Washington, DC: National Association for the Education of Young Children.

Mitchell, L. C. (2004). Making the most of creativity in activities for young children with disabilities. *Young Children 59*(4), 46–49.

Mix, K. S., Huttenlocher, J., & Levine, S. C. (2002). *Quantitative development in infancy and early childhood.* New York, NY: Oxford University Press.

Miyakawa, Y., Kamii, C., & Nagahiro, M. (2005). The development of logico-mathematical thinking at ages 1–3 in play with blocks and an incline. *Journal of Research in Childhood Education, 19*, 292–301.

Monhardt, L., & Monhardt, R. (2006). Creating a context for the learning of science process skills through picture books. *Early Childhood Education Journal, 34*(1), 67–71.

Mooney, C. (2005). *Use your words: How teacher talk helps children learn.* St. Paul, MN: Redleaf Press.

Moore, S. G. (1985). Social effects of peers on curiosity. *Early Report, 12*(3), 1–2.

Morrow, L. (2005). *Literacy development in the early years: Helping children read and write* (5th ed.). Boston: Allyn & Bacon.

Morrow, L. M. (1985). Retelling stories: A strategy for improving children's comprehension, concept of story structure, and oral language complexity. *The Elementary School Journal, 85*, 647–661.

Morrow, L. M. (1990). Preparing the classroom environment to promote literacy during play. *Early Childhood Research Quarterly, 5*, 537–554.

Mostow, A. J., Izard, C. E., Fine, S., & Trentacosta, C. J. (2002). Modeling emotional, cognitive, and behavioral predictors of peer acceptance. *Child Development, 73*(6), 1775–1788.

Murphey, D. A., & Burns, C. E. (2002). Development of a comprehensive community assessment of school readiness. *Early Childhood Research and Practice, 2.* Retrieved June 16, 2007, from http://ecrp.uiuc.edu/v4n2/murphey.html

Murphy, K. L., DePasquale, R., & McNamara, E. (2003). Meaningful connections: Using technology in primary classrooms. *Young Children, 58*(6), 12–18.

Mussen, P. H., Conger, J. J., Kagan, J., & Huston, A. C. (1990). *Child development and personality* (7th ed.). New York: Harper and Row.

National Association for the Education of Young Children. (1996). NAEYC position statement: Responding to linguistic and cultural diversity—Recommendations for effective early childhood education. *Young Children, 52*(2), 4–12.

National Association for the Education of Young Children. (2005a). *Screening and assessment of young English-language learners: Supplement to the NAEYC position statement on early childhood curriculum, assessment, and program evaluation.* Washington, DC: Author.

National Association for the Education of Young Children. (2005b). *Where we stand on the screening and assessment of young English-language learners.* Washington, DC: Author.

National Center for Education Statistics (NCES). (1993). *Public school kindergarten teachers' views on children's readiness for school.* Washington, DC: Author. Retrieved July 6, 2007, from http://nces.ed.gov/surveys/frss/publications/93410/index.asp?sectionID=3

National Center for Education Statistics (NCES). (2000). *Special analysis 2000. Entering kindergarten: A portrait of American children when they begin school.* Retrieved September 12, 2007, from http://nces.ed.gov/programs/coe/2000/essay/e03g.asp

National Center for Education Statistics (NCES). (2002). *Children's reading and mathematics achievement in kindergarten and first grade.* Washington, DC: Author. Retrieved July 6, 2007, from http://nces.ed.gov/pubs2002/kindergarten/24.asp?nav=4

National Committee on Science Education Standards and Assessment, National Research Council (1996). *National Science Education Standards.* Retrieved October 20, 2008, from http://books.nap.edu/openbook. php?record_id=4962&page=105

National Council of Teachers of Mathematics (NCTM). (2000). *Principles and standards for school mathematics.* Reston, VA: Author.

National Council of Teachers of Mathematics (NCTM). (2006). *Curriculum focal points for prekindergarten through grade 8 mathematics: A quest for coherence.* Reston, VA: Author.

National Early Literacy Panel. (2004). *A synthesis of research on language and literacy.* Retrieved June 2004, from http://www.famlit.org/ProgramsandInitiatives/ FamilyPartnershipinReading/index.cfm

National Early Literacy Panel. (2008). *Developing early literacy: Report of the National Early Literacy Panel.* Retrieved January 2009, from http://www.nifl.gov/nifl/ publications/pdf/NELPReport09.pdf

National Institute of Child Health and Human Development. (2000). *Report of the national reading panel. Teaching children to read: An evidence-based assessment of the scientific research literature on reading and its implications for reading instruction* (NIH Publication No. 00-4769). Washington, DC: U.S. Government Printing Office.

National Institute on Deafness and Other Communication Disorders (NIDCD). (2000, April.) *Speech and language developmental milestones.* Retrieved July 21, 2007, from http://www.nidcd.nih.gov/health/ voice/speechandlanguage.asp/

National Reading Panel. (2000). *Teaching children to read: An evidence-based assessment of the scientific research literature on reading and its implications for reading instruction.* NIH Publication No. 00-4769. Washington, DC: National Institute of Child Health and Human Development.

National Research Council. (1998). *Preventing reading difficulties.* Washington, DC: National Academy Press.

National Research Council. (1998). *Starting out right.* Washington, DC: National Academy Press.

National Research Council. (2009). *Mathematics learning in early childhood: Paths toward excellence and equity.* Committee on Early Childhood Mathematics, C. T. Cross, T. A. Woods, and H. Schweingruber, Eds. Center for Education, Division of Behavioral and Social Sciences and Education. Washington, DC: The National Academies Press.

National Scientific Council on the Developing Child. (2004). *Children's emotional development is built into the architecture of their brain: Working paper no. 2.* Retrieved August 31, 2007, from www.developingchild.net/pubs/ wp/emotional_development_is_built.pdf

Neuman, S., & Roskos, K. (1990). Play, print and purpose: Enriching play environments for literacy development. *Reading Teacher, 44*(3), 214–221.

Neuman, S., & Roskos, K. (1993). Access to print for children of poverty: Differential effects of adult mediation and literacy-enriched play settings on environmental and functional print tasks. *American Educational Research Journal, 30,* 95–122.

Neuman, S., Copple, C., & Bredekamp, S. (2000). *Learning to read and write: Developmentally appropriate practices for young children.* Washington, DC: National Association for the Education of Young Children.

Neuman, S. B. (2003). From rhetoric to reality: The case for high-quality compensatory prekindergarten programs. *Phi Delta Kappan, 85*(4), 286–291.

Newman, L. S. (1990). Intentional and unintentional memory in young children: Remembering vs. playing. *Journal of Experimental Child Psychology, 50,* 243–258.

Nicolopoulou, A., & Richner, E. S. (2007). From actors to agents to persons: The development of character representation in young children's narratives. *Child Development, 78,* 412–429.

Nilges, L., & Usnick, V. (2000). The role of spatial ability in physical education and mathematics. *Journal of Physical Education, Recreation & Dance, 71*(6), 29–35.

Nobes, G., Moore, D. G., Martin, A. E., Clifford, B. R., Butterworth, G., Panagiotaki, G., et al., (2003). Children's understanding of the earth in a multicultural community: Mental model or fragments of knowledge? *Developmental Science, 6*(1), 72–85.

Normandeau, S., & Guay, F. (1998). Preschool behavior and first-grade school achievement: The mediational role of cognitive self-control. *Journal of Educational Psychology, 90*, 111–121.

Northwest Educational Technology Consortium, Northwest Region Educational Laboratory. (2002). 5 effective ways for young children to use technology. Portland, OR: Author.

Nourot, P. M., & Van Hoorn, J. L. (1991). Research in review: Symbolic play in preschool and primary settings. *Young Children, 46*(6), 40–50.

O'Reilly, A. W., & Bornstein, M. H. (1993). Caregiver-child interaction in play. *New Directions in Child Development, 59*, 55–66.

Ohman-Rodriquez, J. (2004). Music from inside out: Promoting emergent composition with young children. *Young Children, 59*(4), 50–55.

Oller, D. K., & Eilers, R. E. (Eds.). 2002. *Language and literacy in bilingual children*. Bristol, UK: Multilingual Matters.

Ontai, L. & Thompson, R. A. (2002). Patterns of attachment and maternal discourse effects on children's emotion understanding from 3 to 5 years of age. *Social Development, 11*(4), 433–450.

Ostrov, J. M., Woods, K. E., Jansen, E. A., Casas, J. F., & Crick, N. R. (2004). An observational study of delivered and received aggression, gender, and social-psychological adjustment in preschool: "This white crayon doesn't work…" *Early Childhood Research Quarterly, 19*, 355–371.

Owens, C. V. (1999). Conversational science 101A: Talking it up! *Young Children, 54*(5), 4–9.

Páez, M. M., Tabors, P. O., & López, L. M. (2007). Dual language and literacy development of Spanish-speaking preschool children. *Journal of Applied Developmental Psychology, 28*(2), 85–102.

Palermo, F., Hanish, L. D., Martin, C. L., Fabes, R. A., & Reiser, M. (2007). Preschoolers' academic readiness: What role does the teacher-child relationship play? *Early Childhood Research Quarterly, 22*, 407–422.

Palmer, H. (2001). The music, movement, and learning connection. *Young Children, 56*(5), 13–17.

Parish-Morris, J., Hennon, E. A., Hirsh-Pasek, K., Golinkoff, R. M., & Tager-Flusberg, H. (2007). Children with autism illuminate the role of social intention in word learning. *Child Development, 78*, 1265–1287.

Parker, J. G. & Asher, S. R. (1987). Peer relations and later personal adjustment: Are low-accepted children at risk? *Psychological Bulletin, 102*, 357–389.

Pauen, S. (2002). The global-to-basic level shift in infants' categorical thinking: First evidence from a longitudinal study. *International Journal of Behavioral Development, 26*, 492–499.

Payne, J. N., & Huinker, D. M. (1993). Early number and numeration. In R. J. Jensen (Ed.), *Research ideas for the classroom: Early childhood mathematics* (pp. 43–71). New York: Macmillan.

Payne, V. G., & Rink, J. E. (1997). Physical education in the developmentally appropriate integrated curriculum. In C. H. Hart, D. C. Burts, & R. Charlesworth (Eds.), *Integrated curriculum and developmentally appropriate practice: Birth to age eight*, pp. 145–170. Albany, New York: SUNY Press.

Pearson, B., & Fernández, S. (1994). Patterns of interaction in the lexical growth in two languages of bilingual infants and toddlers. *Language Learning, 44*(4), 617–653.

Pearson, B., Fernández, S., Lewedeg, V., & Oller, D. K. (1997). The relation of input factors to lexical learning by bilingual infants. *Applied Psycholinguistics, 18*, 41–58.

Peisner-Feinberg, E. S., Burchinal, M. R., Clifford, R. M., Culkin, M. L., Howes, C., & Kagan, S. L., et al. (1999). The children of the cost, quality, and outcomes study go to school: Technical report. Chapel Hill: University of North Carolina at Chapel Hill, Frank Porter Graham Child Development Center.

Pellegrini, A. D., & Galda, L. (1982). The effects of theme-fantasy play training on the development of children's story comprehension. *American Educational Research Journal, 19*, 443–452.

Peña, E. D., & Mendez-Perez, A. (2006). Individualistic and collectivistic approaches to language learning. *Zero to Three, 27*(1), 34–41.

Perry, M. W. (2006). A splash of color. *Young Children, 61*(2), 83.

Petersen, S., & Wittmer, D. (2008). Relationship-based infant care: Responsive, on demand, and predictable. *Young Children, 63*(3), 40–42.

Peterson, S. M., & French, L. (2008). Supporting young children's explanations through inquiry science in preschool. *Early Childhood Research Quarterly, 23*(3), 395–408.

Pettit, G. S., & Harrist, A. W. (1993). Children's aggressive and socially unskilled playground behavior with peers: Origins in early family relations. In C. H. Hart (Ed.), *Children on playgrounds: Research perspectives and applications*. Albany, NY: SUNY Press.

Piaget, J., & Inhelder, B. (1967). *The child's conception of space* (F. J. Langdon & J. L Lunzer, Trans.). New York: Norton.

Pianta, R. C. (1999). *Enhancing relationships between children and teachers*. Washington, DC: American Psychological Association.

Pianta, R. C., & Stuhlman, M. W. (2004). Teacher-child relationships and children's success in the first years of school. *School Psychology Review, 33*, 444–458.

Pica, R. (1997). Beyond physical development: Why young children need to move. *Young Children, 52*(6), 4–11.

Pica, R. (2006). Physical fitness and the early childhood curriculum. *Young Children, 61*(3), 12–19.

Pickett, L. (1998). Literacy learning during block play. *Journal of Research in Childhood Education, 12*(2), 225–230.

Pierce, K. L., & Schreibman, L. (1994). Teaching daily living skills to children with autism in unsupervised settings through pictorial self-management. *Journal of Applied Behavioral Analysis 27*(3), 471–481.

Piker, R. A., & Rex, L. A. (2008). Influences of teacher-child interactions on English language development in a Head Start classroom. *Early Childhood Education Journal, 36*, 187–193.

Pinciotti, P. (1993). Creative drama and young children: The dramatic learning connection. *Arts Education Policy Review, 94*(6), 24–28.

Plumert, J. M., & Hawkins, A. M. (2001). Biases in young children's communication about spatial relations: Containment versus proximity. *Child Development, 72*, 22–36.

Ponitz, C. E. C., McLelland, M. M., Jewkes, A. M., Conner, C. M., Farris, C. L., & Morrison, F. J. (2008). Touch your toes! Developing a direct measure of behavioral regulation in early childhood. *Early Childhood Research Quarterly, 23*(2), 141–158.

Poole, C., & Miller, S. A. (n. d.) *Problem solving in action*. Retrieved February 1, 2009, from http://www2.scholastic.com/browse/article.jsp?id=3746479

Pope, C. E., & Springate, K. W. (1995). Creativity in early childhood classrooms. *ERIC Digest*. ED389474 1995-12-00. Retrieved July 16, 2007, from www.eric.ed.gov

Preissler, M. A., & Carey, S. (2004). Do both pictures and words function as symbols for 18- and 24-month old children? *Cognition and development, 5*(2), 185–212.

Public Broadcasting System. (n. d.) *Child Development and Early Child Development Advice/PBS parents: Child development tracker*. Retrieved September 7, 2007, from www.pbs.org/parents/childdevelopment/

Putallaz, M. & Gottman, J.M. (1981). Social skills and group acceptance. In S. R. Asher & J. M. Gottman (Eds.), *The development of children's friendships* (pp. 116–149). New York: Cambridge University Press.

Putallaz, M., & Wasserman, A. (1990). Children's entry behavior. In S. R. Asher & J. D. Coie (Eds.), *Peer rejection in childhood* (pp. 60–89). New York: Cambridge University Press.

Ramsey, P. G. (2003). Growing up with the contradictions of race and class. In C. Copple (Ed.), *A world of difference: Readings on teaching young children in a diverse society* (pp. 24–28). Washington, DC: National Association for the Education of Young Children.

Ratner, N. B. (2001). Atypical language development. In J. B. Gleason (Ed.), *The development of language* (pp. 369–406). Boston: Allyn & Bacon.

Raver, C. C., & Zigler, E. F. (1997). Social competence: An untapped dimension in evaluating Head Start's success. *Early Childhood Research Quarterly, 12*, 363–385.

Rawson, R. M., & Goetz, E. M. (1983). *Reading-related behavior in preschoolers: Environmental factors and teacher modeling.* Unpublished manuscript.

Ray, A., Bowman, B., & Brownell, J. O. (2006). Teacher-child relationships, social-emotional development, and school achievement. In B. Bowman & E. K. Moore (Eds.), *School readiness and social-emotional development: Perspectives on cultural diversity* (pp. 7–22). Washington, DC: National Black Child Development Institute, Inc.

Reio, T. G., Jr., Petrosko, J. M., Wiswell, A. K., & Thongsukmag, J. (2006). The measurement and conceptualization of curiosity. *The Journal of Genetic Psychology, 16*(2), 117–135.

Resources for exploring the creative arts with young children. (2004). *Young Children, 59*(4), 58–59.

Richard, B. A., & Dodge, K. A. (1982). Social maladjustment and problem-solving in school aged children. *Journal of Consulting and Clinical Psychology, 50,* 226–233.

Richardson, K., & Salkeld, L. (1995). Transforming mathematics curriculum. In S. Bredekamp & T. Rosegrant (Eds.), *Reaching potentials: Transforming early childhood curriculum and assessment,* Vol. 2. Washington, DC: National Association for the Education of Young Children.

Richgels, D. J. (1986). An investigation of preschool and kindergarten children. *Journal of Research and Development in Education, 19*(4), 41–47.

Riley, D., San Juan, R. R., Klinkner, J., & Ramminger, A. (2008). *Social & emotional development: Connecting science and practice in early childhood settings.* St. Paul, MN and Washington, DC: Redleaf Press and National Association for the Education of Young Children.

Riley, J. (1996). *The Teaching of Reading.* London: Paul Chapman.

Rimm-Kaufman, S., Pianta, R. C., & Cox, M. (2000). Teachers' judgments of problems in the transition to school. *Early Childhood Research Quarterly, 15*(2), 147–166.

Robert, D. L. (1999). *The effects of a preschool movement program on motor skill acquisition, movement concept formation, and movement practice behavior.* (Doctoral dissertation, West Virginia University). Retrieved August 10, 2008 from http://eidr.wvu.edu/files/1193/Robert_D_Diss.pdf

Roberts, J. E., Burchinal, M., & Durham, M. (1999). Parents' report of vocabulary and grammatical development of African American preschoolers: Child and environmental associations. *Child Development, 70,* 92–106.

Robinson, C. C., Anderson, G. T., Porter, C. L., Hart, C. H., & Wouden-Miller, M. (2003). Sequential transition patterns of preschoolers' social interactions during child-initiated play: Is parallel-aware play a bidirectional bridge to other play states? *Early Childhood Research Quarterly, 18,* 3–21.

Robinson, L. (2003). Technology as a scaffold for emergent literacy: Interactive storybooks for toddlers. *Young Children, 58*(6), 42–48.

Rodger, L. (1996). Adding movement throughout the day. *Young Children, 51*(3), 4–7.

Rodriguez, R. (1983). *Hunger of memory: The education of Richard Rodriguez.* New York: Bantam Books.

Rogoff, B., Mistry, A., Goncu, A., & Mosier, C. (1993). Guided participation in cultural activity by toddlers and caregivers. *Monographs of the Society for Research in Child Development, 58,* Serial No. 236.

Rosenow, N. (2008). Learning to love the Earth… and each other. *Young Children, 63*(1), 10–13.

Roskos, K., Tabors, P., & Lenhart, L. (2004). *Oral language and early literacy in preschool.* Newark, DE: International Reading Association.

Ross, M. E. (2000). Science their way. *Young Children, 55*(2), 6–13.

Rowe, M. B. (1987). Wait time: Slowing down may be a way of speeding up. *American Educator, 11,* 38–43, 47.

Rubin, K. H., Bukowski, W., & Parker, J. G. (1998). Peer interactions, relationships, and groups. In W. Damon & N. Eisenberg (Eds.), *Handbook of child psychology,* Vol. 3: *Social, emotional, and personality development* (pp. 619–700). New York: John Wiley & Sons.

Rule, A. C. (2007). Mystery boxes: Helping children improve their reasoning. *Early Childhood Education Journal, 35*(1), 13–18.

Rule, A. C., & Stewart, R. A. (2002). Effects of practical life materials on kindergartners' fine motor skills. *Early Childhood Education Journal, 30*(1), 9–13.

Russell, S. J. (1991). Counting noses and scary things: Children construct their ideas about data. In D. Vere-Jones (Ed.), *Proceedings of the third international conference on teaching statistics* (pp. 158–164). Voorburg, Netherlands: International Statistical Institute.

Russo, M. (with Colurciello, S. G. & Kelly, R.). (2008). For the birds! Seeing, being, and creating the bird world. *Young Children, 63*(1), 26–30.

Sacha, T. J., & Russ, S. W. (2006). Effects of pretend imagery on learning dance in preschool children. *Early Childhood Education Journal, 33*(5), 341–345.

Salmon, M., & Akaran, S. E. (2005). Cross-cultural e-mail connections. *Young Children, 60*(5), 36.

Saltz, E., Dixon, D., & Johnson, H. (1997). Training disadvantaged preschoolers on various fantasy activities: Effects on cognitive functioning and impulse control. *Child Development, 48,* 367–380.

Saltz, E., Dixon, D., & Johnson, H. (1997). Training disadvantaged preschoolers on various fantasy activities: Effects on cognitive functioning and impulse control. *Child Development, 48,* 367–380.

Sanders, S. W. (2002). *Active for life: Developmentally appropriate movement programs for young children.* Washington, DC: National Association for the Education of Young Children.

Sanders, S. W. (2006). Physical education in kindergarten. In D. F. Gullo (Ed.), *K today: Teaching and learning in the kindergarten year* (pp. 127–137). Washington, DC: National Association for the Education of Young Children.

Sarama, J., & Clements, D. H. (2003). Early childhood corner: Building blocks of early childhood mathematics. *Teaching Children Mathematics, 9*(8), 480–484.

Sarama, J., & Clements, D. H. (2004). *Building Blocks* for early childhood mathematics. *Early Childhood Research Quarterly, 19*, 181–189

Sarama, J., & Clements, D. H. (2006). Mathematics in kindergarten. In D. F. Gullo (Ed.), *K Today: Teaching and learning in the kindergarten year* (pp. 85–94). Washington, DC: National Association for the Education of Young Children.

Satchwell, L. (1994). Preschool physical education class structure. *Journal of Physical Education, Recreation, and Dance, 65*(6), 34–36.

Saunders, G. (1988). *Bilingual children: From birth to teens.* Philadelphia: Multilingual Matters.

Saville-Troike, M. (1987). Dilingual discourse: The negotiation of meaning without a common code. *Linguistics, 25*, 81–106.

Saville-Troike, M. (1988). Private speech: Evidence for second language learning strategies during the "silent" period. *Journal of Child Language, 15*(3), 567–590.

Scarborough, H., & Dobrich, W. (1994). On the efficacy of reading to preschoolers. *Developmental Review, 14*, 245–302.

Scharmann, M. W. (1998). We are friends when we have memories together. *Young Children, 53*(2), 27–29.

Schickedanz, J. A. (1999). *Much more than the abc's: The early stages of reading and writing.* Washington, DC: National Association for the Education of Young Children.

Schickedanz, J. A., & Casbergue, R. M. (2009). *Writing in preschool: Learning to orchestrate meaning and marks.* (2nd ed.). Newark, DE: International Reading Association.

Schickedanz, J. A., Schickedanz, D. I., Forsyth, P. D., & Forsyth, G. A. (2001). *Understanding children and adolescents* (4th ed.). Boston: Allyn & Bacon.

Schmidt, D. (1985). Adult influences on curiosity in children. *Early Report, 12*(3), 2–3.

Schmidt, H. M., Burts, D. C., Durham, R. S., Charlesworth, R., & Hart, C. H. (2007). Impact of developmental appropriateness of teacher guidance strategies on kindergarten children's interpersonal relations. *Journal of Research in Childhood Education, 21*, 290–301.

Schultz, D., Izard, C. E., & Ackerman, B. P. (2000). Children's anger attribution bias: Relations to family adjustment and social adjustment. *Social Development, 9*, 284–301.

Seefeldt, C. (1995). Transforming curriculum in social studies. In S. Bredekamp & T. Rosegrant (Eds.), *Reaching potentials: Transforming early childhood curriculum and assessment,* Vol. 2. (pp. 109–124). Washington, DC: National Association for the Education of Young Children.

Seefeldt, C. (1997). Social studies in the developmentally appropriate integrated curriculum. In C. H. Hart, D. C. Burts, & R. Charlesworth (Eds.), *Integrated curriculum and developmentally appropriate practice: Birth to age eight* (pp. 171–199). Albany, NY: SUNY Press.

Segatti, L., Brown-DuPaul, J., & Keyes, T. L. (2003). Using everyday materials to promote problem solving in toddlers. *Young Children, 58*(5), 12–16, 18.

Seo, K. (2003). What children's play tells us about teaching mathematics. *Young Children, 58*(1), 28–33.

Share, D. L., & Jaffe-Gur, T. (1999). How reading begins: A study of preschoolers' print identification strategies. *Cognition and Instruction, 17,* 177–213.

Shipman, K. L., & Zeman, J. (2001). Socialization of children's emotion regulation in mother-child dyads: A developmental psychopathology perspective. *Development and Psychopathology, 13,* 317–336.

Shonkoff, J. P., & Phillips, D. A. (Eds). (2000). *From neurons to neighborhoods: The science of early childhood development.* Washington, DC: National Academy Press.

Shore, R. & Strasser, J. (2006). Music for their minds. *Young Children, 61*(2), 62–67.

Shure, M. B. (1997). Interpersonal cognitive problem solving: Primary prevention of early high-risk behaviors in the preschool and primary years. In G. W. Albee & T. P. Gullota (Eds.), *Primary prevention works* (pp. 167–190). Thousand Oaks, CA: Sage Publications.

Sigman, M. & Ruskin, E. (1999). Continuity and change in the social competence of children with autism, Down syndrome, and developmental delay. *Monographs of the Society for Research in Child* Development, 64 (1, Serial No. 256).

Silvern, S., Williamson, P., & Waters, B. (1983). Play as a mediator of comprehension: An alternative to play training. *Educational Research Quarterly, 7,* 16–21.

Slaby, R. G., Roedell, W. C., Arezzo, D., & Hendrix, K. (1995). *Early violence prevention: Tools for teachers of young children.* Washington, DC: National Association for the Education of Young Children.

Smetana, J. G. (1984). Toddlers' social interactions regarding moral and conventional transgressions. *Child Development, 55,* 1767–1776.

Smidts, D. P., Jacobs, R., & Anderson, V. (2004). The object classification task for children (OCTC): A measure of concept generation and mental flexibility in early childhood. *Developmental Neuropsychology, 26*(1), 385–401.

Smilansky, S., & Shefatya, L. (1990). *Facilitating play: A medium for promoting cognitive, socio-emotional, and academic development in young children.* Gaithersburg, MD: Psychosocial and Educational Publications.

Smith, H., & Heckman, P. (1995). The Mexican-American war. In E. García & B. McLaughlin (Eds.), *Meeting the challenge of linguistic and cultural diversity in early childhood education* (pp. 64–84). New York: Teachers College Press.

Smith, P. K., & Hart, C. H. (2002). Blackwell handbook of childhood social development. Oxford: Blackwell Publishers.

Smith, S. P. (2006). *Early childhood mathematics* (3rd ed.). Boston: Pearson.

Snow, C. E. (1983a). Age differences in second language acquisition: Research findings and folk psychology. In K. Bailey, M. Long, & S. Peck (Eds.), *Second language acquisition studies* (pp. 141–150). Rowley, MA: Newbury House.

Snow, C. E. (1983b). Literacy and language: Relationships during the preschool years. *Harvard Educational Review, 53*(2), 165–189.

Snow, C. E. (1991). The theoretical basis for relationships between language and literacy development. *Journal of Research in Childhood Education, 6*(1), 5–10.

Snow, C. E., Burns, M. S., & Griffin, P. (Eds.). (1998). *Preventing reading difficulties in young children.* Washington, DC: National Academy Press.

Snow, C. E., & Hoefnagel-Hohle, M. (1977). Age differences in the pronunciation of foreign sounds. *Language and Speech, 20,* 357–365.

Snow, C. E., & Van Hemel, S. B. (Eds.). (2008). *Early childhood assessment: Why, what, and how? Report of the National Research Council of the National Academies.* Washington, DC: National Academies Press. http://www.nap.edu/catalog/12446.html

Son, S. H., & Meisels, S. J. (2006). The relationship of young children's motor skills to later school achievement. *Merrill-Palmer Quarterly, 52*, 755–778.

Spaulding, C., Gottlib, N. H., & Jensen, J. (2008). Promoting physical activity in low-income preschool children. *Journal of Physical Education, Recreation & Dance, 79*(5), 42–47.

Spivak, G., & Shure, M. B. (1974). *Social adjustment of young children: A cognitive approach to solving real-life problems.* San Francisco: Jossey-Bass.

Stadler, M. A., & Ward, G. C. (2005). Supporting the narrative development of young children. *Early Childhood Education Journal, 33*(2), 73–80.

Staley, L., & Portman, P. A. (2000). Red Rover, Red Rover, it's time to move over. *Young Children, 55*(1), 67–72.

Stark, R. (1978). Features of infant sounds: The emergence of cooing. *Journal of Child Language, 5*, 1–12.

Starkey, P., Klein, A., & Wakely, A. (2004). Enhancing young children's mathematical knowledge through a pre-kindergarten mathematics intervention. *Early Childhood Research Quarterly, 19*, 99–120.

Steglin, D. A. (2005). Making the case for play policy: Research-based reasons to support play-based environments. *Young Children, 60*(2), 76–85.

Stetson, C., Jablon, J., & Dombro, A. L. (2009). *Observation: The key to responsive teaching.* Washington, DC: Teaching Strategies, Inc.

Stevenson, H. W., & Newman, R. S. (1986). Long-term prediction of achievement and attitudes in mathematics and reading. *Child Development 57*, 646–659.

Stewart, R. A., Rule, A. C., & Giordano, D. A. (2007). The effect of fine motor skill activities on kindergarten student attention. *Early Childhood Education Journal, 35*, 103–109.

Stipek, D. (2002). *Motivation to learn: Integrating theory and practice* (4th ed.). Boston: Allyn & Bacon.

Stipek, D., Recchia, S, & McClintic, S. (1992). Self-evaluations in young children. *Monographs of the Society for Research in Child Development, 57*(1), Serial No. 226.

Stipek, D. J., Feiler, R., Byler, P., Ryan, R., Milburn, S., & Salmon, J. M. (1998). Good beginnings: What difference does the program make in preparing young children for school? *Journal of Applied Psychology, 19*(1), 41–66.

Stoel-Gammon, C., & Menn, L. (2004). Phonological development: Learning sounds and sound patterns. In J. B. Gleason (Ed.), *The development of language* (7th ed.). Boston: Allyn & Bacon.

Strickland, D. S. (2006). Language and literacy in kindergarten. In D. F. Gullo (Ed.), *K today: Teaching and learning in the kindergarten year* (pp. 73–84). Washington, DC: National Association for the Education of Young Children.

Strickland, D. S., & Riley-Ayers, S. (2007). *Literacy leadership in early childhood: The essential guide.* New York: Teacher's College Press.

Strickland, D. S., & Schickedanz, J. A. (2004). *Learning about print in preschool: Working with letters, words, and beginning links with phonemic awareness.* Newark, DE: International Reading Association.

Strickland, D. S., & Shanahan, T. (2004). Laying the groundwork for literacy. *Educational Leadership, 61*(6), 74–77.

Stuart, M. (1995). Prediction and qualitative assessment of five- and six-year-old children's reading: A longitudinal study. *British Journal of Educational Psychology, 65*, 287–296.

Sulzby, E. (1985).Children's emergent reading of favorite storybooks: A developmental study. *Reading Research Quarterly, 20*(4), 464.

Sutterby, J. A., & Frost, J. L. (2002). Making playgrounds fit for children and children fit on playgrounds. *Young Children, 57*(3), 36–42.

Szechter, L. E., & Liben, L. S. (2007). Children's aesthetic understanding of photographic art and the quality of art-related parent–child interactions. *Child Development, 78*(3), 879–894.

Tabors, P. O. (1998, November). What early childhood educators need to know: Developing effective programs for linguistically and culturally diverse children and families. *Young Children, 53*(6), 20–26.

Tabors, P. O. (2002). Language and literacy for *all* children. *Head Start Bulletin, 74,* 10–14.

Tabors, P. O. (2008). *One child, two languages: A guide for early childhood educators of children learning English as a second language* (2nd ed.). Baltimore: Paul H. Brookes.

Tabors, P. O., Aceves, C., Bartolomé, L., Páez, M., & Wolf, A. (2000). Language development of linguistically diverse children in Head Start classrooms: Three ethnographic portraits. *NHSA Dialog, 3*(3), 409–440.

Tabors, P. O., Beals, D. E., & Weizman, Z. O. (2001). "You know what oxygen is?" Learning new words at home. In D. K. Dickinson & P. O. Tabors (Eds.), *Beginning literacy with language: Young children learning at home and school* (pp. 93–110). Baltimore: Paul H. Brookes.

Tabors, P. O., & López, L. M. (2005). How can teachers and parents help young children become (and stay) bilingual? *Head Start Bulletin, 78,* 14–17.

Tabors, P. O., Páez, M., & López, L. (2003). Dual language abilities of bilingual four-year olds: Initial findings from the Early Childhood Study of Language and Literacy Development of Spanish-speaking Children. *NABE Journal of Research and Practice, 1*(1), 70–91. Retrieved August 16, 2007, from http://www.uc.edu/njrp/pdfs/Tabors.pdf

Tabors, P. O., & Snow, C. (1994). English as a second language in preschools. In F. Genesee (Ed.), *Educating second language children: The whole child, the whole curriculum, the whole community* (pp. 103–125). New York: Cambridge University Press.

Tabors, P. O., & Snow, C. E. (2001). *Young bilingual children and early literacy development.* In S. B. Neuman & D. K. Dickinson (Eds.), *Handbook of early literacy research,* Vol. 1 (pp. 159–178). New York: Guilford.

Taeschner, T. (1983). *The sun is feminine: A study of language acquisition in bilingual children.* New York: Springer-Verlag.

Taylor, D. (1983). *Family literacy.* Exeter, NH: Heinemann.

Taylor, I. (1981). Writing systems and reading. In G. E. Mackinnon & T. G. Waller (Eds.), *Reading research: Advances in theory and practice* (Vol. 2), New York: Academic Press.

Taylor-Cox, J. (2003). Algebra in the early years? Yes. In D. Koralek (Ed.), *Spotlight on young children and math* (pp. 7–13). Washington, DC: National Association for the Education of Young Children.

Teaching and learning about science (2002). *Young Children, 57*(5), pp. 10–47.

Teaching and learning about social studies (2005). *Young Children, 60*(5), pp. 10–60.

Teale, W., & Yokota, J. (2000). Beginning reading and writing: Perspectives on instruction. In D. S. Strickland & L. M. Morrow (Eds.), *Beginning reading and writing: Language and literacy series* (pp. 3–21). Newark, DE: International Reading Association.

Tenenbaum, H. R., & Callanan, M. A. (2008). Parents' science talk to their children in Mexican-descent families residing in the United States. *International Journal of Behavioural Development, 32*(1), 1–12.

Tenenbaum, H. R., Rappolt-Schlichtmann, G., & Zanger, V. V. (2004). Children's learning about water in a museum and in the classroom. *Early Childhood Research Quarterly, 19*(1), 40–58.

Thatcher, D. H. (2001). Reading in the math class: Selecting and using picture books for math investigations. *Young Children, 56*(4), 20–26.

Thompson, C. M. (1995). Transforming curriculum in the visual arts. In S. Bredekamp & T. Rosegrant (Eds.), *Reaching potentials: Transforming early childhood curriculum and assessment,* Vol. 2 (pp. 81–98). Washington, DC: National Association for the Education of Young Children.

Thompson, R. A., & Lagattuta, K. H. (2006). Feeling and understanding: Early emotional development. In K. McCartney & D. Phillips (Eds.), *Blackwell handbook of early childhood development* (pp. 317–337). Malden, MA: Blackwell Publishing.

Thompson, S. C. (2005). *Children as illustrators: Making meaning through art and language.* Washington, DC: National Association for the Education of Young Children.

Torquati, J., & Barber, J. (2005). Dancing with trees: Infants and toddlers in the garden. *Young Children, 60*(3), 40–47.

Trawick-Smith, J. (1998). An analysis of metaplay in the preschool years. *Early Childhood Research Quarterly, 13,* 433–452.

Trawick-Smith, J. (1998). Why play training works: An integrated model for play intervention. *Journal of Research in Childhood Education, 12,* 117–129.

Trawick-Smith, J. (2006). *Early childhood development: A multicultural perspective* (4th ed.). Upper Saddle River, NJ: Pearson.

Tsybina, I., Girolametto, L. E., Weitzman, E., & Greenberg, J. (2006). Recasts used with preschoolers learning English as their second language. *Early Childhood Education Journal, 34,* 177–185.

Tu, T. (2006). Preschool science environment: What is available in a preschool classroom? *Early Childhood Education Journal, 33*(4), 245–251.

Ulrich, B. D., & Ulrich, D. (1985). The role of balancing ability in performance of fundamental motor skills in 3-, 4-, 5-year-old children. In J. E. Clark & J. H. Humphrey (Eds.), *Motor development: Current selected research* (Vol. 1), pp. 87–97. Princeton: Princeton Book Company.

Van Hiele, P. M. (1986). *Structure and insight: A theory of mathematics education.* Orlando, FL: Academic Press.

Varol, F., & Farran, D. C. (2006). Early mathematical growth: How to support young children's mathematical development. *Early Childhood Education Journal, 33,* 381–387.

Verschueren, K., Buyck, P., & Marcoen, A. (2001). Self-representations and socioemotional competence in young children: A 3-year longitudinal. *Developmental Psychology, 37,* 126–134.

Vlach, H. A., & Carver, S. M. (2008). The effects of observation coaching on children's graphic representations. *Early Childhood Research and Practice, 10*(1). Retrieved April 7, 2009 from http://ecrp.uiuc.edu/v10n1/vlach.html

VORT Corporation. (2004). *HELP for preschoolers— Assessment strands: Ages 3–6 years.* Palo Alto, CA: Author.

VORT Corporation. (2004). *Revised HELP Checklist: Birth to three years.* Palo Alto, CA: Author.

Vukelich, C. (1990). Where's the paper? Literacy during dramatic play. *Childhood Education, 55*(4), 205–209.

Vygotsky, L. (1997). *The history of the development of higher mental functions.* In R. W. Rieber (Ed.), *The collected works of L. S. Vygotsky* (M. J. Hall, Trans., Vol. 4). New York: Plenum Press.

Wagner, R. K., Torgesen, J. K., Laughon, P., Simmons, K., & Rashotte, C. A. (1993). The development of young readers' phonological processing abilities. *Journal of Educational Psychology, 30,* 73–87.

Wagner, R. K., Torgesen, J. K., Rashotte, C. A., Hecht, S. A., Barker, T. A., Burgess, S. R., et al. (1997). Changing causal relations between phonological processing abilities and word-level reading as children develop from beginning to fluent readers: A 5-year longitudinal study. *Developmental Psychology, 33,* 468–479.

Wang, J. H. T. (2004). A study of gross motor skills of preschool children. *Journal of Research in Childhood Education, 19*(1), 32–43.

Wang, W. Y., & Ju, Y. H. (2002). Promoting balance and jumping skills in children with Down syndrome. *Perceptual Motor Skills, 94,* 443–438.

Washington state early learning and development benchmarks (2005). Retrieved May 23, 2007, from http://www.k12.wa.us/EarlyLearning/pubdocs/EarlyLearningBenchmarks.pdf

Webster-Stratton, C., & Herbert, M. (1994). *Troubled families—Problem children: Working with parents: A collaborative process.* Chichester, England: Wiley.

Weitzman, E., & Greenberg, J. (2002). *Learning language and loving it.* Toronto, Ontario: The Hanen Centre.

Wells, G. (1985). Preschool literacy-related activities and success in school. In D. R. Olance, N. Torrance, & A. Hildyard (Eds.), *Literacy, language, and learning* (pp. 229–255). Cambridge, England: Cambridge University Press.

Wells, G. (1986). *The meaning makers: Children learning language and using language to learn.* Portsmouth, NH: Heinemann.

Wentzel, K., & Asher, S. (1995). The academic lives of neglected, rejected, popular, and controversial children. *Child Development, 66,* 754–763.

West, J., Denton, K., & Germino-Hausken, E. (2000). *America's kindergartners: Findings from the early childhood longitudinal study, kindergarten class of 1998–99, Fall 1998.* Retrieved July 16, 2007, from http://ceep.crc.uiuc.edu/eecearchive/digests/ed-cite/ed438089.html

Whitehurst, G. J., & Fischel, J. (1994). Practitioner review: Early developmental language delay: What, if anything, should the clinician do about it? *Journal of Child Psychology and Psychiatry, 35,* 613–648.

Whitin, P. (2001). Kindness in a jar. *Young Children, 56*(5), 18–22.

Whitin, P., & Whitin, D. J. (2003). Developing mathematical understanding along the yellow brick road. In D. Koralek (Ed.), *Spotlight on young children and math* (pp. 25–28). Washington, DC: National Association for the Education of Young Children.

Whiting, B. B., & Edwards, C. P. (1988). *Children of different worlds.* Cambridge, MA: Harvard University Press.

Whiting, B. B., & Whiting, J. W. M. (1975). *Children of six cultures: A psycho-cultural analysis.* Cambridge, MA: Harvard University Press.

Wien, C. A., Keating, B., Coates, A., & Bigelow, B. (2008). Moving into uncertainty: Sculpture with three- to five-year-olds. *Young Children, 63*(4), 78–86.

Wiggins, D. G. (2007). Pre-K music and the emergent reader: Promoting literacy in a music-enhanced environment. *Early Childhood Education Journal, 35*(1), 55–64.

Williams, A. E. (2008). Exploring the natural world with infants and toddlers in an urban setting. *Young Children, 63*(1), 22–25.

Williams, K. C., & Cooney, M. H. (2006). Young children and social justice. *Young Children, 61*(2), 75–82.

Wishard, A. G., Shivers, E. M., Howes, C., & Ritchie, S. (2003). Child care program and teacher practices: Associations with quality and children's experiences. *Early Childhood Research Quarterly, 18,* 65–103.

Wong Fillmore, L. (1976). *The second time around: Cognitive and social strategies in second language acquisition.* Unpublished doctoral dissertation, Stanford University, Palo Alto.

Wong Fillmore, L. (1979). Individual differences in second language acquisition. In C. J. Fillmore, D. Kempler, & W. S-Y. Wang (Eds.), *Individual differences in language ability and language behavior* (pp. 203–228). New York: Academic Press.

Wong Fillmore, L. (1985). *Second language learning in children: A proposed model.* In *English Language Development. Proceedings of a conference on issues in English language development for minority language education.* Washington, DC: ERIC Clearinghouse on Languages and Linguistics. (ERIC Document Reproduction Service No. ED273149)

Wong Fillmore, L. (1991a). Language and cultural issues in the early education of language minority children. In S. Kagan (Ed.), *The care and education of America's young children: Obstacles and opportunities. 90th yearbook of the National Society for the Study of Education, Part I* (pp. 30–49). Chicago: University of Chicago Press.

Wong Fillmore, L. (1991b). When learning a second language means losing the first. *Early Childhood Research Quarterly, 6*(3), 323–346.

Woodard, C., Haskins, G., Schaefer, G., & Smolen, L. (2004). Let's talk: A different approach to oral language development. *Young Children, 59*(4), 92–95.

Worden, P. E., & Boettcher, W. (1990). Young children's acquisition of alphabet knowledge. *Journal of Reading Behavior, 20*(3), 277–295.

Wright, C., Bacigalupa, C., Black, T., & Burton, M. (2008). Windows into children's thinking: A guide to storytelling and dramatization. *Early Childhood Education Journal, 35*(4), 363–369.

Wu, P., Robinson, C. C., Yang, C, Hart, C. H., Olsen, S. F., Porter, C. L., et al. (2002). Similarities and differences in mothers' parenting of preschoolers in China and the United States. *International Journal of Behavioral Development, 26*, 481–491.

Yamamoto, J., & Kubota, M. (1983). Emotional development of Japanese-American children. In G. J. Powell (Ed.), *The psychosocial development of minority children* (pp. 237–247). New York: Brunner/Mazel.

Yeats, K. O., Schultz, L. H., & Selman, R. L. (1991). The development of interpersonal negotiation strategies in thought and action: A social-cognitive link to behavioral adjustment and social status. *Merrill-Palmer Quarterly, 37*, 369–405.

Yen, C. J., Konold, T. R., & McDermott, P. A. (2004). Does learning behavior augment cognitive ability as an indicator of academic achievement? *Journal of School Psychology, 42*, 157–169.

Yoon, J., & Onchwari, J. A. (2006). Teaching young children science: Three key points. *Early Childhood Education Journal, 33*(6), 419–423.

Young, D., & Behounek, L. M. (2006). Kindergartners use PowerPoint to lead their own parent–teacher conferences. *Young Children, 61*(2), 24–26.

Youngblade, L. M., & Dunn J. (1995). Individual differences in young children's pretend play with mother and sibling: Links to relationships and understanding of other people's feelings and beliefs. *Child Development, 66*, 1472–1492.

Younger, B. A., & Johnson, K. E. (2004). Infants' comprehension of toy replicas as symbols for real objects. *Cognitive Psychology, 18*, 207–242.

Youngstrom, E., Wolpaw, J. M., Kogos, J. L., Schoff, K., Ackerman, B., & Izard, C. (2000). Interpersonal problem solving in preschool and first grade: Developmental change and ecological validity. *Journal of Clinical Child Psychology, 29*, 589–602.

Yuzawa, M., Bart, W. M., Yuzawa, M., & Junko, I. (2005). Young children's knowledge and strategies for comparing sizes. *Early Childhood Research Quarterly, 20*, 239–253.

Zachopoulou, E., Tsapakidou, A., & Derri, V. (2004). The effects of a developmentally appropriate music and movement program on motor performance. *Early Childhood Research Quarterly, 19*, 631–642.

Zaslow, M., & Martinez-Beck, I. (Eds.). (2005). *Critical issues in early childhood professional development.* Baltimore: Paul H. Brookes.

Zill, N., Collins, M., West, J., & Hausken, E.G. (1995). *Approaching kindergarten: A look at preschoolers in the United States.* Washington, DC: U.S. Department of Education, Office of Education.

Zimmerman, E., & Zimmerman, L. (2000). Art education and early childhood education: The young child as creator and meaning maker within a community context. *Young Children, 55*(6), 87–92.

Zur, O., & Gelman, R. (2004). Young children can add and subtract by predicting and checking. *Early Childhood Research Quarterly, 19*, 121–137.

Optional Dimensions for Physical Objectives 4–6

Objective 4. Demonstrates traveling skills

  a. Walks

  b. Runs

  c. Gallops and skips

Objective 5. Demonstrates balancing skills

  a. Sits and stands

  b. Walks on beam

  c. Jumps and hops

Objective 6. Demonstrates gross-motor manipulative skills

  a. Throws

  b. Catches

  c. Kicks

Objective 4 Demonstrates traveling skills

Optional Dimensions:

a. Walks

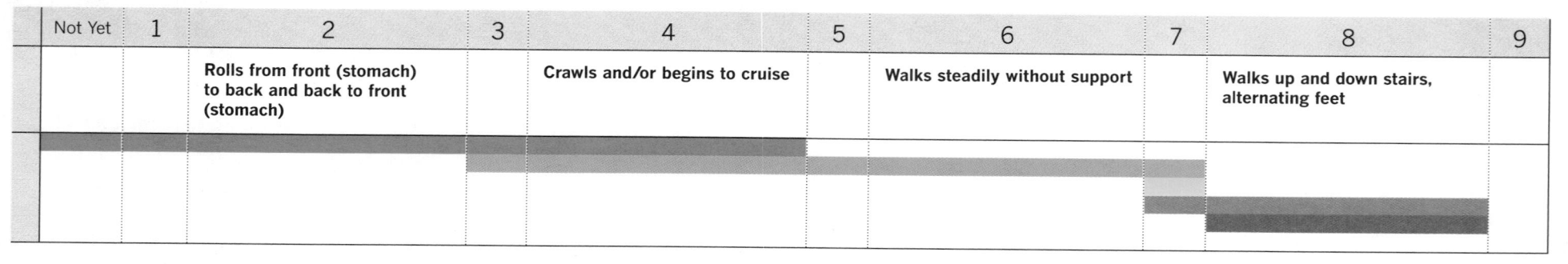

Not Yet	1	2	3	4	5	6	7	8	9
		Rolls from front (stomach) to back and back to front (stomach)		Crawls and/or begins to cruise		Walks steadily without support		Walks up and down stairs, alternating feet	

b. Runs

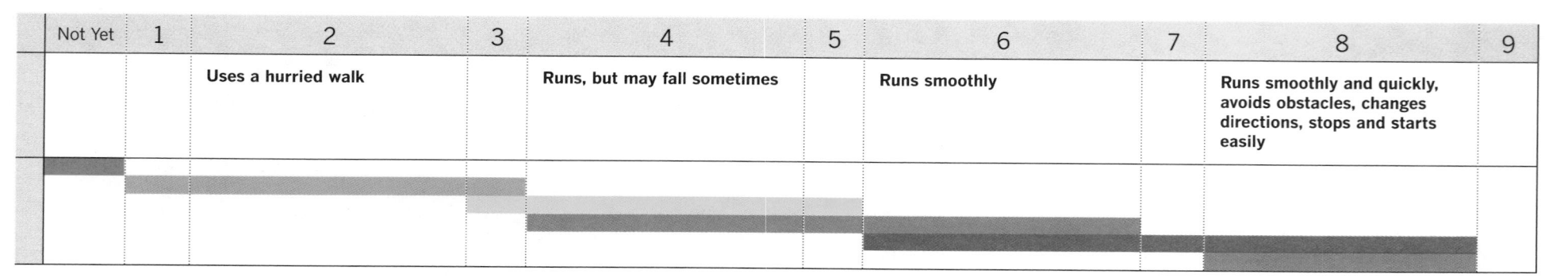

Not Yet	1	2	3	4	5	6	7	8	9
		Uses a hurried walk		Runs, but may fall sometimes		Runs smoothly		Runs smoothly and quickly, avoids obstacles, changes directions, stops and starts easily	

c. Gallops and skips

Not Yet	1	2	3	4	5	6	7	8	9
		Gallops, but not smoothly		Gallops smoothly, always leading with the same foot		Uses a one-footed skip (not alternating feet)		Skips smoothly (alternating leading feet)	

See pages 60–62 of *Child Assessment Portfolio.*

Objective 5 Demonstrates balancing skills

Optional Dimensions:

a. Sits and stands

Not Yet	1	2	3	4	5	6	7	8	9
		Sits unsupported; pulls to a standing position		Reaches for a toy without falling over while sitting; stands unsupported		Stands on one foot briefly while holding on		Stands on one foot for 5–10 seconds without support	

b. Walks on beam

Not Yet	1	2	3	4	5	6	7	8	9
		Walks on a line on the ground or a balance beam lying flat on the floor		Walks on a low, wide beam, watching feet; leads with same foot		Walks on a low, wide beam, alternating feet		Walks forward easily on a 2- to 3-inch-wide beam	

c. Jumps and hops

Not Yet	1	2	3	4	5	6	7	8	9
		Jumps off floor with both feet		Jumps over small objects; hops up to 3 times on one foot		Jumps forward landing on both feet; hops 4–6 times on same foot; attempts to jump rope		Hops 7–10 times on same foot; jumps rope	

See pages 63–65 of *Child Assessment Portfolio.*

Objective 6 Demonstrates gross-motor manipulative skills

Optional Dimensions:

a. Throws

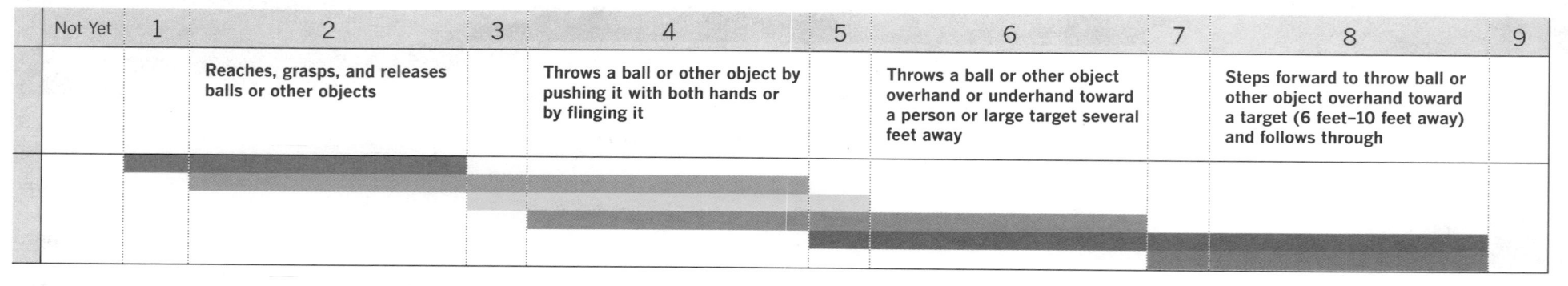

Not Yet	1	2	3	4	5	6	7	8	9
		Reaches, grasps, and releases balls or other objects		Throws a ball or other object by pushing it with both hands or by flinging it		Throws a ball or other object overhand or underhand toward a person or large target several feet away		Steps forward to throw ball or other object overhand toward a target (6 feet–10 feet away) and follows through	

b. Catches

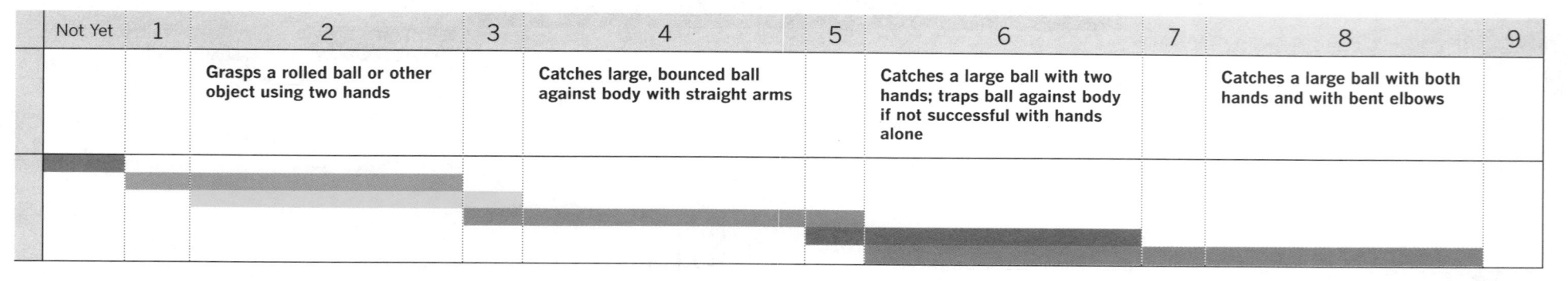

Not Yet	1	2	3	4	5	6	7	8	9
		Grasps a rolled ball or other object using two hands		Catches large, bounced ball against body with straight arms		Catches a large ball with two hands; traps ball against body if not successful with hands alone		Catches a large ball with both hands and with bent elbows	

c. Kicks

Not Yet	1	2	3	4	5	6	7	8	9
		Pushes against ball with foot		Kicks a ball with a straight leg, not bending knee, and with stiff body movement		Kicks stationary ball forward, stepping or running up to it, bending the kicking leg at the knee		Kicks moving ball by stepping forward, swinging leg back, and using full range of motion	

See pages 66–68 of *Child Assessment Portfolio.*

Spanish Language and Literacy Objectives (8–10 and 15–19)

Objetivo 8. Escucha y comprende lenguaje cada vez más complejo

    a. Comprende el lenguaje

    b. Sigue instrucciones

Objetivo 9. Usa el lenguaje para expresar lo que piensa y lo que necesita

    a. Usa un vocabulario cada vez más rico y expresivo

    b. Habla con claridad

    c. Usa la gramática convencional

    d. Habla acerca de otro momento o lugar

Objetivo 10. Usa destrezas apropiadas para conversar y comunicarse

    a. Participa en conversaciones

    b. Sigue las reglas sociales del lenguaje

Objetivo 15. Demuestra conciencia fonológica

    a. Nota y diferencia la rima

    b. Nota y diferencia la aliteración

    c. Nota y diferencia unidades cada vez más pequeñas del sonido

Objetivo 16. Demuestra conocimiento del alfabeto

    a. Identifica y nombra las letras

    b. Usa el conocimiento de las letras y sus sonidos

Objetivo 17. Demuestra conocimiento del lenguaje escrito y sus usos

    a. Usa y aprecia los libros

    b. Usa los conceptos del lenguaje escrito

Objetivo 18. Comprende los libros u otros textos y responde a ellos

    a. Interactúa durante las lecturas en voz alta y las conversaciones sobre libros

    b. Usa destrezas iniciales de lectura

    c. Relata de nuevo los cuentos

Objetivo 19. Demuestra destrezas iniciales de escritura

    a. Escribe su nombre

    b. Escribe para comunicar significado

Objetivo 8 Escucha y comprende lenguaje cada vez más complejo

a. Comprende el lenguaje

Todavía no	1	2	3	4	5	6	7	8	9

Muestra interés en el habla de los demás

- Vuelve la cabeza para mirar a las personas que están hablando.
- Reconoce una voz familiar antes de que el adulto entre en la habitación.
- Mira hacia un juguete favorito cuando un adulto lo nombra y lo señala.
- Responde a su nombre propio.

Identifica personas, animales, y objetos conocidos cuando se le pide que lo haga

- Toma su taza cuando se le pregunta: "¿Dónde está tu taza?"
- Se dirige al lavabo cuando se le pide que se lave las manos.
- Se toca diferentes partes del cuerpo cuando le cantan una canción que las nombra.

Responde apropiadamente al vocabulario específico y a enunciados, preguntas y cuentos sencillos

- Encuentra su ilustración preferida en un libro de cuentos cuando se le pide.
- Escucha a un compañero que cuenta cómo se cortó un dedo y después se dirige al área de juego dramático para buscar una curita.
- Muestra con gestos el tamaño relativo de tres hojas de árboles.

Responde apropiadamente a enunciados, preguntas, vocabulario y cuentos complejos

- Responde apropiadamente cuando se le pregunta: "¿Cómo crees que se movería el carro si tuviera ruedas cuadradas?"
- Desarrolla ideas acerca de cómo reparar el vagón roto.
- Representa con acciones el ciclo de vida de una mariposa después de que el maestro lee un cuento sobre el tema.

b. Sigue instrucciones

Todavía no	1	2	3	4	5	6	7	8	9

Responde a pedidos sencillos acompañados con gestos o un tono especial de voz

- Dice adiós con la mano cuando la mamá le dice: "Dime adiós", mientras ella también hace el gesto.
- Se cubre los ojos cuando un adulto dice: "¿Dónde está Lucy?"
- Deja caer un juguete cuando el maestro extiende la mano y dice: "Por favor, dámelo".

Sigue pedidos sencillos que no están acompañados con gestos

- Lanza la basura en un cubo cuando se le pide: "¿Puedes botar esto, por favor?"
- Coloca las pelotas en la canasta cuando se le dice: "Pon todas las pelotas en la canasta, por favor".
- Va al casillero cuando el maestro dice: "Es hora de ponerse los abrigos para salir".

Sigue instrucciones de dos o más pasos, que se relacionan con objetos y experiencias familiares

- Se lava y se seca las manos después de que se le recuerda la secuencia correspondiente.
- Completa una secuencia de tareas: "Toma la caja de los libros y colócala sobre la mesa. Luego trae el papel y los crayones".

Sigue instrucciones detalladas de varios pasos

- Sigue las indicaciones para navegar por un programa de computación.
- Sigue la orientación del maestro: "Para alimentar a los peces, primero toma el alimento. Abre el frasco y esparce una pizca de alimento sobre el agua. Ponle la tapa al frasco y vuelve a ponerlo en el estante".

Objetivo 9 Usa el lenguaje para expresar lo que piensa y lo que necesita

a. Usa un vocabulario cada vez más rico y expresivo

Todavía no	1	2	3	4	5	6	7	8	9

Vocaliza y hace gestos para comunicarse
- Hace sonidos de satisfacción cuando está contento.
- Llora después de intentar varias veces obtener un juguete fuera de su alcance.
- Agita la mano frente a su cara para apartar la cuchara cuando se le alimenta.
- Usa gestos de la mano para señalar o indicar "más".

Nombra personas, animales y objetos conocidos
- Dice una palabra como "Bela" cuando la abuela entra en la habitación.
- Nombra la vaca, el caballo, el pollito, el cerdo, la oveja y la cabra al verlos en el paseo a la granja.

Describe y menciona el uso de muchos objetos conocidos
- Al hacer panqueques, dice: "Esta es la batidora. Déjame batir los huevos con él".
- Responde: "Usamos el paraguas rojo grande para poder taparnos los dos".

Incorpora palabras nuevas, menos conocidas o técnicas en las conversaciones cotidianas
- Usando un dispositivo de comunicación para niños que tengan discapacidades, dice: "Mi pájaro fue al veterinario. Tiene una enfermedad. Se le caen las plumas".
- Dice: "No creo que pueda armarlo. Es complicado".

b. Habla con claridad

Todavía no	1	2	3	4	5	6	7	8	9

Produce sucesiones de sonidos consonánticos sencillos y combina sonidos
- Dice: "m-m-m"; "d-d-d".
- Dice: "ba-ba-ba".
- Produce series de sonidos cuya entonación imita la de una oración.

Usa algunas palabras y sonidos parecidos a palabras y le entiende la mayoría de las personas conocidas
- Se refiere a la abuelita como "Bela".
- Pregunta: "¿Dónde abija?", y un amigo le trae su cobija.
- Dice: "¡No va!" para indicar que no quiere entrar.

La mayoría de las personas le entiende; puede pronunciar mal palabras nuevas, largas o inusuales
- Dice: "Vi hormigas y un montesalta" (saltamontes).
- Habla de manera que le entiende una persona que visite la escuela.

Pronuncia correctamente palabras polisílabas o inusuales
- Dice: "Oh, esa tiene capas, es una roca *sedimentaria*".
- Pregunta: "¿Qué significa *desterrados*?" después de oír una lectura en la cual aparece la palabra.

See pages 72–73 of *Child Assessment Portfolio*.

Objetivo 9 Usa el lenguaje para expresar lo que piensa y lo que necesita

c. Usa la gramática convencional

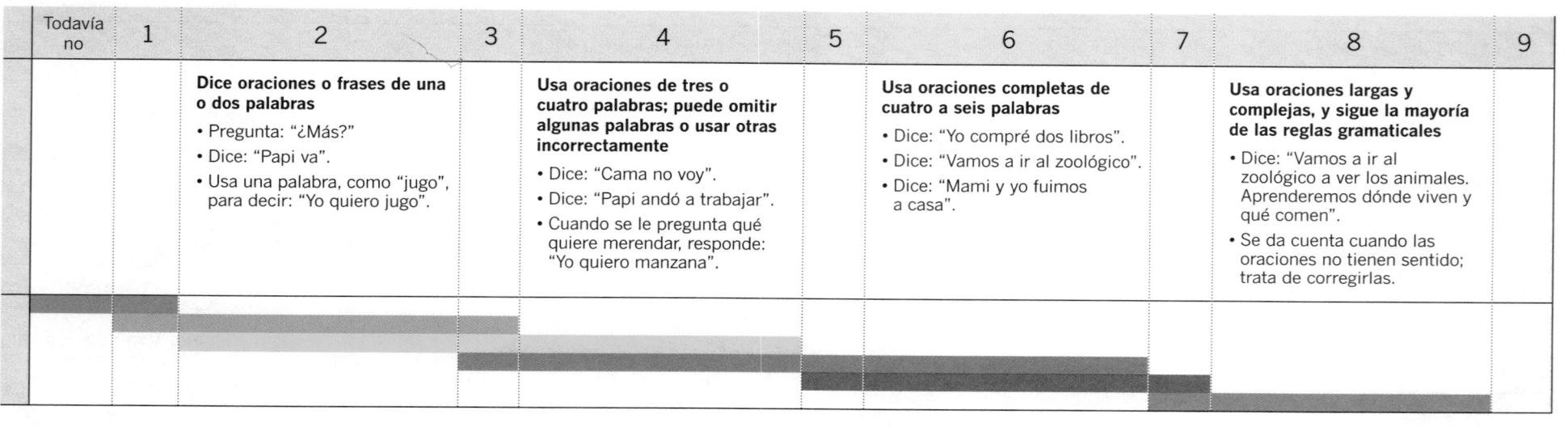

Todavía no	1	2	3	4	5	6	7	8	9

Dice oraciones o frases de una o dos palabras
- Pregunta: "¿Más?"
- Dice: "Papi va".
- Usa una palabra, como "jugo", para decir: "Yo quiero jugo".

Usa oraciones de tres o cuatro palabras; puede omitir algunas palabras o usar otras incorrectamente
- Dice: "Cama no voy".
- Dice: "Papi andó a trabajar".
- Cuando se le pregunta qué quiere merendar, responde: "Yo quiero manzana".

Usa oraciones completas de cuatro a seis palabras
- Dice: "Yo compré dos libros".
- Dice: "Vamos a ir al zoológico".
- Dice: "Mami y yo fuimos a casa".

Usa oraciones largas y complejas, y sigue la mayoría de las reglas gramaticales
- Dice: "Vamos a ir al zoológico a ver los animales. Aprenderemos dónde viven y qué comen".
- Se da cuenta cuando las oraciones no tienen sentido; trata de corregirlas.

d. Habla acerca de otro momento o lugar

Todavía no	1	2	3	4	5	6	7	8	9

Hace enunciados simples sobre acontecimientos recientes y sobre personas y objetos conocidos que no están presentes
- Dice: "Tengo zapatos".
- Escucha a un helicóptero, se detiene y dice: "Cótero".
- Dice: "Abu vive lejos".

Narra relatos sencillos sobre objetos, acontecimientos y personas que no están presentes; no incluye muchos detalles y sus relatos no tienen un principio, un desarrollo y un final convencionales
- Dicta un relato sencillo con pocas conexiones entre los personajes y los sucesos.
- Dice: "Tengo zapatos nuevos. Fui a la tienda".

Narra relatos sobre otros momentos y lugares, que tienen un orden lógico y que incluyen detalles importantes
- Cuenta experiencias pasadas y menciona los sucesos principales en una secuencia lógica.
- Dice: "Fui a la tienda con mi abuelita. Compramos dos pares de zapatos".

Narra relatos detallados que se refieren a otros momentos y lugares
- Dicta un relato detallados sobre su reciente visita a la zapatería, e incluye detalles sobre quién, qué, cuándo, por qué y cómo.
- Cuenta muchos detalles mientras representa su reciente visita a la zapatería.

See pages 74–75 of *Child Assessment Portfolio*.

Objetivo 10 Usa destrezas apropiadas para conversar y comunicarse

a. Participa en conversaciones

Todavía no	1	2	3	4	5	6	7	8	9

Participa en intercambios sencillos con los demás

- Dirige un sonido a un adulto, que responde con una frase como "Miguelito me está hablando, sí". Repite el sonido y el adulto lo imita.
- Dice "No" con la cabeza; mueve la mano para despedirse.
- Participa en juegos como en el cual el adulto se tapa y luego sorprende al bebé al reaparecer, o en el que se dan palmadas al ritmo de una rima.

Inicia conversaciones breves y les presta atención

- Dice: "Perrito". El maestro responde: "Ves un perrito". El niño dice: "Perrito guau".
- Pregunta al maestro: "¿Casa ahora?" El maestro responde: "Sí, me voy para mi casa".
- Mira al maestro y señala la ilustración de un auto. El maestro responde: "No, me voy a mi casa caminando".

Participa en conversaciones de al menos tres intercambios

- No cambia de tema durante las conversaciones.
- Continúa la conversación repitiendo lo que la otra persona dice o haciendo preguntas.

Participa en conversaciones complejas y largas (cinco o más intercambios)

- Ofrece comentarios interesantes (con un dispositivo de comunicación, si lo necesita).
- Amplía la conversación pasando gradualmente de un tema a otro relacionado.

b. Sigue las reglas sociales del lenguaje

Todavía no	1	2	3	4	5	6	7	8	9

Responde a la persona que habla, mirándola; está atento a señales de que le entienden cuando se comunica

- Escucha una sirena y le dice al adulto: "Amión bombeo" (camión de bomberos)
- Mira al adulto y dice "pelota" varias veces hasta que el adulto dice: "Pelota. ¿Quieres la pelota?"

Hace contacto visual y pausas cuando corresponde, y usa fórmulas verbales sencillas cuando se requieren

- Presta atención a la persona que habla durante la conversación.
- Hace una pausa después de preguntar para esperar una respuesta.
- Dice "por favor" y "gracias" aunque a veces haya que recordárselo.

Usa un lenguaje aceptable y sigue reglas sociales cuando se comunica con los demás; puede necesitar recordatorios

- Se turna en las conversaciones pero puede interrumpir o dirigir la charla hacia él.
- Usa el grado correcto de formalidad cuando habla con compañeros y con adultos ("usted", o "tú", según corresponda).
- Baja el volumen de su voz cuando se le recuerda.

Usa un lenguaje aceptable y sigue reglas sociales durante la comunicación con los demás

- Habla en voz más baja con sus compañeros en la biblioteca y con un tono más fuerte en el patio.
- Responde "Hola" al curador del museo durante una excursión.

See pages 76–77 of *Child Assessment Portfolio.*

Objetivo 15 Demuestra conciencia fonológica

a. Nota y diferencia la rima

Todavía no	1	2	3	4	5	6	7	8	9

Participa en actividades con canciones y juegos basados en la rima

- Cuando se canta una canción, tararea y dice algunas palabras que riman.
- Canta en grupo canciones que riman.

Aporta la palabra que rima que hacía falta; dice palabras que riman espontáneamente

- Adivina qué palabra viene al repetir la rima.
- Entona espontáneamente palabras o sonidos que riman.

Decide si dos palabras riman

- Decide si riman dos palabras que presenta el maestro.
- Decide si riman las palabras de dos tarjetas con ilustraciones que presenta el maestro.

Cuando se le da una palabra, dice otras que riman con ella

- Dice: "flan, van, Juan" cuando el maestro le pregunta qué palabras riman con "dan".

b. Nota y diferencia la aliteración

Todavía no	1	2	3	4	5	6	7	8	9

Repite trabalenguas, rimas y canciones en los cuales se repite el mismo sonido inicial

- Repite canciones y rimas que contienen los mismos sonidos iniciales.

Muestra conciencia de que algunas palabras comienzan con el mismo sonido

- Dice: "María y Miguel: nuestros nombres comienzan igual".

Identifica palabras con los mismos sonidos iniciales

- Agrupa objetos o dibujos cuyos nombres comienzan con el mismo sonido.
- Indica un payaso cuando le preguntan: "¿Qué palabra empieza igual que *pie, papá* y *pulpo*?"

Aísla e identifica el sonido inicial de una palabra

- Dice: "/l-l-l/" cuando el maestro le pregunta cuál es el sonido inicial de *leche*.
- Dice: "/b/" cuando el maestro le pregunta cuál es el sonido inicial de *barco, bombero* y *burro*.

See pages 78–79 of *Child Assessment Portfolio*.

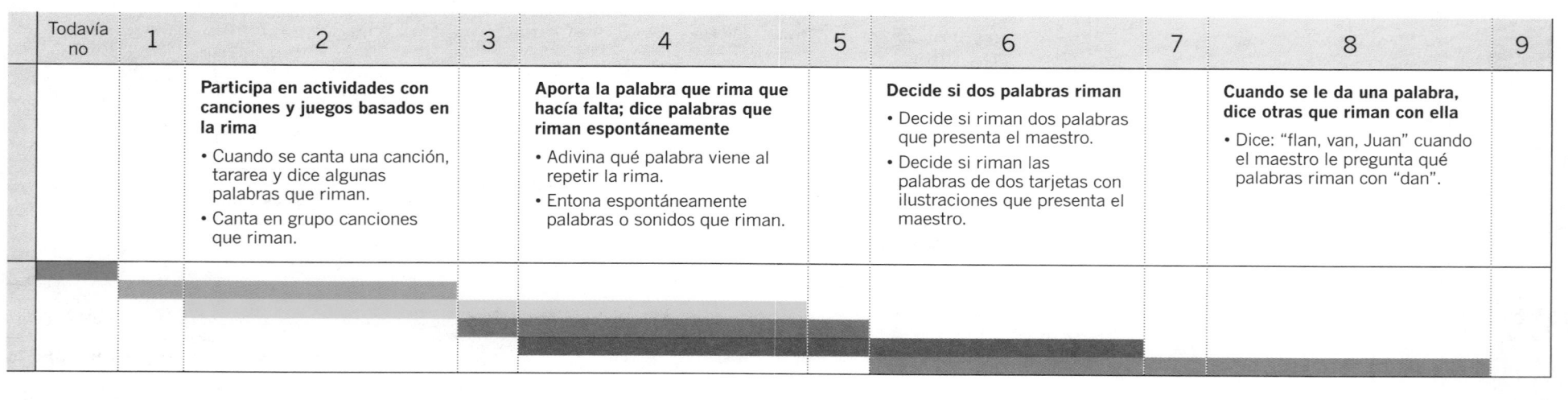

Objetivo 15 Demuestra conciencia fonológica

c. Nota y diferencia unidades cada vez más pequeñas del sonido

Todavía no	1	2	3	4	5	6	7	8	9
		Sabe que existen distintas palabras en las oraciones y puede diferenciarlas cuando las oye • En un grupo, da una palmada con cada palabra al recitar: "Yo soy un niño". • Salta al escuchar una palabra específica en un cuento.		**Sabe que existen distintas sílabas en las palabras y puede diferenciarlas cuando las oye** • Da una palmada por cada sílaba de la palabra *si-lla*. • Une las sílabas "si" y "lla" para decir *silla*. • Une las sílabas "li" y "bro" para decir *libro*.		**Puede separar cada sílaba en su sonido inicial y su sonido final** • Puede separar los sonidos en la sílaba "pa" diciendo /p/ y /a/. • Puede separar los sonidos en la sílaba "mar" diciendo /m/ y /ar/.		**Puede separar cada fonema de la palabra** • Separa la palabra *sol* por fonema /s/ /o/ /l/. • Dice *mar* después de oír /m/ /a/ /r/.	

See page 80 of *Child Assessment Portfolio.*

Objetivo 16 Demuestra conocimiento del alfabeto

a. Identifica y nombra las letras

Todavía no	1	2	3	4	5	6	7	8	9
		Reconoce y nombra algunas letras de su nombre		Reconoce y nombra hasta 10 letras, sobre todo las de su nombre		Reconoce y nombra de 11 a 20 letras mayúsculas y de 11 a 20 letras minúsculas presentadas al azar		Reconoce y nombra todas las letras mayúsculas y minúsculas presentadas al azar	

b. Usa el conocimiento de las letras y sus sonidos

Todavía no	1	2	3	4	5	6	7	8	9
		Identifica los sonidos de algunas letras		Produce los sonidos correctos de 10 a 20 letras		Muestra comprensión de que una secuencia de letras representa una secuencia de sonidos hablados		Aplica la correspondencia letra-sonido cuando intenta leer y escribir	

Muestra comprensión de que una secuencia de letras representa una secuencia de sonidos hablados

• Al escribir, pregunta: "¿Cómo se escribe *libro*?"

Aplica la correspondencia letra-sonido cuando intenta leer y escribir

• Ve la palabra *gato* y combina lentamente los sonidos de cada letra para pronunciar la palabra entera: /g/ /a/ /t/ /o/.
• Crea un letrero: "ABRTA" para indicar que su tienda imaginaria está abierta.

See pages 81–82 of *Child Assessment Portfolio.*

a. Usa y aprecia los libros

Todavía no	1	2	3	4	5	6	7	8	9

Muestra interés en los libros
- Mira las páginas de un libro.
- Le lleva un libro a un adulto para que se lo lea.

Orienta el libro correctamente; pasa las páginas comenzando por las primeras; reconoce libros conocidos por sus cubiertas
- Le entrega un libro al maestro y dice: "¡Vamos a leer *Abuelas!*"

Conoce algunas características de un libro (título, autor, ilustrador); relaciona libros específicos con los autores
- Dice: "Hoy quiero leer este libro de Alma Flor Ada".
- Dice: "Pat Mora escribió este libro. Ella es la autora".

Usa distintos tipos de libros para sus propósitos
- Elige un libro sobre insectos para identificar las mariposas que vio en el patio.

b. Usa los conceptos del lenguaje escrito

Todavía no	1	2	3	4	5	6	7	8	9

Demuestra que entiende que el texto tiene un significado y que se puede leer
- Señala las palabras en un cartel junto a la pecera y dice: "¡Hay que darle poquita comida!"

Indica dónde empezar a leer y qué dirección seguir
- Señala el comienzo del texto en la página cuando simula que lee y mueve el dedo de izquierda a derecha al bajar por la página.

Muestra conciencia de las distintas características del lenguaje escrito: letras, palabras, espacios, letras mayúsculas y minúsculas y algunos signos de puntuación
- Señala la palabra *hipopótamo* y dice: "Esa es una palabra larga".
- Señala un punto al final de una oración y dice: "Eso quiere decir que paramos de leer".

Relaciona una palabra escrita con una palabra hablada, pero puede que no sea la palabra escrita correspondiente; sigue el lenguaje escrito desde el final de un renglón hasta el comienzo del siguiente
- Toca cada palabra en la página mientras recita el texto de *Oso pardo, Oso Pardo, ¿qué ves ahí?*
- Levanta el dedo y lo coloca al inicio del siguiente renglón cuando simula que lee.

See pages 83–84 of *Child Assessment Portfolio.*

Objetivo 18 Comprende los libros u otros textos y responde a ellos

a. Interactúa durante las lecturas en voz alta y las conversaciones sobre libros

Todavía no	1	2	3	4	5	6	7	8	9
		Aporta en el momento apropiado determinadas palabras tomadas del libro • Cuando el maestro hace una pausa en *La mariquita malhumorada*, dice: "No eres lo bastante grande".		**Hace y responde preguntas sobre el cuento; se remite a las ilustraciones** • Responde: "Estaba enojado. Tiró el sombrero al piso".		**Identifica problemas, sucesos y soluciones relacionados con el cuento, en conversaciones con un adulto** • Cuando se le pregunta, dice: "A Jorge lo llevaron a la cárcel. Salió por la puerta y se escapó".		**Recrea el cuento usando imágenes, texto y accesorios; comienza a hacer inferencias y a sacar conclusiones** • Participa en la conversación sobre el cuento y luego dice: "Creo que Max estaba enojado porque lo mandaron a dormir sin cenar".	

b. Usa destrezas iniciales de lectura

Todavía no	1	2	3	4	5	6	7	8	9
		Finge leer un libro conocido, tratando cada página como una unidad independiente; nombra y describe lo que está en cada página usando las ilustraciones como claves		**Finge leer usando algo de lo que está escrito en el texto; describe la acción que sucede a lo largo de las páginas usando las ilustraciones para ordenar los sucesos; puede necesitar indicaciones de un adulto**		**Finge leer, recita palabras que se relacionan estrechamente con el texto de cada página y usa una entonación parecida a la lectura**		**Trata de relacionar el lenguaje hablado con las palabras de la página; señala las palabras mientras lee; usa estrategias diferentes (por ejemplo, pronunciar el sonido de cada letra, recordar palabras conocidas o hallar patrones) para entender el texto**	

See pages 85–86 of *Child Assessment Portfolio.*

c. Relata de nuevo los cuentos

Todavía no	1	2	3	4	5	6	7	8	9
		Cuenta de nuevo algunos sucesos de un cuento conocido con la ayuda constante del adulto • Cuando el maestro pregunta: "¿Qué hace el primer cerdito con la paja?"; dice: "El cerdito construye una casa con la paja". Luego, cuando el maestro pregunta: "¿Qué le hace el lobo a la casa?"; contesta: "El lobo sopla y la derriba".		**Cuenta de nuevo cuentos conocidos usando ilustraciones o accesorios como estímulos** • Cuenta de nuevo los sucesos básicos de *Los tres cerditos* usando piezas de fieltro sobre una pizarra de fieltro.		**Cuenta de nuevo un cuento conocido en la secuencia correcta, e incluye los sucesos y los personajes principales** • Cuenta de nuevo *Los tres cerditos:* empieza cuando los cerditos se despiden de su madre; recuerda el orden correcto en que los cerditos construyen las casas y termina cuando el lobo baja por la chimenea y se cae en la olla de agua hirviendo.		**Cuenta de nuevo cuentos con muchos detalles sobre los personajes, los sucesos y los argumentos** • Cuenta de nuevo *Los tres cerditos,* e incluye detalles sobre cómo se siente la madre cuando sus tres hijos dejan el hogar, las personalidades de los cerditos y por qué es mejor construir una casa con ladrillos que con paja o ramas.	

See page 87 of *Child Assessment Portfolio.*

Objetivo 19 Demuestra destrezas iniciales de escritura

a. Escribe su nombre

Todavía no	1	2	3	4	5	6	7
	Garabatos o marcas • Hace garabatos deliberadamente. • Hace marcas que a los adultos les dan la impresión de estar en un orden aleatorio.	**Garabatos lineales controlados** • Garabatea líneas, círculos o zigzags en hileras. • A menudo repite la acción y las formas.	**Imita letras o formas parecidas a letras** • Escribe líneas que se parecen a una parte de la forma de una letra; por ejemplo, rayas y curvas. • Puede usar demasiadas líneas para hacer una letra; por ejemplo, cinco líneas horizontales en la letra "E". • Puede que no oriente correctamente las líneas de las letras.	**Sucesiones de letras** • Escribe algunas letras correctamente. • Escribe letras según un orden no convencional.	**Nombre parcialmente exacto** • Escribe todas las letras de su propio nombre, aunque puede que algunas no estén en la secuencia correcta. • Escribe todas las letras de su propio nombre, pero algunas de las letras no están formadas ni orientadas correctamente.	**Nombre exacto** • Escribe todas las letras de su propio nombre, con la secuencia, la forma y la orientación correctas. • Usa letras mayúsculas o minúsculas (o una combinación de ambas) cuando escribe su nombre.	
	Carina	Lilly	Paola	Lourdes	Marco	Adelia	

See page 88 of *Child Assessment Portfolio.*

b. Escribe para comunicar significado

Todavía no	1	2	3	4	5	6	7
	Garabatos o marcas	**Garabatos lineales controlados**	**Imita letras o formas parecidas a letras**	**Sucesiones de letras**	**Escritura inventada (etapa inicial)**	**Escritura inventada (más desarrollada)**	

1 — Garabatos o marcas
- Hace garabatos deliberadamente.
- Hace marcas que a los adultos les dan la impresión de estar en un orden aleatorio.

2 — Garabatos lineales controlados
- Garabatea líneas, círculos o zigzags en hileras.
- A menudo repite la acción y las formas.

3 — Imita letras o formas parecidas a letras
- Escribe líneas que se parecen a una parte de la forma de una letra; por ejemplo, rayas y curvas.
- Puede usar demasiadas líneas para hacer una letra; por ejemplo, cinco líneas horizontales en la letra "E".
- Puede que no oriente correctamente las líneas de las letras.

4 — Sucesiones de letras
- Escribe sucesiones de letras.
- Escribe algunas letras correctamente.
- Escribe las letras según un orden no convencional.
- Empieza a separar grupos de letras con espacios.
- Puede que copie el material escrito que hay en el entorno.

5 — Escritura inventada (etapa inicial)
- Usa la primera letra de la palabra para representar la palabra completa.
- Escribe los sonidos iniciales o finales de una palabra para representar la palabra completa.

Nota: La escritura inventada (etapa inicial) puede estar compuesta principalmente de vocales.

6 — Escritura inventada (más desarrollada)

Empieza a incluir los sonidos iniciales, medios y finales de las palabras.

Representa la mayoría de los sonidos que escucha en las palabras en el orden correcto.

Maya dijo: "Mira, mami. Lee esto".

Carolina dijo: "Ese es mi número de teléfono. Puedes llamarme".

Erica dijo: "Estoy escribiendo mi abecedario, como mi hermana".

Octavio dijo: "¡Aquí tienes una entrada! ¡Vamos al cine!".

Jorge escribió: "Quiero a mi mami".

Javier dijo: "Eso dice es mi perro".

See page 89 of *Child Assessment Portfolio.*